The Engineering Design Primer

The Engineering Design Primer

KEITH L. RICHARDS

CRC Press
Taylor & Francis Group
Boca Raton London New York

CRC Press is an imprint of the
Taylor & Francis Group, an **informa** business

First published in paperback 2024

CRC Press
4 Park Square, Milton Park, Abingdon, Oxon, OX14 4RN

and by CRC Press
2385 NW Executive Center Drive, Suite 320, Boca Raton FL 33431

Library of Congress Cataloging-in-Publication Data
Names: Richards, Keith L., author. Title: The engineering design primer / authored by K.L. Richards. Description: Boca Raton, FL : CRC Press/Taylor & Francis Group, 2020. | Includes bibliographical references and index. Identifiers: LCCN 2019040887 (print) | LCCN 2019040888 (ebook) | ISBN 9780367210137 (hardback ; acid-free paper) | ISBN 9780429264917 (ebook) Subjects: LCSH: Product design. | Engineering design. Classification: LCC TS171 .R48 2020 (print) | LCC TS171 (ebook) | DDC 658.5/752--dc23 LC record available at https://lccn.loc.gov/2019040887 LC ebook record available at https://lccn.loc.gov/2019040888

ISBN: 978-0-367-21013-7 (hbk)
ISBN: 978-1-03-283885-4 (pbk)
ISBN: 978-0-429-26491-7 (ebk)

DOI: 10.1201/9780429264917

Visit the Taylor & Francis Web site at
http://www.taylorandfrancis.com

and the CRC Press Web site at
http://www.crcpress.com

Contents

Preface

The philosophy behind the engineering design primer is to introduce student engineers to the world of engineering design. Most student engineers start in the drawing office as draughtsmen and the majority stay there for the duration of their working lives with little thought of progressing into design engineering. From the author's experience, the drawing office lays a very good foundation for a career in design and allows the student to explore the many facets of design.

The first part of the book introduces the student to the workings of the drawing office together with the working principles of producing a drawing having sufficient detail to enable the part to be manufactured. Chapter 3 covers the principles of the design process followed by the design specification or PDS. This is the singular most important document in the design process as it lays down the definition of the design in so far as what the company will produce and most importantly what the customer is expecting.

Chapter 6 covers 'Design for "X"' discussing such items as manufacture, reliability, robustness, maintainability and serviceability. Life cycle costing is also discussed in this chapter.

Quality is discussed in Chapters 6 and 11. It is important for the producer that the customer has the utmost confidence that the product they buy will meet all their expectation.

I make no apology for discussing probabilities and engineering statistics as these items are important when discussing reliability.

The book is rounded off with chapters on material selection, mathematical modelling and configuration management, the later covering change controls. Communication is an important attribute for the budding designer to stand up and confidently and clearly to put his case across for the adaptation of his/her design.

The author wishes the readers every success in their respective design careers and hopes it will provide them many years of employment as, it has for him.

About the Author

Keith L. Richards is a retired mechanical engineer with industry experience of over 55 years. He served an indentured apprenticeship with BSA Tools that manufactured a wide range of machine tools including the Acme Gridley, a multi-spindle automatic lathe built under licence, and single-spindle automatic lathes; these were built in Britain and widely exported all around the world.

On leaving the BSA, he served as a freelance engineering designer in a wide range of industries, including aluminium rolling mill design, industrial fork lift trucks and was a lead engineer for the mooring system for the Hutton tension leg platform. In later years he became more involved in stress analysis that led to working in the aerospace industry covering landing gear and environmental control systems for both military and commercial aircraft and trailing wing components for the Airbus A380.

1

Organisation and Structure of the Drawing Office

1.1 Introduction

Over the last few years the 'drawing office' has seen a massive revolution. Digital draughting has replaced the original method of paper and manual drawing, and alongside this major change there has been a technological revolution in the way drawing prints are now processed and the way data is now transferred to the multi-axis machining centres on the shop floor.

Drawing offices used to be quite noisy with general chatter and heated discussions, now all this has been replaced by a quiet environment with only the clatter of keyboards to be heard. Any major discussions are carried out in side offices to the main drawing area.

Figures 1.1 to 1.5 show typical drawing offices from 1900 to the present day, and the changes that have taken place can be seen. This has been reflected across the engineering industry in the United Kingdom.

1.2 The Purpose of the Drawing Office

The purpose of the drawing office has not measurably changed over the years. In a manufacturing organisation it still serves as the hub between the sales, service, procurement, engineering and manufacturing, as shown in Figure 1.6. Its prime function is to provide working drawings, for the designs developed by the engineering department, to be transmitted to the manufacturing departments.

The drawing office has a number of responsibilities including:

- The preparation of working drawings to a consistent standard
- Checking drawings
- The register of drawing numbers
- Maintaining a register of all drawing revisions and modifications
- Maintaining a reprographics section
- Printing and issuing drawings
- Ensuring quality control is maintained within the department

FIGURE 1.1
A drawing office in early 1900s.

FIGURE 1.2
1923 drawing office.

FIGURE 1.3
1963 drawing office.

FIGURE 1.4
A typical computer-aided design (CAD)/computer-aided manufacturing (CAM) drawing office in 1986.

FIGURE 1.5
A computer-aided design (CAD)/computer-aided manufacturing (CAM) drawing office in 1991.

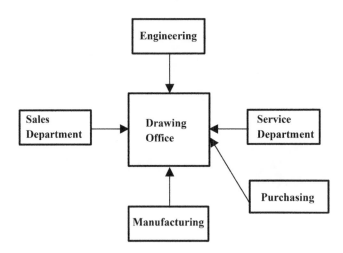

FIGURE 1.6
Relationship between the drawing office and other departments.

- Preparing and maintaining drawing standards
- Preparing data sheets
- Drawing issue and drawing transmittal outside the department
- Drawing storage
- Drawing security
- Maintaining and keeping up to date a technical and standards library

The earliest British Standard relating to engineering appeared in 1903 and covered a range of sizes for metal bars, sheet, nuts and bolts and flanges, etc. The first British Standard relating to drawing office practice was published in 1927 and covered the following factors:

- Sizes of drawings, tracings and widths of tracing cloth and paper
- Position of drawing number, date and name of draughtsman
- Indication of scale
- Method of projection
- Types of line and text
- Colour of lines
- Dimensioning figures
- Relative importance of dimensions
- Indication of materials used
- A variety of degrees of finish
- Screw threads
- Flats and squares
- Machine tapers
- Abbreviations used on drawings

In addition to the above, there were five figures depicting:

- Methods of projection
- Types of lines
- Views and sections
- Screw threads
- Tapers

First angle projection was the preferred method for the illustrations, and the publication was printed on A5 sheets of paper.

In the early days prior to World War I, manufacturers simply fitted components together without due regard to future replacement when any wear took place. The dimensions used were those as used in the prototype part. When manufacturing industry was faced with the introduction of quantity production as led by the gun trade where components had to be manufactured at various manufacturing sites, measurements had to be more precise and methods devised to measuring the parts more easy. As each factory had developed its own standard methods, it became clear and imperative that a National Standard was essential. British Standards published a comprehensive Limits and Fits standard. The National Physical Laboratory was first founded in 1900 and it was obvious that this should be the custodian of the measuring standards. All companies were required to have their measuring equipment certified and calibrated by the laboratory to ensure a consistent measuring system is applied across the industry.

There are two clear aspects that need to be considered for the specification of a component drawing:

1. The drawing is required to show all relevant dimensions for the part in three planes projections.
2. The metrologist produces an evaluation of the part with regard to limits and fits.

1.3 The Importance of the Drawing Office

The drawing office is considered to be the centre of any manufacturing organisation and is generally responsible for the following activities:

1. Development
2. Research
3. Manufacturing investigations, including metallurgy, heat treatments, etc.
4. Project planning
5. Field testing of products

Sales and marketing:

The drawing office may receive requests for assistance in connection:

1. General assembly drawings or layouts for prospective customers
2. Illustrations for technical publications

3. Modifications to an existing product to meet a specific customer request

4. Installation diagrams

5. Feasibility studies

Service:

The service department provides a prompt and efficient response to any service calls. Any work the drawing office receives from this department is associated with:

1. Maintenance tools and special equipment and tooling

2. Service kits for any overhauls

3. Repair or modification work resulting from field knowledge

Manufacturing:

This department is the recipient of all the drawing office manufacturing drawings that have been approved for manufacture. The drawing office supplies all working drawings, schedules and purchase requests for all proprietary items.

1. Working drawings of all the company's current products

2. Amended or revised drawings

3. Drawings of any jigs and fixtures to aid production

1.4 Organisation of a Typical Drawing Office

Figure 1.7 depicts a typical organisation structure of a drawing office. The function of the chief draughtsman is to take overall control of all the activities carried out within the office and to monitor the work being currently carried out. He/she receives all the work coming into the office, sets all the timescales and distributes the work to the section leaders.

The section leader is responsible for all the work carried out within the section by the team of draughtsmen under his/her direct control. The team is made up of a range of skills of various grades from senior to junior levels.

When the work has been carried out to his/her satisfaction the work is then passed over to the checking section. The Standard section scrutinises each drawing to ensure that all the appropriate standards have been addressed correctly.

All the administration work is carried out by the technical clerks who produce all the schedules, lists of equipment relating to the design and general routine work. When all the work has been completed and is ready for approval, it is passed back to the chief draughtsman by the individual section leader.

These days the majority of drawings are produced digitally using computer-aided design (CAD) and these are stored on the servers. It is the responsibility of the IT department to ensure all the files are safely and securely backed up using a number of redundant servers as appropriate. It is not unusual for paper prints to be stored as belts and bracers in the event of a power failure and inability to access the servers. It is not unheard of a computer file being lost and the paper print coming to the rescue.

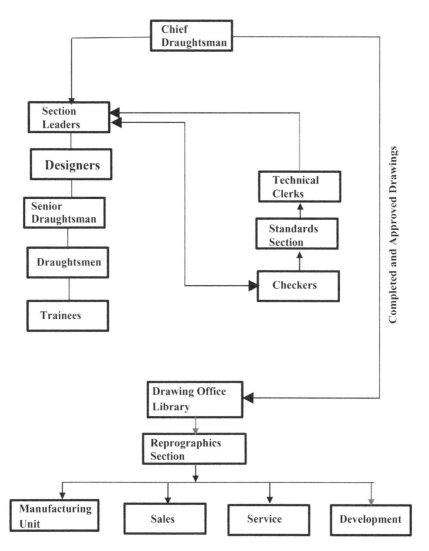

FIGURE 1.7
Organisation of a typical drawing office.

It is not a practice to permit original drawings to leave the drawing office. Only copies are allowed. In some cases a drawing may take several weeks to be produced and represents a significant investment by the company.

The reprographics section distributes copies of all the relevant drawings to the planning, procurement and manufacturing departments to the authorised parties.

2

Engineering Drawing Principles

2.1 Introduction

The objective of this chapter is to give the student studying mechanical engineering design the foundations for producing engineering drawings that are to be used in the manufacture of an engineering artefact or component. Engineering drawings are important to manufacturing engineers for all the information that is required to manufacture the part and includes information such as dimensions and tolerances, including surface finishes and material specifications.

These days, as companies operate over several continents, engineering drawings need to be understood in a number of countries where English is not the first language. It is, therefore, important that the drawings follow the rules that are defined and embodied in the publications of the standards organisations such as the British Standards Institute (BSI) in the United Kingdom, the American National Institute (ANSI) in the United States of America and the Deutsches Institut für Normung (DIN) in Germany. The most important one is the International Standards Organisation (ISO), as this is the world's overarching standards organisation that determines the standards which subscribing countries adopt in preference to their domestic ones.

2.1.1 Technical Product Documentation

Technical Product Documentation is the term used by the ISO to describe the whole area of design communication, covering the information sufficient for the manufacture of a product and can be described in a number of ways including traditional paper-based drawings. The full title of the ISO Technical Product Documentation (TPD) standard is ISO 29845:2011 TPD.

This standard has been adopted by the British Standards Institute (United Kingdom) as BS ISO 29845:2011, and at the time of writing (2017) it was under review. The BSI has a policy that when any ISO standard is published that is relevant to TPD, it is automatically adopted and rebadged as a British Standard.

2.1.2 BS 308

BS 308 was introduced in 1927 to unify all the individual drawing standards being used at the time.

BS 308 became widely used throughout the British Commonwealth. The standard was in use in India, Canada, Australia, New Zealand, parts of Africa, and many other countries.

BS 308 was developed, revised and expanded over the years. Changes to the standard came about as it was extended to cover new areas, and to keep abreast of technological development and changes in working practice. In 1972, it was split into the three parts that many engineers and designers are familiar with.

Part 1: Recommendations and General Principles

Part 2: Recommendations for Dimensioning and Tolerancing for Size

Part 3: Recommendations for Geometrical Tolerancing

BS 308 was withdrawn in 2000 and replaced by BS 8888.

2.1.3 BS 8888:2000

BS 8888 is the current *British standard* that has been developed by the *BSI Group* for technical product documentation, geometric product specification, geometric tolerance specification and engineering drawings. It replaces BS 308 that was the standard since 1927. Over a period of 73 years it was expanded and edited until its withdrawal in 2000 being replaced by BS 8888.

When BS 8888 was first published, it was originally just a long list of ISO standards and gave virtually no guidance on how to produce a specification. Where BS 308 had provided guidance, explanations and examples on various topics, BS 8888 simply listed the ISO standards which now dealt with that topic. It was in effect just an expensive shopping list.

In recent years, BSI has changed their approach. In some ways, BS 8888 has returned to its original BS 308 format and is once again a document which provides rules, definitions and guidance for those involved in creating or interpreting technical specifications.

2.2 Classification of Engineering Drawings

There are a number of different types of engineering drawings, each of which meets a particular purpose. There are typically nine types of drawings in common use which will be discussed in the following sections.

2.2.1 A Design Layout Drawing (or a Design Scheme)

This type of drawing that is generally to scale depicts the basic layout of a proposed design, meeting the requirements of the design brief. There may be a number of layout drawings covering various proposals.

2.2.2 A Detailed Drawing

This drawing is also referred to as a component drawing and contains all the necessary information for the part to be manufactured, e.g., dimensions, tolerances, surface finishes and treatments.

2.2.3 Tabular Drawing

A tabular drawing covers a component that has a common form but can be manufactured in a range of sizes. The variable dimensions are listed in a tabular form.

2.2.4 Assembly Drawing

This type of drawing shows the individual parts that make up the assembly combined together. Generally, an item list is included on the drawing or is referred to. Only information relating to the assembly is included on the drawing such as fitting instructions or dimensions that must be adhered to are allowed on this type of drawing.

2.2.5 Combined Drawing

In some cases this may be drawn as a combined part and assembly drawing together with all the manufacturing details and a tabulated parts list. This type of drawing is restricted to fairly simple type of drawings.

2.2.6 Arrangement Drawing

This type of drawing shows the arrangement of assemblies and parts. It should include important information as well as performance requirement features. An installation drawing is a particular variation of an arrangement drawing that provides the necessary details to affect installation of the associated equipment.

2.2.7 Diagram Drawing

This is a drawing that depicts the function of a system, typically electrical, electronic, hydraulic or pneumatic schemes.

2.2.8 Items List (Also Referred to as a Parts List)

An item list is a list that includes all the component parts that make up the assembly. An item list will either be included on an assembly drawing or as a separate drawing that the assembly drawing refers to.

2.2.9 Drawing List

This type of list is used when a variety of parts make up an assembly and each separate part or component is detailed on a separate drawing. All the drawings and items list will be cross-referenced on a drawing list.

2.3 Drawing Sheet Sizes

Engineering drawings are prepared on standard-size drawing sheets. The current sheet sizes are based on the ISO sheet sizes, as detailed in Table 2.1 ranging from A0 down to A5. Historically, the original drawing sheet sizes were based on imperial sizes.

2.3.1 Metric Sheet Sizes

The standard for drawing sheet sizes is the 'A' series. The basic size in this series is the A0 size (841 mm × 1189 mm), which has an area of approximately 1.0 m^2. The sides of every sheet size in this series are in the ratio $\sqrt{2}:1 = 1.414:1$ and each size will be half the area of the preceding size (see Figure 2.1).

TABLE 2.1

Drawing Sheet Sizes

Sheet Designation	Drawing Sheet Size (mm)	Drawing Sheet Size (inches)	Drawing Space (±0.5 mm)
A0	841 × 1189	33.11 × 46.81	821 × 1159
A1	594 × 841	23.39 × 33.11	574 × 811
A2	420 × 594	16.55 × 23.39	400 × 564
A3	297 × 420	11.69 × 16.55	277 × 390
A4	210 × 297	8.27 × 11.69	180 × 277
A5	148 × 210	5.84 × 8.27	118 × 200

2.3.2 Requirements of Drawing

A blank drawing sheet should contain the following features (see Figure 2.2):

1. Title block (mandatory)
2. Frame for containing drawing space (mandatory)
3. Centring marks (mandatory)

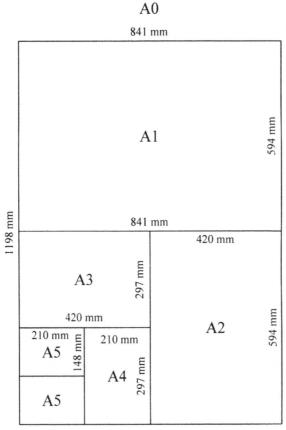

FIGURE 2.1
Drawing sheet sizes.

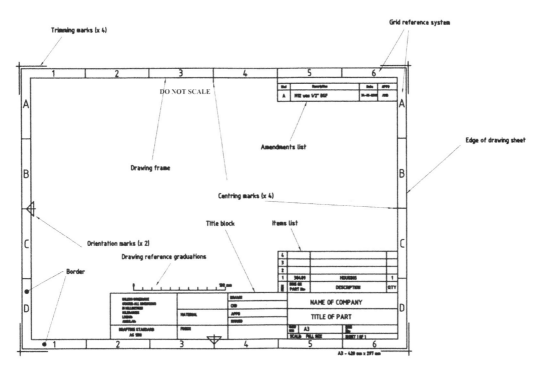

FIGURE 2.2
A typical drawing sheet.

 4. Orientation marks (non-mandatory)
 5. Metric reference graduations (non-mandatory)
 6. Grid reference system (non-mandatory)
 7. Trimming marks (non-mandatory)

2.3.3 Title Blocks

The title block is located in a designated area of the drawing sheet, usually in the bottom right-hand corner (see Figure 2.3) and contains information pertaining to the identification, administration and interpretation of the drawing. The drawing may be prepared in either a landscape or a portrait format. The portrait format is generally limited to the A4 and A5 sheet sizes.

It is recommended the title block should contain (as a minimum):

The name of the company or organisation, drawing number, title, date, name of the draughtsman, drawing scale, copyright, projection symbol, measurement units, sheet number and number of sheet and issue information.

The following supplementary information may be provided on the drawing if thought to be necessary.

Material specification, heat treatment, surface finish, tolerances and geometrical tolerances, superseded by any appropriate warning notes.

2.3.4 Borders and Frames

A border is to define the extent of the drawing region and should have a minimum width of 20 mm for the A0 sheet size, see Table 2.2 for all sheet sizes.

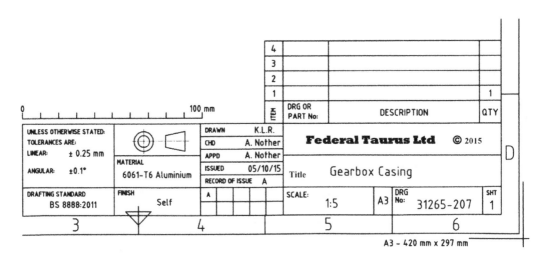

FIGURE 2.3
A typical completed title block.

The suggested border is proportional to the sheet size with the A0 sheet size having a border width of 20 mm and incrementally reducing down to 5 mm for the A4 sheet size.

2.3.5 Trimming Marks

Trimming marks may be added at the edges of the drawing to facilitate the trimming of the paper. There should be four trimming marks located at each corner.

Ideally the trimming marks should be spaced approximately 5 mm outside the border line. This is to ensure the border is within the cut size of the sheet, as shown in Figure 2.4.

2.3.6 Centring Marks

It will help if centring marks are added to the drawing; this mark will facilitate the positioning of the drawing within the drawing frame. They can take the form of a dash that is placed in the centre of each side and extends slightly into the drawing frame, as shown in Figure 2.5.

2.3.7 Orientation Marks

These may be provided on two sides of the drawing sheet, as shown in Figure 2.5. These consist of a triangle coinciding with the centring marks. Two such orientation marks should be provided if used with one pointing towards the draughtsman's viewing position.

TABLE 2.2

Border Sizes

Sheet Size	Border Size (mm)	Internal Frame Size (mm)
A0	20	801×1133
A1	14	566×801
A2	10	400×566
A3	7	283×400
A4	5	200×283

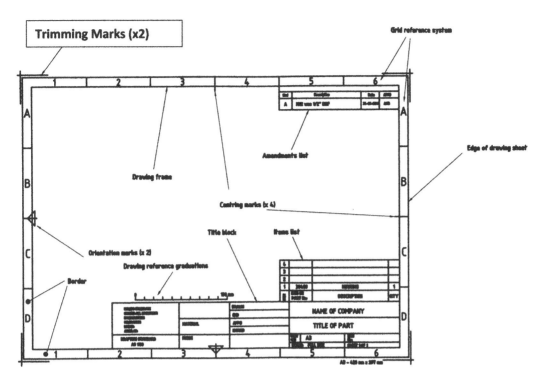

FIGURE 2.4
Trimming marks.

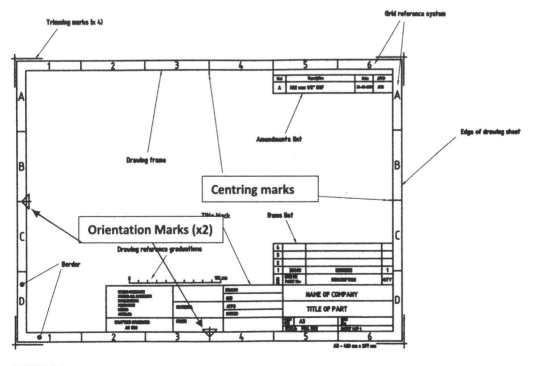

FIGURE 2.5
Centring marks and orientation marks.

2.3.8 Alphanumeric Reference Graduations

The Alphanumeric Reference Graduation system is very useful for all drawings as it permits the easy location of any detail within the drawing frame. The number of divisions should be in multiples of two. The number of divisions should be based on the size of the drawing. Capital letters being used on one side of the drawing and numericals on the other side. ISO 5457:1980 recommends that the length of any one of the reference zones should not be less than 25 mm and not more than 75 mm.

2.3.9 Drawing Scales

Not all drawings are drawn full size; in most instances the drawing is scaled to show the full size part. For example, a house is drawn to scale as it would be impossible to draw it full size.

The preferred scales used in drawing are 1:1, 1:2, 1:5, 1:10, 1:20, 1:50 and 1:100.

These scales cover the majority of drawings that the student may be involved with, although in certain cases some components may need to be drawn to a larger scale, in this case the scales are the reciprocal of the preferred scale: 2:1, 5:1, 10:1, 20:1, etc.

2.4 Engineering Drawing Numbers

Engineering numbers should be a unique identifier for a specific engineering drawing. It would be a disaster for the company to have more than one drawing associated with a particular drawing number. It would cause severe confusion within the company, particularly within the manufacturing and service departments.

It is usually a technical clerk's responsibility to allocate individual drawing numbers that are listed in a secure file and the draughtsman has to request the next available number(s).

The drawing number should be simple, usually no more than seven characters long and should identify the part to a particular design group. The drawing number can be a combination of alphanumeric characters; ideally the best systems use only numeric characters.

For best practice, part numbers should be short, numeric and non-significant. The advantages are:

- Unambiguous in almost any font style and size
- Simple to assign
- Never in conflict with the part description or other attributes
- Consistent in length and format, making it easier to identify missing or extra characters
- Faster to enter into computer systems
- Less subject to clerical transposition errors
- Easier to recall from short-term memory
- Simple to reserve in large blocks for contract design, and to receive numbers back without requiring review
- More clearly communicated in noisy environments and in written communications
- Not artificially constrained to a specific product, project, plant or customer
- Always correct when marked directly on parts
- Simple to merge with an acquired or legacy part number system
- Difficult to invent 'on the fly' outside of normal design release procedures
- Unhelpful for deciphering proprietary information

2.4.1 Revision Numbers

Part revision numbers are an important part of any drawing number system and may be separated from the prime drawing number with a dash, where the part number is applied to the component by either engraving or photo etching. This helps in identifying the actual part and obtaining a replacement.

2.4.2 Group Technology

As early as 1924, it was recognised that using product-oriented departments to manufacture standardised products in machine companies leads to reduced transportation. This can be considered the start of group technology (GT). Parts are classified and parts with similar features are manufactured together with standardised processes. As a consequence, small 'focused factories' are being created as independent operating units within large facilities.

The principle of group technology is to divide the manufacturing facility into small groups or cells of machines. The term cellular manufacturing is often used in this regard. Each of these cells is dedicated to a specified family or set of part types. Typically, a cell is a small group of machines (as a rule of thumb not more than five). An example would be a machining centre with inspection and monitoring devices, tool and part storage, a robot for part handling, and the associated control hardware.

GT is an approach in which similar parts are identified and grouped together in order to take advantage of the similarities in design and production. Parts having similar features permit them to be classified into part families.

The advantage of GT can be divided into three groups:

1. Engineering
2. Manufacturing
3. Process planning

Disadvantages of GT manufacturing are as follows:

1. Involves less manufacturing flexibility
2. Increases the machine downtime, as machines are grouped as cells which may not be functional throughout the production process

2.4.3 Classification and Coding

The purpose of classification and coding is to classify components by some specific feature and to code that feature so that components having similar code numbers are grouped together. There are three basic features on the basis of which components can be classified:

1. Shape
2. Function
3. Manufacturing operations and tooling

Different classification systems use distinctive features or combinations of these features. There is a wide variety of classification and coding systems available for identifying similar families of components.

With the advent of computer aided design and draughting, the advantage of using a classification and coding method for drawing control is that it saves having to redraw the part several times to be used in various other products within the company. Other advantages include:

- Reduced machine set-up times
- Reduced inventory controls
- Material saving

2.5 Manual and Digital Draughting

2.5.1 Manual Draughting

In previous times manual draughting was the only method that could be used to produce a drawing.

There are two methods for producing an engineering drawing:

- Freehand sketches
- Formal drawing

2.5.1.1 Freehand Sketches

This is an informal method of explaining the requirements for an engineering part. It may or may not be to scale.

2.5.1.2 Formal Drawing

Formal drawings can be produced either manually or digitally. In the former, the drawings are prepared using either pencil or ink on translucent paper. The image is transferred onto the light-sensitive paper using a special printer that exposes the paper to an arc light and then developed using ammonia fumes. Originally the resultant image was a negative image in blue, hence the term '*Blue-Print*'.

In manual draughting, the various lines required to define a component or assembly are drawn on the paper using draughting equipment. A simple draughting equipment would consist of a plane surface to draw on with either pencil or ink pens, with the aid of a horizontal ruler that can be moved vertically up or down the board, as shown in Figure 2.6. More industrial draughting equipment would again consist of a plane drawing surface attached to a rigid floor-mounted frame. The draughting equipment being attached to the board, the equipment would be a pantograph machine holding horizontal and vertical rulers that may be rotated using a protractor, as shown in Figure 2.7, or an orthogonal drawing machine, as shown in Figure 2.8, where a horizontal channel is attached to the top edge of the board and a vertical channel sliding in this horizontal channel carries the protractor that carries the vertical and horizontal rulers; this machine is shown in Figure 2.9.

As shown in Figures 1.1 and 1.2 in Chapter 1, depicting an photograph showing an old-style drawing office of pre-1960s.

FIGURE 2.6
A simple student-style draughting board.

FIGURE 2.7
A pantograph draughting machine.

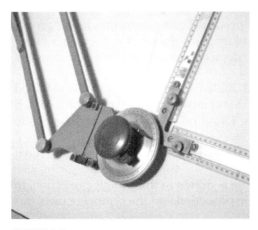

FIGURE 2.8
Drafting machine protractor head.

FIGURE 2.9
Track style draughting machine.

2.5.2 A Precautionary Tale

When the author was serving his apprenticeship in the machine design office during the late 1950s, a draughtsman who was using a pantograph-type draughting machine (similar to that shown in Figure 2.7) with the board in a slightly off-vertical position suffered an unusual accident. The balance weight retained by a fastener failed causing the counter-balance weight to rotate around its pivot striking the poor draughtsman on the side of the head and knocking him unconscious. Fortunately he did not sustain any major injury other than a dented ego.

2.6 Projection Methods

There are a number of projection methods that the student needs to be aware of, including:

- Orthographic projection
  - First angle
  - Third angle
- Axonometric projection
  - Isometric
  - Trimetric
  - Dimetric
  - Oblique
- Perspective projection
  - Single-point perspective
  - Second-point perspective
  - Three-point perspective

These methods will be discussed further.

2.6.1 Orthographic Projection

The greater majority of engineering drawings are produced using the orthographic projection (also referred to as the orthogonal projection) and is a means of conveying a three-dimensional object in two dimensions. Figure 2.10 depicts a three -dimensional component drawn in the first angle projection.

Figure 2.11 shows a component drawn in third-angle projection. A symbol is included in the drawing depicting the projection method, this symbol is a standard and is adopted to show the projection method used and will be found on all engineering drawings to minimise any confusion.

Third-angle projection is the method of choice in the United Kingdom and the United States.

In Figure 2.11 the symbol shows that the drawing is drawn in third-angle projection. In Figure 2.12, the drawing is produced in first-angle projection and the symbol depicts this projection method.

Questions often arise in the students' minds that 'why are first- and third-angle projections so named?' The reason for their naming is connected with geometry.

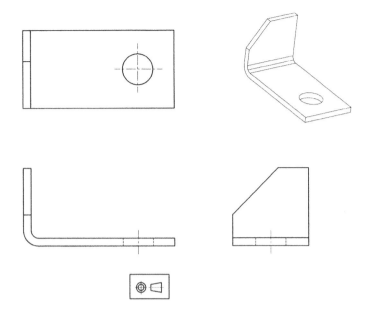

FIGURE 2.10
A typical orthogonal drawing.

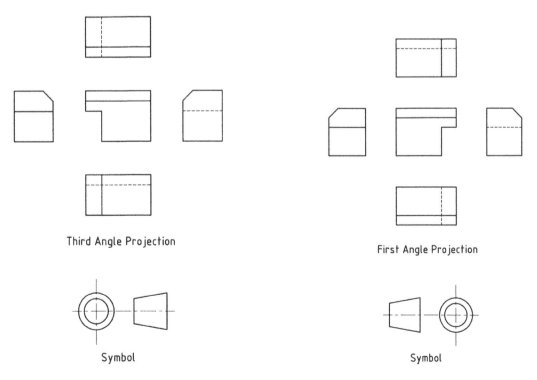

Third Angle Projection

Symbol

FIGURE 2.11
Third-angle projection method.

First Angle Projection

Symbol

FIGURE 2.12
First-angle projection method.

Figure 2.12 shows the four quadrants given by the planes 'OA', 'OB', 'OC' and 'OD'. When a part is placed in either of these four quadrants, its outline can be projected onto either the horizontal plane or the vertical plane. These projections are produced by viewing the part from either the right-hand side or from above as indicated by the arrows in the figure.

For the first-angle projection, the view is projected backwards onto the planes 'OA' and 'OB'. The two views as seen in the first quadrant will be in the first-angle projection arrangement.

When the part is placed in the third quadrant and again viewed from the right-hand side and above, the view will be projected (in this case) forward onto the planes 'OC' and 'OD'. It is clearly seen that the projection will be in the third angle.

If the part is placed in the second quadrant and the horizontal plane is rotated at 90° in a clockwise direction, the two orthographic views will overlap each other, and it will be difficult to determine which part is on the front and which is on the top. Similarly, if the part is placed in the fourth quadrant, a comparable observation will be made. It is for this reason alone why second-and fourth-angle projections are not used.

2.6.1.1 Principal View

The principal view on which all the other views on the drawing is based upon is selected as the view being the most informative. This may be the view which is easily recognised during manufacture or use, i.e., the side view of an aircraft or the front view of a house.

2.6.2 Axonometric Projection

Axonometric projections show all three principal dimensions using a single drawing view, approximately as they appear to an observer. These projections are often called pictorial drawings. Since a pictorial drawing shows only the appearance of an object, it is not usually suitable for completely describing and dimensioning complex or detailed forms. Pictorial drawings are also useful in developing design concepts. They can help to picture the relationships between design elements and quickly generate several solutions to a design problem (Figure 2.13).

2.6.2.1 Isometric

In an isometric projection, all angles between the axonometric axes formed with the plane of projection are equal and are therefore foreshortened equally. To produce an isometric projection (isometric means 'equal measure'), the edges of a cube are projected so, that they all measure the same and the object is oriented so that its principal edges (or axes) make equal angles with each other (of 120°), as shown in Figure 2.14.

2.6.2.2 Trimetric

A trimetric projection is an axonometric projection of an object oriented so that no two axes make equal angles with the plane of projection (Figure 2.15). In other words, each of the three axes and the lines parallel to them have different ratios of foreshortening. If the three axes are selected in any position on paper so that none of the angles is less than 90°, and they are not an isometric or a dimetric projection, the result will be a trimetric projection.

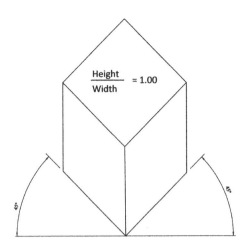

FIGURE 2.13
Axonometric projection.

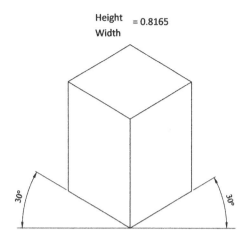

FIGURE 2.14
Isometric projection.

2.6.2.3 Dimetric

A dimetric projection is an axonometric projection of an object where two of its axes make equal angles with the plane of projection and the third axis makes either a smaller or a greater angle (Figure 2.16). The two axes making equal angles with the plane of projection are foreshortened equally, while the third axis is foreshortened in a different proportion.

2.6.2.4 Oblique

Oblique drawing is also the crudest '3D' drawing method but the easiest to master. One way to draw using an oblique view is to draw the side of the object you are looking at in two dimensions, i.e., flat, and then draw the other sides at an angle of 45° (see Figure 2.17), but instead of drawing the sides full size they are only drawn with half the depth creating 'forced depth' – adding an element of realism to the object. Even with this 'forced depth', oblique drawings look very unconvincing to the eye. For this reason oblique is rarely used by professional designers and engineers.

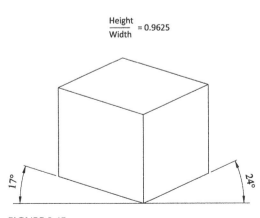

FIGURE 2.15
Trimetric projection.

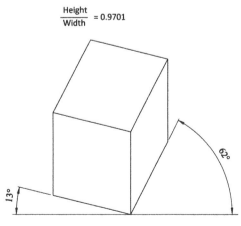

FIGURE 2.16
Dimetric projection.

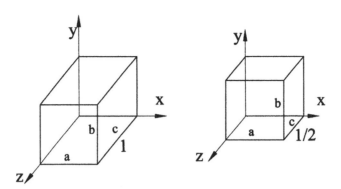

FIGURE 2.17
Oblique projection.

2.6.3 Perspective Projections

Perspective drawing gives a three-dimensional feeling to a picture. In art, it is a system of representing the way that objects appear to get smaller and closer together the further away they are in the scene.

2.6.3.1 Single-Point Perspective

In one-point perspective, the horizontals and verticals which run across the field of view remain parallel, as their vanishing points are at 'infinity'. Horizontals, which are perpendicular to the viewer, vanish towards a point near the centre of the image (see Figure 2.18a).

2.6.3.2 Second-Point Perspective

In the two-point perspective, the viewer is positioned so that objects (such as boxes or buildings) are viewed from one corner. This creates two sets of horizontals which diminish towards vanishing points at the outer edges of the picture plane, while only verticals remain perpendicular.

It is slightly more complex, as both the front and back edges and the side edges of an object must be diminished towards vanishing points. Two-point perspective is often used when drawing buildings in the landscape (see Figure 2.18b).

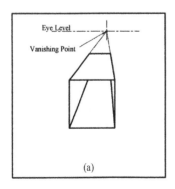
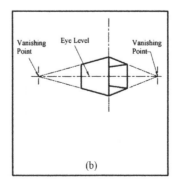
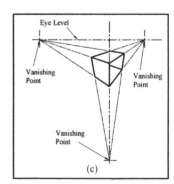

(a)   (b)   (c)

FIGURE 2.18
a, b and c Perspective projection methods.

TABLE 2.3

Line Types and Thicknesses

Engineering Drawing Lines									
Continuous Lines				Discontinuous Lines					
Thick		Thin		Thick		Thin			Thick & Thin
Straight	Wavy	Straight	Non-straight	Dash	Chain	Dash	Chain		
			Curved	Zigzag				Single	Double
ǀ	none	ǀ	)	⌇	∣	⋮	∣	⋮	⋮	⋮
ISO 128 Classification of Line Types 'A' to 'K'									
A	none	B	C	D	E	J	F	G	K	H

2.6.3.3 Three-Point Perspective

In *three-point perspective*, the viewer is looking up or down so that the verticals also converge on a vanishing point at the top or bottom of the image (see Figure 2.18c).

2.7 Line Types and Thicknesses

The standard ISO 128-24:2014 gives 10 line types identified as 'A' to 'K' (excluding the letter 'I').

Tables 2.3 and 2.4 depict these lines as thick, thin, continuous, straight, curved or zigzag. Discontinuous dotted and discontinuous chain dotted is also included in the standard.

TABLE 2.4

Applications of Engineering Drawing Line Types

Type of line	Used in drawing	Sample line
Continuous thick	Visible outlines	———
Continuous thin	Dimension line, leader line, extensions, construction lines and hatching lines.	———
Continuous thin (drawn free hand)	Irregular boundary line, short break lines.	⌒
Continuous thin with zigzag	Long break lines	—⋀—⋀—
Short dashes (hidden line)	Invisible edges	– – – – –
Long chain (thin)	Centre lines	—·—·—·—
Long chain (thick at ends and thin else where)	Cutting plane	━—·—·—·—━

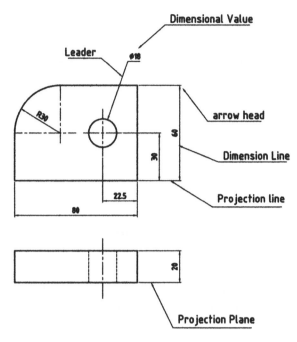

FIGURE 2.19
Examples of leader line terminations.

Each line type has a definite meaning on the drawing where various types of lines are used to represent different parts or portions of an object. These are defined in Table 2.4. See also Figure 2.19 that shows examples of leader line terminations.

2.7.1 Dimension Lines

The basic standard ISO 129-1:2004 covers the application of dimension lines. A dimension consists of at least four parts:

- Two projection lines that extend from the component showing the beginning and end of the actual dimension. It is usual to leave a small gap between the part drawing and beginning of the dimension line, as shown in Figure 2.20.
- The dimension line is of type 'B' (thin, continuous and straight). The dimension lines are the length of the dimension itself, unless the drawing is to a specified scale.
- When dimensioning an angle, the dimension line will be part of a radius (as shown in Figure 2.21)
- A numerical value specifying the length or the angle is stated adjacent to the dimension line, as shown in Figure 2.20.
- Two terminators indicating the beginning and end of the dimension line. There are four types of arrowheads allowed in the ISO standard, these are shown in Figure 2.21a.

The normal arrowhead used in engineering drawings is the *'filled'* in arrowhead that is shown in Figure 2.21a.

An alternative to an arrowhead is the oblique stroke, as shown in Figure 2.21b. These are generally seen on architectural or civil engineering drawings.

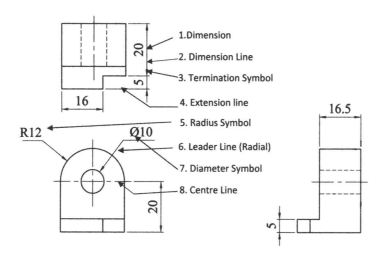

FIGURE 2.20
Examples of dimension lines.

An open circle is used to indicate the datum dimension when dimensioning a chain dimension (Figure 2.21c).

2.7.2 Leader Lines

A leader line connects a feature with an identification or an instruction note, as shown in Figure 2.22. The leader line consists of two parts:

1. A type 'B' line (thin, continuous and straight) going from the feature to the instruction note.
2. A terminator which can be either a dot if the line terminates within the outline of the part, an arrow if the leader line touches the outline of the feature or the centre line of the feature or without a dot or arrow if the line terminates a dimension.

Examples of leader line terminators are shown in Figure 2.28.

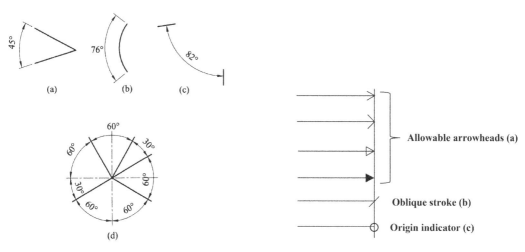

FIGURE 2.21
Angular dimensioning.

FIGURE 2.22
Styles of dimension line terminators.

2.7.3 The Decimal Marker

For many years the decimal point was indicated as a single dot approximately half the height of the adjacent text. The continental preference is for a comma, and at one point British Standards had special dispensation to continue using the decimal point, but later British Standards elected to use the comma to indicate the decimal point. The student will see in older drawing books and drawings the decimal point indicated as a single dot.

As an example 'π' is written as 3,142 and not as 3.142. Similarly the practice of using the comma as a separator in long numbers is no longer recommended; a space should be used instead. Thus, one million is written as 1 000 000 instead of 1,000,000.

2.8 Sectional Views

There will be some instances where, due to the complexity of the internal geometry of the part, a local section will be required to indicate the relationship between the internal and external features. It is allowable to include the local section as part of the orthographic views.

2.9 Lettering, Symbols and Abbreviations

2.9.1 Basic Requirements of Lettering

The lettering style is an important part of engineering drawing. It gives information regarding size and instructions in the form of notes and dimension. It is important that it is readable and clear.

The text is identified by the nominal height (h), and the preferred sizes are listed below in mm:

1,8, 2,8, 3,5, 5,0, 7,0, 10,0, 14,0, 20,0.

The current BS EN ISO stipulates that the comma now replaces the decimal point.

2.9.2 Classification of Lettering

There are two types of lettering most commonly used in engineering drawing viz. Gothic lettering and Roman lettering.

1. Gothic lettering
2. Roman lettering

In Gothic lettering, all the alphabets and numerals are of equal thickness and may be written vertically or in italics.

Roman lettering uses thick and thin line elements and may be written vertically or in italics.

2.9.3 Height of Lettering

The height 'h' of the capital letter is taken as the base of dimensioning.

The main requirement of lettering on engineering drawings are legibility, uniformity, ease and rapidity in execution.

TABLE 2.5

Recommended Sizes of Lettering

Paper Size	Notes & Dimensions	Titles	Headings
A0	3.5	5	7
A1	2.5	3.5	5
A2	2.5	3.5	5
A3	2.5	3.5	5
A4	1.8	2.5	3.5

Both upright and inclined letters are suitable for general use. All letters should be capital, except where lower-case letters are accepted internationally for abbreviations.

Table 2.5 gives the recommended sizes of lettering.

Item	Size h, mm
Drawing number in title block and letters denoting cutting plane section	10, 12
Title of drawing	6, 8
Sub-titles and headings	3, 4, 5, 6
Notes, such as legends, schedules, material list, dimensioning	3, 4, 5
Alteration, entries and tolerances	2, 3

2.10 Dimensioning

The requirement of a drawing is to provide a complete specification of the part ensuring the design will meet all stages of manufacture. Dimensions are essential to specify all features of size, position, geometric control and surface texture required for the part to meet its intended purpose. It should not be necessary for the craftsman to either scale the drawing or deduce any dimensions by the addition or subtraction of other dimensions to determine the position of the feature.

It is important to understand that each dimension stated on the drawing is not an absolute value and will contain some degree of error. The amount of error that is allowable is a decision that has to be made by the designer. The amount of error that is allowable is indicated on the drawing by either a general note or a tolerance applied to individual dimensions (see Section 1.9 for more details of drawing tolerances). As the acceptable tolerance becomes smaller, there will be an impact on the increase in the cost of manufacture.

There are a number of dimensioning methods used to describe size requirements. These methods are discussed in the following sections.

2.10.1 Unidirectional

Unidirectional dimensioning requires that all dimensions, figures and notes are placed horizontally and be read from the bottom of the drawing sheet (see Figure 2.23).

2.10.2 Aligned

Aligned dimensioning requires that all dimensions, figures and notes are aligned with the dimension line to be read from either the bottom or right-hand side of the drawing sheet (see Figure 2.24).

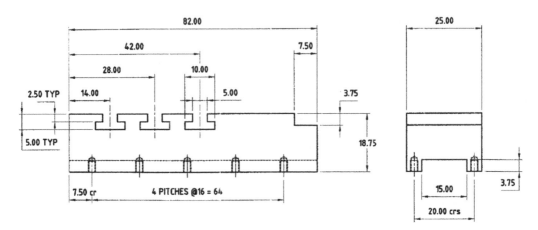

FIGURE 2.23
Unidirectional dimensioning.

2.10.3 Tabular

In tabular dimensioning, the coordinates and sizes of holes and features are given in the form of a table (see Figure 2.25).

British Standards 8888 covers all the ISO rules applicable to dimensioning and if these are adhered to, it is reasonable to expect that the finished drawing will be to a good professional standard.

2.10.4 The Rules for Dimensioning

The following rules should be considered when dimensioning a drawing:

1. Dimensions and extension lines are narrow, continuous lines of a thickness dictated by the size of the drawing and where possible clearly placed outside the outline of the drawing. Ensure the drawing outline is of a thickness defined by the drawing sheet size and gives a clear distinction with the dimension lines.

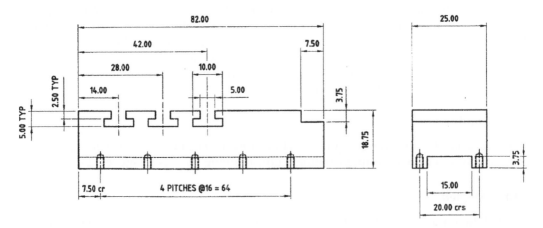

FIGURE 2.24
Aligned dimensioning.

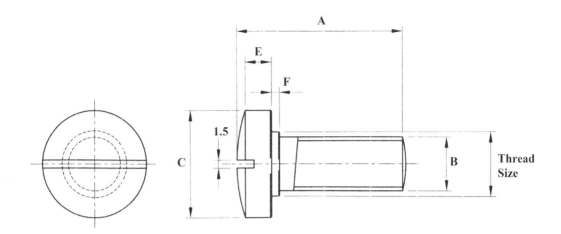

Ident	A	B	C	D	E	F	Thread
	mm	mm	mm	mm	mm	mm	Size
1	16.0	10.0	14.0	1.5	3.5	6.0	M6
2	25.0	12.0	16.0	1.5	4.8	6.0	M8
3	35.0	12.0	20.0	1.5	5.0	9.0	M10

FIGURE 2.25
Tabular dimensioning.

2. The extension lines should not touch the outline of the drawing feature and a small gap should be left between the edge of the dimension line and the edge of the drawing feature, approximately 2 to 3 mm depending on the size of the drawing sheet. The extension line should continue for a similar distance past the dimension line.

3. Arrowheads should be approximately triangular with a length of three units and its width approximately 1 unit. In every case the arrowhead should touch the dimension line to which they refer. Arrowheads should be filled in.

4. Centre lines should never be used as dimension lines and must be left clear and distinct. They can be extended, however, with the use of extension lines.

5. In metric drawings, all dimensions are specified in millimetres. The use of mm should be avoided by giving a general note 'All dimensions are in mm'.
   In the case of decimal dimensions, always use a '0' before the decimal marker. This may not be noticed on a drawing print that has a poor line definition. Hence write 0,5 and not ,5.
   It should be stated that the comma is used as a decimal marker and positioned on the baseline between the figures; for example, 5,2 instead of the previous 5•2 with the decimal marker midway.

6. To enable dimensions to be read clearly they should be placed so that they can be read from the bottom of the drawing, or by turning the drawing in a clockwise direction, so that the dimension can be read from the right-hand side.

7. Datum dimensions should be given from a baseline, an important hole or a finished feature that may be readily established by the inspection department.

8. Dimensions should be quoted once in one view only to minimise the risk of dimensioning misinterpretation.

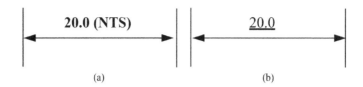

(a)   (b)

FIGURE 2.26
Dimensions not to scale. (a). Not to scale dimension. (b). Alternative method of indicating a 'not to scale' dimension.

9. Overall dimensions should be placed outside the intermediate dimensions.
10. Dimension or extension lines should not cross. Where this is unavoidable the extension line should be broken where it passes over a dimension line.
11. When there are a number of dimension lines, the shorter dimension should be nearer the view.
12. Leaders should not be drawn curved or made free hand.

2.10.5 Features That Are Not Drawn to Scale

In some instances a dimension may have to be modified. Rather than redrawing the drawing it is permissible to underline the dimension, as in Figure 2.26. This is useful where the local dimensional change has no effect on the understanding of the drawing.

2.10.6 Chain Dimensioning

Great care should be taken when considering the use of chain dimensioning in a drawing (Figure 2.27). It should only be used where the accumulation of tolerances will not have a deleterious effect on the component.

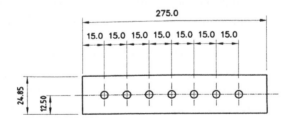

Alternatively, if the hole pitches are equal, the part can be dimensioned as follows.

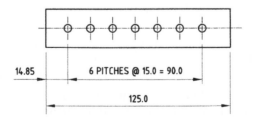

FIGURE 2.27
Chain dimensioning.

2.10.7 Parallel Dimensioning

Positional accuracy is significantly improved by dimensioning more than one feature from a common datum, as shown in Figure 2.28a. It is more prudent to dimension the hole (or feature) from the edge of the component with a single dimension and the parallel dimensions taken from the datum hole (or feature), as depicted in Figure 2.28b.

2.10.8 Running Dimensioning

It is possible to simplify the parallel dimensioning that has the advantage of requiring less drawing space. The common origin is indicated as in Figure 2.29 using a small circle

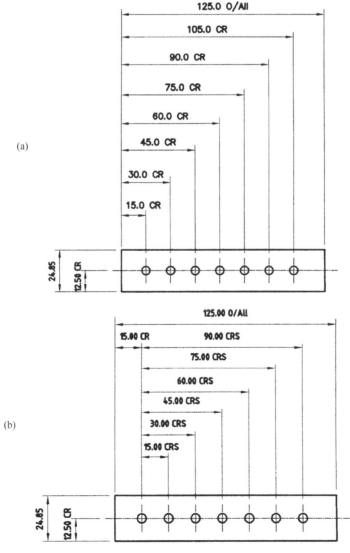

FIGURE 2.28
Parallel dimensioning. (a) Parallel dimensioning from a part edge. (b) Parallel dimensioning from datum feature.

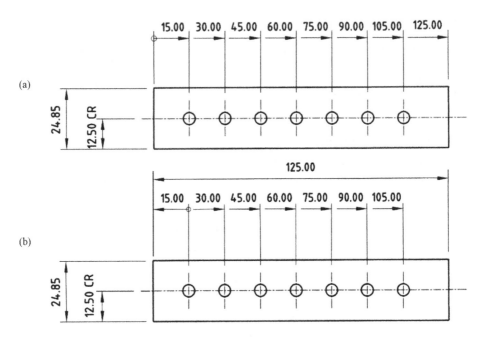

FIGURE 2.29
Running dimensioning. (a) Running dimension from a part edge. (b) Running dimensions from a datum feature.

in place of a dimensional arrow and the subsequent dimensions placed adjacent to the respective arrowheads.

A further method of parallel dimensioning is shown in Figure 2.28 when the feature pitches are equal and an overall dimension is given between the first and last hole (or feature) with a note giving the pitch dimensions.

2.10.9 Staggered Dimensioning

To improve the clarity of a drawing, it may be more convenient to express the dimensions as shown in Figures 2.28a and b. In Figure 2.28, the dimensions are offset from the centre line and it is seen that in the case where a tolerance is applied to the dimension it avoids the dimensions running into each other. In the case of Figure 2.30, this method avoids a number of leader lines, again helping to improve the clarity of the drawing.

2.10.10 Dimensioning Circles and Diameters

When dimensioning diameters, the symbol 'Ø' is placed in front of the dimension text. The symbol should be as large as the text, e.g., Ø120.0. Optional methods of dimensioning diameters are shown in Figure 2.31. The position of the dimension will be dictated by the size of the feature and space available for the dimension.

2.10.11 Dimensioning Radii

Alternate methods of dimensioning radii that do not require the centre to be located is shown in Figure 2.32. In the examples shown, it should be noted that the dimension line is drawn through the centre of the arc (or fillet) and that the arrowhead touches the feature.

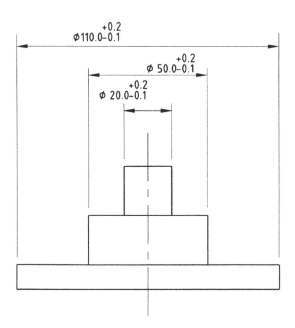

FIGURE 2.30
Staggered dimensioning.

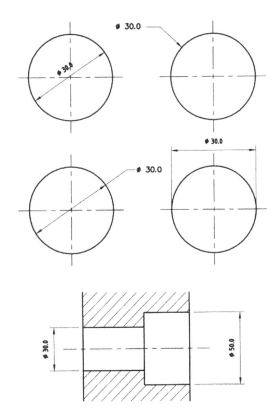

FIGURE 2.31
Dimensioning circles and diameters.

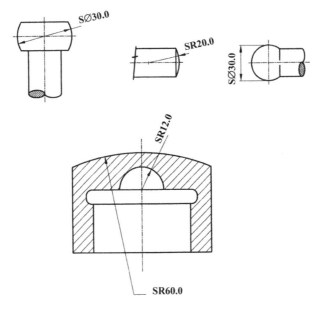

FIGURE 2.32
Dimensioning spherical diameters and radii.

2.10.12 Dimensioning Spherical Radii

Figure 2.32 denotes the method of dimensioning spherical radii. The letter 'S' precedes the symbol 'Ø' (diameter) or the letter 'R' (radii) whichever is appropriate.

2.10.13 Dimensioning Curves

When a curve is constructed from several radii, the radii together with the centres of curvature should be clearly marked as indicated in Figure 2.33.

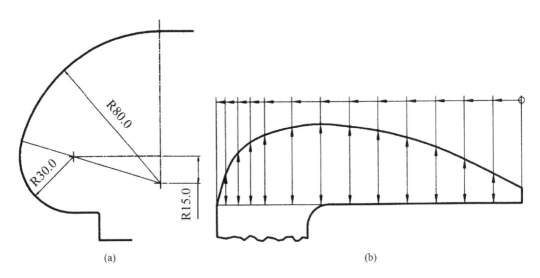

(a)   (b)

FIGURE 2.33
Dimensioning curves. (a) Complex curves. (b) Continuous curve.

2.10.14 Unidirectional and Aligned Dimensions

Unidirectional dimensions are drawn parallel with the bottom edge of the drawing sheet and any associated notes also use this method (Figure 2.34a).

Aligned dimensions are produced in parallel with their related dimension line and the text is positioned such that it can be read from either the bottom of the drawing or from the right-hand side, as shown in Figure 2.34b.

2.10.15 Angular Dimensions

Conventionally, angular dimensions are expressed in the following forms:

1. Degrees, i.e., 40°.
2. Degrees and minutes, i.e., 40° 20′
3. Degrees, minutes and seconds, i.e., 30° 20′ 30″

A full space is left between the degree symbol and the minute symbol and also between the minute and second symbol.

In the situation where the angle is less than 1° it should be preceded by 0°, e.g., 0° 30′.

Various ways the angular dimensions may be shown is depicted in Figure 2.35.

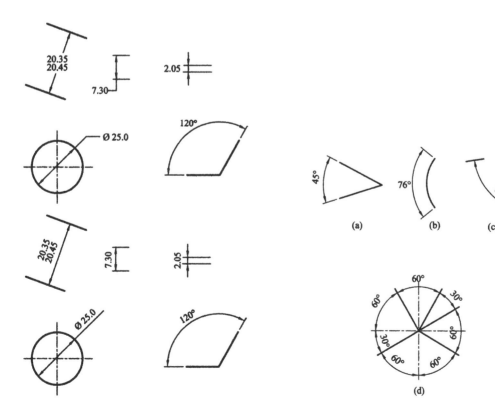

FIGURE 2.34
a and b Unidirectional and aligned dimensions.

FIGURE 2.35
a, b, c and d Angular dimensioning.

2.10.16 Dimensioning Tapers

A tapered feature requires the size, form and position to be defined using one of the following combinations:

1. The rate of taper or the included angle to be specified.
2. Either the diameter or the width at the larger end.
3. The diameter or width at the smaller end to be defined.
4. The length of the tapered feature to be indicated.
5. The diameter or width at a specified cross-section to be specified. This may lie either within or outside the feature concerned.
6. The location dimension from a datum to the cross-section referred to above.

To avoid confusion, only sufficient dimensions should be shown on the drawing as necessary. If a reference dimension is included this should be shown in brackets, i.e., (1:7 taper).

Examples of the methods used to specify the size, form and position of tapered features are shown in Figure 2.36.

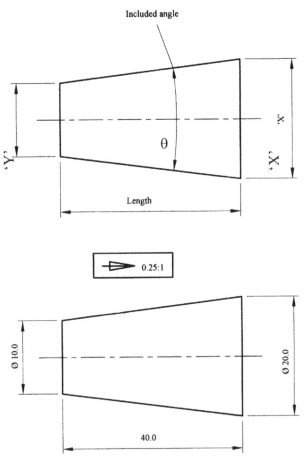

FIGURE 2.36
Dimensioning tapered features.

2.10.17 Dimensioning Two Mating Tapers

In some instances, the tapered feature may be required to fit a corresponding taper in another feature. In this case a note may be added to the drawing with the following information:

1. 'TO FIT PART No. AAA'.
2. 'TO FIT GAUGE (PART No. BB)'.

In the case when note 2 is added to the drawing, it is implied that a specific gauge is to be used that will give acceptable marking when wiped with 'engineering blue'. The functional requirement where the taper is located within the gauge will determine the method and choice of dimensioning.

One example of the dimensioning two mating tapers where the end-wise location is important is shown in Figure 2.37.

Geometric dimensioning and a specified datum is recommended for a more accurate and repeatable location of the taper. See Section 2.12 for further details of geometric dimensioning.

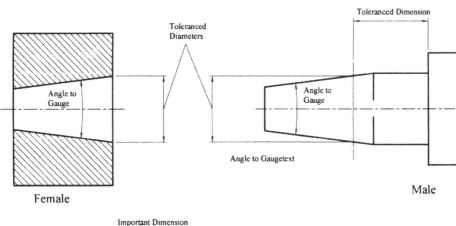

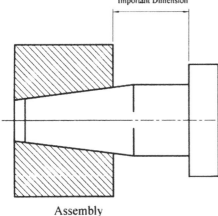

FIGURE 2.37
Dimensioning two mating tapers.

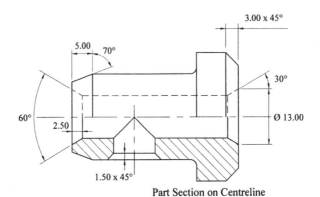

FIGURE 2.38
Dimensioning chamfers.

2.10.18 Dimensioning Chamfers

There are a number of methods for dimensioning either internal or external chamfers and these are presented in Figure 2.38.

2.10.19 Dimensioning Flats or Squares

Where a flat is machined on a circular component as in Figure 2.39a or a square is produced at the end of a shaft as in Figure 2.39b, for rotating using a spanner. A narrow

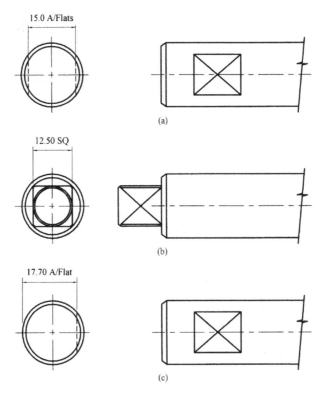

FIGURE 2.39
Dimensioning flats and squares.

diagonal lines are added to indicate a flat surface. When dimensioning such features the abbreviation 'A/F' follows the dimension indicating across flats. In the case where a cotter pin retains the shaft, only a single flat is required and it is dimensioned as indicated in Figure 2.39c.

2.10.20 Dimensioning Holes

Generally holes come in two forms:

1. Plain holes
2. Threaded holes

2.10.20.1 Plain Holes

Plain holes are defined by:

a. Diameter
b. Depth

It is common practice to consider a hole is to be drilled using a conventional fluted drill and the surface finish of the hole to be acceptable 'as finished'. If the surface finish is important then a note is appended to the dimension that the hole should be 'reamed' to ensure that the surface finish is within acceptable standards in such cases where a shouldered bolt is to be fitted or the part is to be located using dowel pins.

Holes to be produced for flanges are generally positioned on a pitch circle and these may be spaced either on the main centre lines of the component, or at angular positions around the centre of the component, as shown in Figure 2.40a and b. Generally, if the part is not required to be explicitly orientated, then the hole pattern can be equally spaced around the pitch circle. Unless there is a requirement that the component is to be 'handed', one of the holes can be produced to ensure the part has to be correctly fitted as indicated in Figure 2.40b.

The depth of a drilled hole unless stated in a note form is generally assumed to go through the material. The depth when specified refers to the cylindrical portion of the hole and does not include the drill point unless explicitly referred to in the note form.

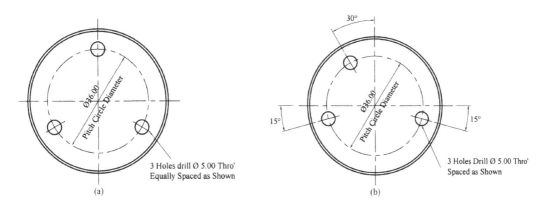

FIGURE 2.40
Dimensioning plain holes. (a). Dimensioning equally spaced holes. (b). Dimensioning unequally spaced holes.

2.10.20.2 Threaded Holes

Threaded holes are predrilled with a tapping drill that is slightly larger than the core diameter of the thread. This is to ensure that the thread of the screw does not 'bind' in the hole.

In most cases it is assumed the tapped hole goes through the material. Where the threaded hole does not clear the material or flange, the depth of the tapping drill is usually 1.5 to 2 pitches deeper than the thread. This allowance is to enable the thread to be produced using threading taps. A typical threaded hole is depicted in Figure 2.41.

2.10.21 Dimensioning Spotfaces, Countersink and Counterbores

Spotfaces, countersinks and counterbores are produced using a drilling machine and all three are dependent upon the accuracy of a predrilled hole.

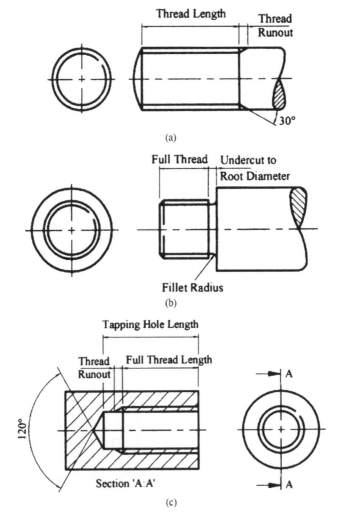

FIGURE 2.41
Dimensioning threaded features. (a) External thread with runout. (b) External thread with undercut. (c) Internal thread.

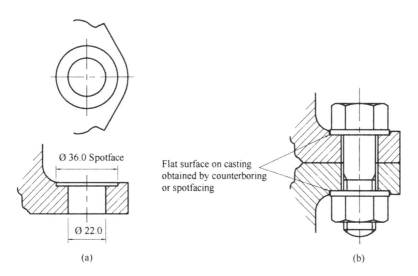

FIGURE 2.42
Dimensioning a spotface.

2.10.21.1 Spotface

A spotface clears material around a hole on a casting to provide a flat surface for a fixing bolt. The method of dimensioning for a spotface is shown in Figure 2.42. Note that the spotface is just sufficient to remove the rough surface over the 35-mm diameter area for a threaded fastener (in this case) to sit on the cast flange.

2.10.21.2 Countersink

Countersinking is carried out to accommodate the heads of countersunk headed screws and rivets. The included angle is usually either 60° or 90° and provides a flush finish for the heads. Figure 2.43 shows typical details for 60° and 90° countersinks.

2.10.21.3 Counterbore

A typical use of a counterbore is to provide a recess for the head of a screw, as depicted in Figure 2.44. The method of dimensioning of a counterbore is shown in Figure 2.45.

Authors Note

When dimensioning for the counterbore of a socket head cap screw, care should be exercised when dimensioning for the clearance hole for the shank of the screw. It is the author's experience that a number of failures involving socket head screws occur when the drilled hole is close fitting to the shank. Figure 2.46 illustrates an example of the interference that would occur under the head of the cap screw where the fillet radius will make contact with the corner of the hole. This generates a stress concentration at the point of contact and further tightening of the screw will generate a stress level that will exceed the strength of the material and lead to a failure with the head shearing off the shank of the screw. This problem will occur in any situation that involves a fillet radius contacting the corner of a close-fitting hole. This type of stress is known as Hertzian contact stresses, and the stresses generated can exceed many times the ultimate compressive stress for the material.

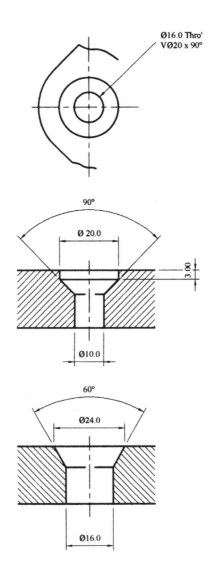

FIGURE 2.43
Dimensioning a countersink.

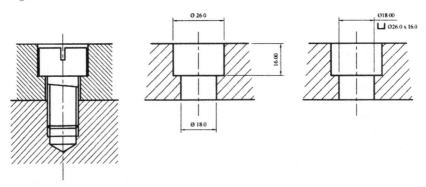

FIGURE 2.44
Dimensioning a counterbore.

gineering Drawing Principles

Engineering Drawing Principles

M16 x 2.0p Socket Head Cap Screw

Ø 26.0

16.00

Ø 17.6 Minimum
Core Drill

Ø17.6

⌴ Ø26.0 x 16.0

FIGURE 2.45
Dimensioning a counterbore for a socket head cap screw.

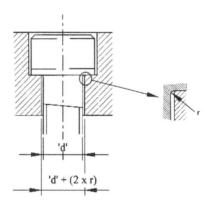

'd'

'd' + (2 x r)

r

Thread Size 'd'	Rad min' 'r'	Clearance Hole 'd' + (2.r)
M1.6	0.1	1.8
M2	0.1	2.2
M2.5	0.1	2.7
M3	0.1	3.2
M4	0.2	4.4
M5	0.2	5.4
M6	0.25	6.5
M8	0.4	8.8
M10	0.4	10.8
M12	0.6	13.2
M16	0.6	17.2
M20	0.8	21.6
M24	0.8	25.6

FIGURE 2.46
Clearance hole for a socket head set screw (fillet radius).

The continental practice is to have a tighter clearance hole and have a small countersink to clear the radius, but it is not easy to machine the depth correctly, and this could lead to either the countersink being too small or too big leading to a reduction of contact land under the socket head.

2.11 Tolerances, Limits and Fits

The early history of using tolerances in engineering manufacture can be attributed to the likes of Colt with the 'Peacemaker' (circa 1873) and Ford with the Model 'T' (circa 1908). Up to this point, craftsmen made individual parts to fit and there was no commitment to interchangeability of parts. The early industrialists recognising the importance of the interchangeability of parts in their visions of mass production took steps to introduce a system of dimensional limits to improve the assembly of parts and reduce costs.

In the United Kingdom, one of the earliest metrology systems developed to standardise structured tolerances was the Newall system. The Newall system provides a range of clearance, transition and interference fits for sizes up to 12″. It is a hole basis system which stipulated two grades of holes, specified with bilateral tolerances, together with 6 grades of shaft tolerances.

This system was superseded by British Standard 1916 which in turn formed the basis of the International Organisation for Standardisation (ISO) 286 198 and 2.1988.

The Newall system is still in limited use today (2018) in a small number of manufacturing organisations.

It has been found that the range covered by the standard can be condensed to a small number of tolerance combinations.

The most commonly applied hole and shaft combinations include:

Selected hole tolerances: H7, H8, H9 and H11.

Selected shaft tolerances: c11, d10, e9, f7, g6, h6, k6, n6, p6, s6 and u6.

The general standard adopted is the basic hole. The measurement of holes is generally controlled using plug gauges having 'go no go' features. Shafts are easily measured using micrometres or gap gauges.

It may be advantageous for a manufacturer to adopt a shaft-based systems in situations where the shaft may be fitted with a variety of accessories including propriety roller bearings, couplings or collars, etc.

Shaft-based systems may also offer advantageous economies where bar-stock material may be available to standard shaft tolerances to the ISO system.

2.11.1 Dimension Tolerances

There are essentially two methods of applying tolerances to dimensions:

- **Universal tolerancing:**
  A general note is added to the drawing stating, 'All tolerances to be within ±0.1 mm'.
      In this case all the features are to be manufactured with their nominal values and the variability allowed are plus or minus (±) 0.1 mm.

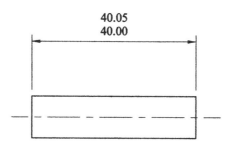

FIGURE 2.47
Alternative toleranced dimension.

The disadvantage of universal tolerancing is that every dimension is subject to this unilateral blanket tolerance and does not take into account any special fitting tolerances such as 'running fits' and fitting of bearings.

A variation of the universal tolerancing is to use different classes of tolerance ranges. One way is the use of the number of zeros after the decimal marker; for example,

Consider all tolerances to be: XX (e.g. 30) means ±0.5 mm.
XX,X (e.g. 30.0) means ±0.1 mm.
XX,XX (e.g. 30.00) means ±0.05 mm.

- **Specific tolerances:**
  To overcome this problem certain critical features have dimensions assigned with specific limits that are different to the universal tolerances. These features may include shafts and spindles that are close running fit.

  An example may include a shaft to be manufactured to a size of 20-mm diameter exactly. The actual final machined size will be slightly different as it is near impossible to machine the shaft to exactly 20-mm diameter; there will always be a tiny variation no matter what machining method is used. If the machine element is to mate with another part, then the dimensions of both parts become important, as they will dictate the nature of the assembly. The allowable variation in the size of the mating parts is called *limits* and the nature of the assembly due to such variations is known as *fits*.

  Figure 2.47 shows a tolerance dimension assigned to a feature, and Figure 2.48 shows alternative ways the tolerance dimension may be displayed.

2.11.2 Limits

The terminologies used to define limits and tolerances are shown in Figure 2.49. The zero line shown in the figure is the basic or nominal size of the feature. For convenience of this discussion, a shaft and a hole combination is chosen to be the mating components.

2.11.2.1 Tolerance

A tolerance is the difference between the maximum and minimum dimensions of a component, i.e., between the upper limit and the lower limit. Depending upon the type of application, the permissible variation of dimension is set as per the tolerance grades (these will be described later in the section).

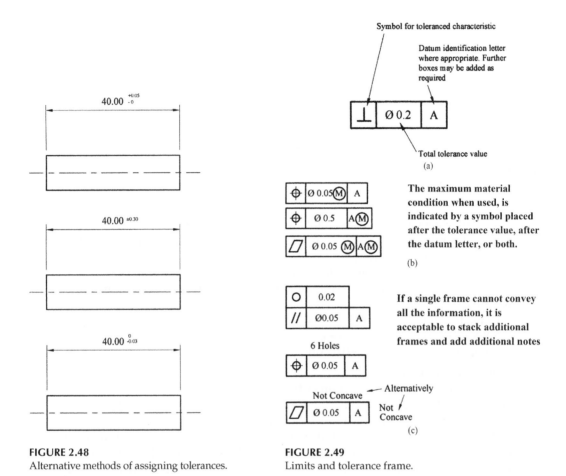

FIGURE 2.48
Alternative methods of assigning tolerances.

FIGURE 2.49
Limits and tolerance frame.

Tolerance is of two types, bilateral and unilateral. When a tolerance is present on both sides of the nominal size, this is termed as bilateral; unilateral tolerance is to one side of the nominal size (see Figure 2.50).

2.11.2.2 Allowance

This is the difference of dimension between two mating parts.

2.11.2.3 Upper Deviation

The upper deviation is the difference of dimension between the maximum possible size of the component and its nominal size.

2.11.2.4 Lower Deviation

Similarly, this is the difference of dimension between the minimum possible size of the component and its nominal size.

2.11.2.5 Fundamental Deviation

This is one of the two deviations which is chosen to define the position of the tolerance zone. Tolerance is defined as the algebraic difference between upper and lower deviations. It is an absolute value.

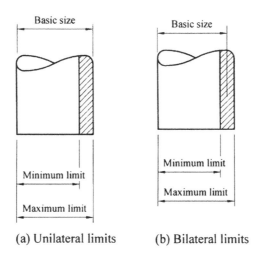

(a) Unilateral limits   (b) Bilateral limits

FIGURE 2.50
Unilateral and bilateral limits.

2.11.3 Fit System

The nature of the assembly of two mating parts can be classified by three types of fit systems:

- Clearance fit
- Transition fit
- Interference fit

These fit systems are shown diagrammatically in Figure 2.51.

There are two ways of representing a fit system. One is the 'hole' basis and the other is the 'shaft' basis. In the hole basis system, the dimension of the hole is considered to be the datum. In the shaft basis system, the shaft is considered to be the datum.

Holes are normally produced by drilling followed by a finishing ream to produce the hole to its finished size. The dimension of the hole is fixed by the nature of the tooling available. The dimension of the shaft is easily controllable using standard manufacturing processes. It is for this reason that the hole-basis system is more popular than the shaft-basis system. Therefore, the hole basis system will only be discussed in the remainder of this section.

2.11.3.1 Clearance Fit

In this fit, the shaft is always smaller than the hole into which it fits (Figure 2.52a).

2.11.3.2 Transition Fit

In this case, the shaft may be either bigger or smaller than the hole into which it fits. It will therefore be possible to have a small degree of interference or clearance in one group of assemblies (as depicted in Figure 2.52b).

2.11.3.3 Interference Fit

In this class of fit, the shaft is always larger than the hole into which it fits; hence, there is always an overlapping of the mating parts, as shown in Figure 2.52c. Interference fit is a form of a tight fit requiring a degree of pressure to achieve a fit between the components.

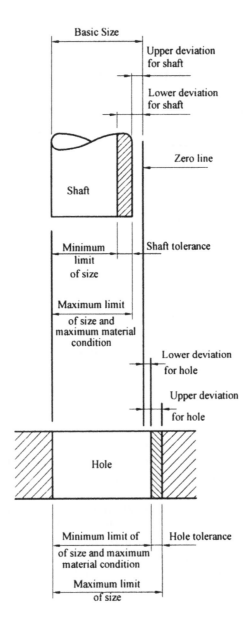

FIGURE 2.51
Terminology used in limits and fits.

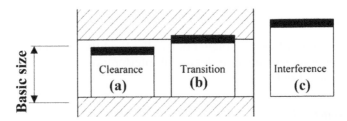

FIGURE 2.52
a, b and c Hole basis fits.

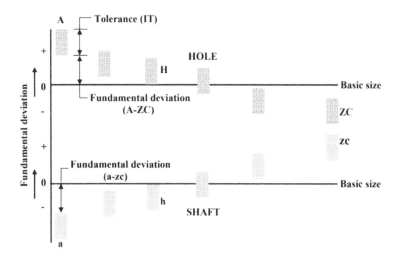

FIGURE 2.53
Schematic view showing standard limits and fits.

2.11.4 Standard Limits and Fits Systems

A schematic view of a standard limits and fits system is shown in Figure 2.53. In this figure tolerances is denoted as IT and there are 18 grades. The fundamental deviations for the hole are denoted by upper-case letters from A to AC having altogether 25 divisions. Correspondingly, the fundamental deviations for the shaft are denoted by lower-case letters from a to zc.

In Figure 2.53, H or h is a typical case, where the fundamental deviation is zero and having a unilateral tolerance of a specified IT grade.

Different elements of a standard limits and fits system are discussed in the following sections.

2.11.4.1 Standard Tolerances

18 grades: IT01, IT0 and IT1–IT 16

2.11.4.2 Fundamental Deviations

25 types: A–ZC (for holes)
a–zc (for shafts)

It is to be noted that the choice of tolerance grade is related to the type of manufacturing process; for example, attainable tolerance grades for lapping are lower than those for plain milling. Similarly, the choice of fundamental deviation will be dependent on the nature of the fit, running fit or tight fit, etc. The approximate zones of fit are shown in Figure 2.54. It is important to bear in mind that manufacturing processes involving lower tolerance zones will be generally costly and as a result the designer has to keep in mind the manufacturing processes to ensure the design is cost effective and inexpensive.

2.11.4.3 Consider the Designation: 50H6/g5

This designation states that the nominal size of the hole and shaft is 50 mm. In this case, 'H' is the nature of the fit for the hole basis system and the fundamental deviation is zero.

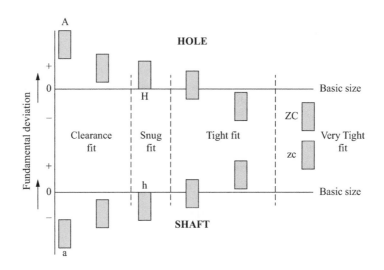

FIGURE 2.54
Zone of fits.

The tolerance grade for making the hole is IT6. For the shaft, the nature of the fit is 'g' where the fundamental deviation is negative, i.e., the dimension is lower than the nominal size and the tolerance grade is IT5.

2.11.4.4 50g6

From the tolerance grade table (Table 2.6), for a basic size of 50.000 mm diameter, the variation between the upper and lower deviations for a grade IT6 will be 0.016 mm and for a grade IT7 will be 0.025 mm.

TABLE 2.6

Tolerance Grade Table

Basic Sizes	Tolerance Grades							
	IT5	IT6	IT7	IT8	IT9	IT10	IT11	IT12
0–3	0.004	0.006	0.010	0.014	0.025	0.040	0.060	0.100
3–6	0.005	0.008	0.012	0.018	0.030	0.048	0.075	0.120
6–10	0.006	0.009	0.015	0.022	0.036	0.058	0.090	0.150
10–18	0.008	0.011	0.018	0.027	0.043	0.070	0.110	0.180
18–30	0.009	0.013	0.021	0.033	0.052	0.084	0.130	0.210
30–50	0.011	0.016	0.025	0.039	0.062	0.100	0.160	0.250
50–80	0.013	0.019	0.030	0.046	0.074	0.120	0.190	0.300
80–120	0.015	0.022	0.035	0.054	0.087	0.140	0.220	0.350
120–180	0.018	0.025	0.040	0.063	0.100	0.160	0.250	0.400
180–250	0.020	0.029	0.046	0.072	0.115	0.185	0.290	0.460
250–315	0.022	0.032	0.052	0.081	0.130	0.210	0.320	0.520
315–400	0.025	0.036	0.057	0.089	0.140	0.230	0.360	0.570
400–500	0.027	0.040	0.063	0.097	0.155	0.250	0.400	0.630

Note: Values in mm.
Source: BS EN 20286-2:1993

From Table 2.7, for Ø50.000 g, the upper deviation is −0.009 mm. The lower deviation will be: −0.009 to 0.016 mm = 0.025 mm.

Hence, the tolerance on a Ø50.000 mm diameter shaft machined to a tolerance grade of g6 is: Ø50.000 mm −0.009/−0.025 mm.

2.11.5 Upper and Lower Deviations

2.11.5.1 Shaft Letter Codes c, d, f, g and h

Upper deviation is equivalent to the fundamental deviation.
Lower deviation is equivalent to:

Upper deviation − Tolerance grade

2.11.5.2 Shaft Letter Codes k, n, p, s and u

Lower deviation is equivalent to the fundamental deviation.
Upper deviation is equivalent to:

Lower deviation + Tolerance grade

TABLE 2.7

Fundamental Deviations for Shafts

Basic Size	Upper Deviation Letter					Lower Deviation Letter				
	c	d	f	g	h	k	n	p	s	u
0–3	−0.060	−0.020	−0.006	−0.002	0	0	0.004	0.006	0.014	0.018
3–6	−0.070	−0.030	−0.010	−0.004	0	0.001	0.008	0.012	0.019	0.023
6–10	−0.080	−0.040	−0.013	−0.005	0	0.001	0.010	0.015	0.023	0.028
10–14	−0.095	−0.050	−0.016	−0.006	0	0.001	0.012	0.018	0.028	0.033
14–18	−0.095	−0.050	−0.016	−0.006	0	0.001	0.012	0.018	0.028	0.033
18–24	−0.110	−0.065	−0.020	−0.007	0	0.002	0.015	0.022	0.035	0.041
24–30	−0.110	−0.065	−0.020	−0.007	0	0.002	0.015	0.022	0.035	0.048
30–40	−0.120	−0.080	−0.025	−0.009	0	0.002	0.017	0.026	0.043	0.060
40–50	−0.130	−0.080	−0.025	−0.009	0	0.002	0.017	0.026	0.043	0.070
50–65	−0.140	−0.100	−0.030	−0.010	0	0.002	0.020	0.032	0.053	0.087
65–80	−0.150	−0.100	−0.030	−0.010	0	0.002	0.020	0.032	0.059	0.102
80–100	−0.170	−0.120	−0.036	−0.012	0	0.003	0.023	0.037	0.071	0.124
100–120	−0.180	−0.120	−0.036	−0.012	0	0.003	0.023	0.037	0.079	0.144
120–140	−0.200	−0.145	−0.043	−0.014	0	0.003	0.027	0.043	0.092	0.170
140–160	−0.210	−0.145	−0.043	−0.014	0	0.003	0.027	0.043	0.100	0.190
160-180	−0.230	−0.145	−0.043	−0.014	0	0.003	0.027	0.043	0.108	0.210
180–200	−0.240	−0.170	−0.050	−0.015	0	0.004	0.031	0.050	0.122	0.236
200–225	−0.260	−0.170	−0.050	−0.015	0	0.004	0.031	0.050	0.130	0.258
225–250	−0.280	−0.170	−0.050	−0.015	0	0.004	0.031	0.050	0.140	0.284
250–280	−0.300	−0.190	−0.056	−0.017	0	0.004	0.034	0.056	0.158	0.315
280–315	−0.330	−0.190	−0.056	−0.017	0	0.004	0.034	0.056	0.170	0.350
315–355	−0.360	−0.210	−0.062	−0.018	0	0.004	0.037	0.062	0.190	0.390
355–400	−0.400	−0.210	−0.062	−0.018	0	0.004	0.037	0.062	0.208	0.435

2.11.5.3 Hole Letter Code 'H'

Lower deviation = 0

Upper deviation = Tolerance grade

2.11.6 Loose Running Fit (Example)

It is required to determine the loose running fit tolerance for a hole and shaft that has a basic diameter of 25.000 mm.

From Table 2.8, the specification for a location clearance fit 25H7/25h6, as detailed in Table 2.9. There are two methods for showing these tolerances.

The first method:

Hole	Shaft
Ø25.000 mm +0.021/−0 mm	Ø25.000 mm +0/+0.031 mm

The second method:

Hole	Shaft
Ø25.000 mm	Ø24.987 mm
Ø25.021 mm	Ø25.000 mm

TABLE 2.8

Fundamental Deviation for Hole

Basic Size	Lower Deviation
	H
0–3	0.000
3–6	0.000
6–10	0.000
10–14	0.000
14–18	0.000
18–24	0.000
24–30	0.000
30–40	0.000
40–50	0.000
50–65	0.000
65–80	0.000
80–100	0.000
100–120	0.000
120–140	0.000
140–160	0.000
160–180	0.000
180–200	0.000
200–225	0.000
225–250	0.000
250–280	0.000
280–315	0.000
315–355	0.000
355–400	0.000

Note: Values in mm.

TABLE 2.9

Preferred Fits Using Basic Hole System

Type of Fit	Symbol	Description
Clearance	H11/ c11	**Loose running fit** For wide commercial tolerance or allowances on external members.
	H9/d9	**Free running fit** Not for use where accuracy is essential but good for large temperature variations, high speed running or heavy journal pressures.
	H8/f7	**Close running fit** For running on accurate machines and for accurate location at moderate speeds and journal pressures.
	H7/g6	**Sliding fit** Where parts are not intended to run freely, but must move and turn freely and locate accurately.
	H7/h6	**Locational clearance fit** Provides a snug fit for location of stationary parts, but can be freely assembled and dismantled.
Transition	H7/k6	**Locational transition fit** For accurate location, a compromise between clearance and interference.
	H7/n6	**Locational transition fit** For more accurate location where greater interference is permissible.
Interference	H7/p6	**Locational interference fit** For parts requiring rigidity and alignment with greater accuracy of location.
	H7/s6	**Medium drive fit** For ordinary steel parts or shrink fit on light sections, the tighter fit is usable with cast iron.
	H7/u6	**Force fit** Suitable for parts that can be highly stressed or for shrink fits where the heavy pressing force required is impracticable.

2.11.7 Surface Finish

One of the limiting features to applying a correct tolerance to a component is the surface finish of the part. It is impractical to apply a close tolerance such as Ø25g6 to a machined shaft that has been turned and has a surface finish of say 12.5 μm.

Table 2.10 gives an indication of the surface finishes that may be obtained by the various manufacturing processes currently found in the majority of machine shops.

2.11.8 Selected ISO Fits – Hole basis

The ISO system provides a wide range of holes and shaft tolerance combinations catering for a great many conditions. Experience has shown that a limited selection of tolerances can cover the majority of fit conditions that are required for normal engineering products. The following selected hole and shaft tolerances have been found to be commonly applied:

Selected hole tolerances: H7, H8, H9, H11

Selected shaft tolerances: C11, d10, e9, f7, g6, h6, k6, n6, p6 and s6

Table 2.11 is a copy extracted from BS4500A and B and show the selected ISO fits for both hole and shaft basis. From the table it is readily seen that it covers from loose clearances to heavy interference and may be found to be suitable for most normal applications.

In some instances, users may find that their needs are met using a further selection within this range.

TABLE 2.10

Surface Texture Obtained by Machining Operations

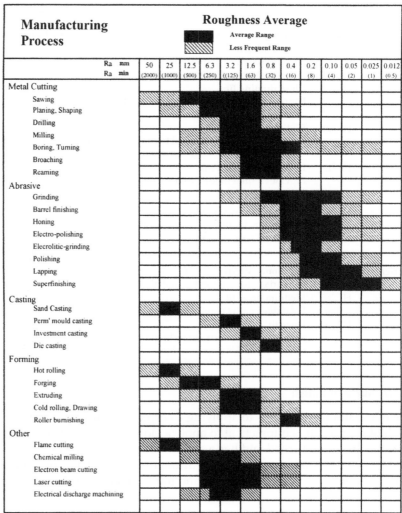

TABLE 2.11

Hole and Shaft Sizes for Location Clearance Fit (H7/h6)

	Hole	Shaft
Tolerance grade	0.021	0.013
Upper deviation	0.021	0.000
Lower deviation	0.000	−0.013
Maximum diameter	25.021	25.000
Minimum diameter	25.000	24.987
Average diameter	25.011	24.994
Maximum clearance	$C_{max} = D_{max} - d_{min} = (25.021 - 24.987) = 0.034$	
Minimum clearance	$C_{min} = D_{min} - d_{max} = (25.000 - 25.000) = 0.000$	

Note: Copied from BS 4500A.

2.11.9 Interpretation of Limits of Size in Relation to Form

There are two methods of interpreting the limits of size of an individual feature which is known as:

1. *The Principle of Independency* where the limits of size apply to local two-point measurements of a feature regardless of the form.

2. *The Envelope Requirements* also known as the Taylor principle, where the limits of size of an individual feature is intended to have a mutual dependency of size and form.

The Principle of Independency is illustrated in Figures 2.55a, b and c.
Figures 2.56a, b, c, d and e illustrate the Envelope Requirements.
The drawing indication in Figure 2.55a shows a linear tolerance followed by the symbol.
Two functional requirements are implied by the use of the symbol.

1. That the surface of the cylindrical feature is contained within the envelope of perfect format the maximum material size of (in this case) Ø120.00

2. That no actual local size shall be less than Ø119.96. An exaggerated view of the feature in Figure 2.55b shows that each actual local diameter of the shaft must remain within the size tolerance of 0.04 and may vary between Ø120.00 and Ø119.96

In the examples that follow, the entire shaft must remain within the boundary of the Ø129.00 envelope cylinder of the perfect form.

It follows, therefore, that the shaft will be perfectly cylindrical when all actual local diameters are at the maximum material size of Ø120.00.

Maximum material condition. It is recommended that ISO 2692 is studied in which it states that: if for functional and economic reasons there is a requirement for the mutual dependency of the size and orientation or location of the feature(s), then the maximum material principle may be applied.

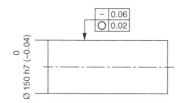

Tolerancing principle ISO 8015

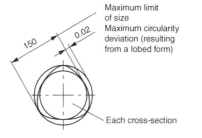

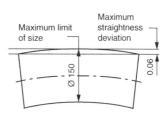

FIGURE 2.55
Principle of independency.

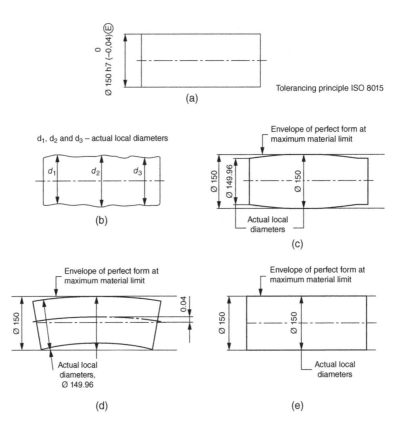

FIGURE 2.56
Envelope requirements.

2.12 Geometrical Dimensioning and Tolerances

2.12.1 Early History

The origin of Geometrical Dimensioning and Tolerances (GD&T) has been credited to a man named Stanley Parker, who in 1938 developed the concept of position or 'true position' as it is referred to today. Mr. Parker, by all accounts, worked in the Royal Torpedo Factory in Alexandria, Scotland.

During his time he encountered individual parts for torpedoes, manufactured in various parts of the country, which were rejected when inspected using traditional tolerance methods. However, he found that many were functional parts and were being sent to production even though they were technically out of specification tolerance. Upon further investigation, he determined that the standard X-Y coordinate tolerances resulted in a square tolerance zone. Some of the dimensions of the working parts fell slightly outside of this zone but were within a circle that encompassed the square's corners. He surmised that if the corners were in spec, in most cases the parts that fell within that circular zone resulting from the application of the same tolerance were just as functional. Mr. Parker later published a book in 1956 entitled *Drawings and Dimensions*. Mr. Parker's determination of position (or true position) has since grown to include other concepts including flatness, profile, run-out, roundness and much more.

The concept of GD&T was adopted by the military in the 1950s and is now in use in multiple industries around the world.

2.12.2 Introduction

GD&T is a symbolic language and is used to specify the shape, size, form, orientation and location of features on a component. Features toleranced using GD&T reflect the actual relationship between mating parts. Drawings having correctly applied geometric tolerancing provide the best opportunity for uniform interpretation and cost-effective assembly. GD&T was created to ensure the correct assembly of mating parts to improve quality and reduce cost. It must be remembered that GD&T is foremost a design tool and before designers can properly apply geometric tolerancing, they must carefully consider the fit and function of each feature of every part.

GD&T can be considered as a checklist to remind the designers to consider all aspects of each feature. Correctly applied geometric tolerancing ensures that each part will assemble every time and allow the designer to specify the maximum available tolerance resulting in the most economical parts.

2.12.3 Application

The application of geometrical tolerances is over and above the normal diametrical tolerances when it is necessary to be more precise regarding the form or shape of a feature of a manufactured part. In the past, the desired qualities would have been covered by a note added to the drawing including expressions such as 'surfaces to be true with one another' or 'surfaces to be flat and parallel', leaving it to the machine shop to provide a satisfactory interpretation of the requirement.

Geometrical tolerances should only be specified when they are essential, otherwise manufacturing and inspection costs will increase. Tolerances should be as large as possible, subject to the design requirements being met. As the GD&T symbols are internationally agreed (see ISO 1101), language problems will not occur. The use of geometrical tolerances does not imply that any particular method of production or inspection is to be used.

2.12.4 Geometrical and Dimensioning and Tolerances

An example of errors of form is shown in Figure 2.57 in which a pin is to fit a bored hole in a block. It is possible to manufacture the parts to the dimensional tolerances specified

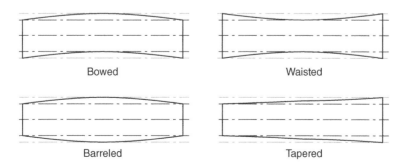

Bowed   Waisted

Barreled   Tapered

FIGURE 2.57
Example of error of form.

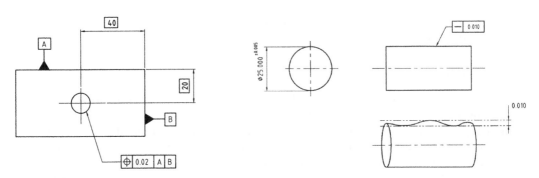

FIGURE 2.58
Example of geometric dimensioning tolerancing.

FIGURE 2.59
A typical tolerance frame showing straightness.

and still discover that the parts will not assemble together as intended. The examples are shown greatly exaggerated for the purposes of illustration.

A further example of geometrical dimensioning and tolerances is shown in Figure 2.58, where the position of the hole is located in respect with the two orthogonal datum faces using boxed dimensions.

2.12.5 Tolerance Frame

Figure 2.59 shows a typical tolerance frame as displayed on drawings indicating a geometrical tolerance.

1. In the first box, the symbol for the characteristic being toleranced is given.
2. The next box contains the tolerance value in the units as used for the linear dimensions. If the tolerance zone is circular or cylindrical, the symbol 'Ø' appears before the tolerance value.
3. The third and succeeding box contains the letters indicating the datum feature or features where there is more than one datum.

Capital letters including 'M', 'P' or 'E' may also appear in the tolerance frame as appropriate, indicating:

- Maximum material condition qualification
- Projected tolerance zone
- Envelope requirements

An example of the maximum material condition is shown in Figure 2.58.

2.13 Examples of the Applications of Geometrical Tolerances

In this section, several examples will be given of the applications of the characteristics on engineering drawings by providing a product requirement and showing the appropriate drawing instruction that needs to be added to the drawing. In the examples shown, the tolerance values shown are only typical figures. The product designer would normally be responsible for selecting these tolerance values.

2.13.1 Straightness

Straightness actually has two very different functions in GD&T depending on how it is called out. In its normal form or surface straightness, is a tolerance that controls the form of a line somewhere on the surface or the feature. Axis straightness is a tolerance that controls how much curve is allowed in the part's axis.

Figure 2.59 shows the symbol for straightness. This is a small straight line.

2.13.2 Flatness

Flatness is a form of control. The flatness control defines how much a surface on a real part may deviate from the ideal flat plane. Tolerance zone: The flatness tolerance zone is the volume between two parallel planes. The distance between the parallel planes is the stated flatness control tolerance value.

To apply a flatness control to a surface, the *Feature Control Frame* (FCF) may point to the surface, or can point to or rest on the extension line that extends from the surface, as indicated in Figure 2.60. The FCF is placed in the view where the surface is viewed as a line. The FCF shown below applies a flatness tolerance to the entire surface. This surface must lie between two parallel planes that are spaced 0.2 mm apart.

2.13.3 Circularity

The circularity symbol is used to describe how close an object should be to a true circle. Sometimes called roundness, circularity is a two-dimensional tolerance that controls the overall form of a circle ensuring it is not too oblong, square or out of round. This tolerance feature is usually displayed on a drawing as shown in Figure 2.61.

2.13.4 Cylindricity

Cylindricity is a three-dimensional tolerance that controls the overall form of a cylindrical feature to ensure that it is round enough and straight enough along its axis. Cylindricity is

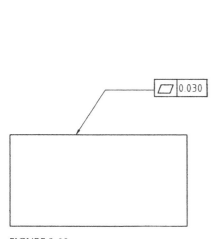

FIGURE 2.60
Example of flatness control.

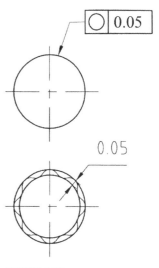

FIGURE 2.61
Example of circularity.

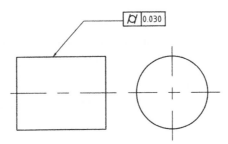

FIGURE 2.62
Example of cylindricity.

independent of any datum feature the tolerance needs to be less than the diameter dimensional tolerance of the part. An example is shown in Figure 2.62.

2.13.5 Profile of a Surface

The profile tolerance of a surface is used to control the ideal form of a surface, this is defined by theoretically exact boxed dimensions and accompanied by a relative-tolerance zone. The tolerance zone, unless and otherwise stated, is taken as a bilateral and is equally disposed about its true-form surface.

An example of a profile tolerance is shown in Figure 2.63. The figure shows the profile tolerance applied to a curved surface. The boxed symbols can be read 'with respect to

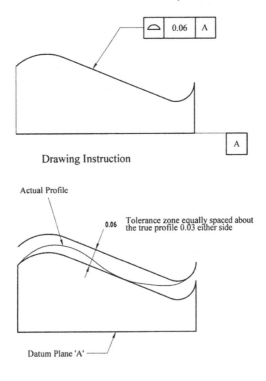

FIGURE 2.63
Profile of a surface.

datum A, this surface must lie between two surface boundaries 0.8 mm apart and spaced equally about the true (or ideal) surface profile'.

2.14 Maximum Material and Least Material Principles

2.14.1 Maximum Material Conditions and Least Material Condition

In GD&T, **maximum material condition (MMC)** refers to a *feature-of-size* that contains the greatest amount of material, yet remains within its tolerance zone. Some examples of MMC include:

- Largest pin diameter
- Smallest hole size

In contrast, **least material condition (LMC)** refers to a feature of size containing the least amount of material, yet remains within its tolerance zone:

- Smallest pin diameter
- Largest hole size

The MMC and LMC symbols are, respectively, the letter M or L inside of a circle. An example use of the MMC symbol applied to a part is shown in Figure 2.64. The boxed symbols can be read as 'the position of these two holes may vary within a cylindrical tolerance zone of 0.1 relative to datums A, B, and C when the holes are at their maximum material condition'. In this case, the maximum material condition for the holes would be at 2.75, or the smallest hole. If the holes were not at their MMC, the GD&T tolerance would be given a bonus tolerance, effectively increasing the position tolerance of the holes.

Consider a Ø25.00/25.10 mm hole having a positional tolerance frame as shown in Figure 2.65. The limit tolerance indicates that the hole size can be as small as Ø25.00 mm (maximum material condition) and as large as Ø25.20 mm (least material condition). The geometric tolerance specifies that the hole can be positioned with a cylindrical tolerance zone of 0.35 mm in diameter when the hole is produced at its maximum material condition. The tolerance zone is orientated perpendicular to datum 'A' and located with basic dimensions to

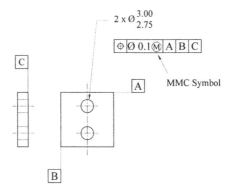

FIGURE 2.64
Example of maximum material condition.

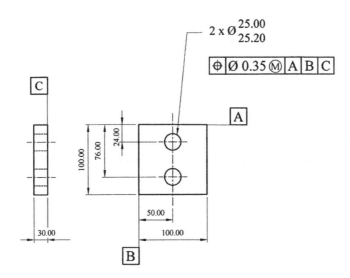

FIGURE 2.65
Positional tolerance applied to a Ø25.00 hole.

datums 'B' and 'C'. As the hole size in Figure 2.65 departs from the maximum material condition to the least material condition, an additional location tolerance, referred to as bonus tolerance, is allowed which is equal to the difference between the maximum material condition and the actual size. If the hole specified by the feature control frame is actually machined as a diameter of 25.15 mm, the total available tolerance is a diameter of 0.50 mm.

Actual feature size: 25.15 mm
Minus the maximum material condition: –25.00 mm
Bonus tolerance: 0.15 mm
Plus the geometrical tolerance: +0.35 mm
Total tolerance: 0.50 mm
The maximum material condition modifier allows the designer to capture all the available tolerance.

2.15 Surface Finish

2.15.1 Introduction

In mechanical engineering, surface finish is an important subject as it controls the degree of friction existing between two surfaces as well as the aesthetic finish of a surface. It also depends upon the degree of accuracy of the component tolerances (Section 1.13).

Table 2.12 gives the surface roughness values that is obtainable using standard manufacturing processes available in most workshops. Surface finish is also known as surface texture or surface topography and is defined by three characteristics: (See Figure 2.66)

- Surface roughness
- Lay
- Waviness

TABLE 2.12

Surface Roughness Values Obtainable Using Standard Manufacturing Processes

	Manufacturing Process	Normally Obtainable	Obtainable with Difficulty	Roughing
Casting	Sand casting	6.3–12.5	0.8–1.6	
	Permanent mould	1.6–6.3		12.5–25
	Die casting	0.8–3.2		
Mechanical	Forging	3.2–25	1.6–3.2	
	Extrusion	0.8–6.3	0.4–0.8	
	Rolling	0.8–3.2	0.4–0.8	
Surface process	Flame cut	25–50		
	Hack saw	6.3–50		
	Band saw	3.2–50		
	Filing	1.6–12.5	0.8–1.6	
	Emery polish	0.4–1.6	0.1–0.4	1.6–3.2
Machining	Shell milling	3.2–25	1.6–3.2	25–50
	Drilling	6.3–25	3.2–6.3	
	Planning and shaping	1.6–12.5		
	Face milling	1.6–12.5	0.8–1.6	12.5–50
	Turning	1.6–6.3	0.2–1.6	6.3–50
	Boring	1.6–6.3	0.2–1.6	6.3–50
	Reaming	0.8–6.3	0.4–0.8	6.3–12.5
	Cylindrical grinding	0.4–3.2	0.025–0.4	3.2–6.3
	Centreless grinding	0.4–3.2	0.05–0.4	
	Internal grinding	0.4–3.2	0.024–0.4	3.2–6.3
	Surface grinding	0.4–3.2	0.025–0.4	3.2–6.3
	Broaching	0.8–3.2	0.2–0.8	3.2–6.3
	Super finishing	0.1–0.4	0.025–0.1	
	Honing	0.1–0.4	0.025–0.1	
	Lapping	0.05–0.4	0.006–0.05	
Gear manufacture	Milling. Spiral bevel	3.2–12.5	1.6–3.2	12.5–25
	Milling with form cutter	3.2–12.5	1.6–3.2	12.5–50
	Hobbing	3.2–12.5	0.8–3.2	12.5–50
	Shaping	1.6–12.5	0.4–1.6	12.5–250
	Planning	1.6–18.5	0.4–1.6	12.5–50
	Shaving	0.8–3.2	0.4–0.8	
	Grinding (criss-cross)	0.8–1.6	0.4–0.8	
	Grinding	0.4–0.8	0.1–0.4	
	Lapping	0.2–0.8	0.05–0.2	

Note: All values in micrometre.

These are small local surface deviations from a perfectly flat ideal plane. As already indicated, surface texture is one of the important factors that control friction between surfaces during sliding. Surface textures can be either isotropic or anisotropic. The stick-slip friction phenomenon has been observed during sliding dependent upon the surface texture.

Not surprisingly, manufacturing processes produces many kinds of surface texture and may require an additional process to modify the initial texture, including grinding (abrasive cutting), polishing, lapping, abrasive blasting honing or other processes.

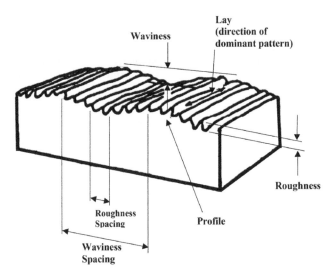

FIGURE 2.66
Characteristics of surface finish.

Table 2.13 shows a comparison chart for ISO Grade Numbers from N1 to N12 and gives the equivalence between the roughness value in mm, Root Mean Square (RMS) and Centre Line Average (CLA) together with the roughness. These are the most common methods of measuring surface roughness.

2.15.2 Types of Surface Finish

2.15.2.1 Surface Roughness

This is usually shortened to roughness and is the measure of the surface irregularities produced by the engineering machining processes. This is generally referred to as 'surface finish'.

TABLE 2.13

Comparison Chart for ISO Grade Numbers

ISO Grade Number	Roughness Value	Roughness Value	Root Mean Square	Centre Line Average	Roughness
N	Ra	Ra	RMS	CLA	Rt
	(mm)	(in)			(mm)
N1	0.025	1	1.1	1	0.3
N2	0.05	2	2.2	2	0.5
N3	0.1	4	4.4	4	0.8
N4	0.2	8	8.8	8	1.2
N5	0.4	16	17.6	16	2
N6	0.8	32	32.5	32	4
N7	1.6	63	64.3	6.3	8
N8	3.2	125	137.5	125	13
N9	6.3	250	275	250	25
N10	12.5	500	550	500	50
N11	25	1000	1100	1000	100
N12	50	2000	2200	2000	200

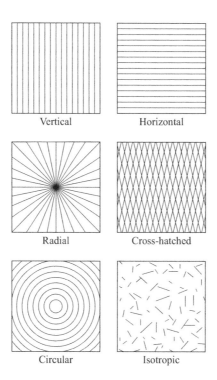

FIGURE 2.67
Various lay patterns.

2.15.2.2 Waviness

Waviness is the measure of the surface irregularities that occur, and the spacing is greater than the surface roughness. These irregularities can occur due to vibration, deflections during machining.

2.15.2.3 Lay

Lay is the direction of the predominant surface pattern generated by the various machining processes. Figure 2.67 shows a selection of various lay patterns produced by different machining processes.

2.15.3 Methods of Indicating Surface Finish and Texture

2.15.3.1 Graphical Symbols to Indicate Surface Texture

The basic graphical symbol is shown in Figure 2.68. The centre line between the lines of unequal length is positioned square to the required surface.

This symbol indicates a surface texture obtained by any manufacturing process (e.g. turning, grinding, plating).

Figure 2.69 is for a surface texture obtained by material removal by machining operation (e.g. turning, drilling, milling, slotting). Note that figure 2.69 is same as table 2.10, which is repeated here for the sake of convenience.

Surface texture obtained WITHOUT removal of material (e.g. casting surfaces, welding faces, procurement size surface) is shown in Figure 2.70.

Symbol	Name	Description
	Basic Symbol	Surface texture obtained by any manufacturing process (e.g., turning, grinding, plating, bending)
	Material Removal by machining required	Surface texture obtained by material removal by machining Operation (e.g., turning, drilling, Milling, slotting)
	Material removal not permitted	Surface texture obtained by WITHOUT removal of material (e.g., casting surfaces, welding faces, Procurement size surface)
	The same finish for all surfaces	Surface finish the same for all surfaces

FIGURE 2.68
Graphical symbols indicating surface finish.

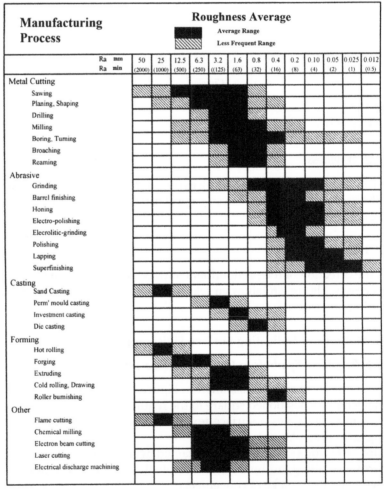

FIGURE 2.69
Surface texture obtained by machining operations.

	Ra	50	25	12.5	6.3	3.2	1.6	0.8	0.4	0.2	0.10	0.05	0.025	0.012
	Ra	(2000)	(1000)	(500)	(250)	((125)	(63)	(32)	(16)	(8)	(4)	(2)	(1)	(0.5)
Non-Machining Operations														
Flame cutting		▨	■	▨										
Chemical milling				▨	■	■	▨							
Electron beam cutting					■	■	■	▨	▨					
Laser cutting					■	■	■	▨	▨					
Electrical discharge machining				▨	▨		▨							

FIGURE 2.70
Surface texture obtained by non-machining operations.

With the exception of the symbol of 'Without removal of material', both the other symbols are defined with value of Ra required for a particular manufacturing process.

Meaning of complete surface finish symbol is given below and in Figure 2.71.

a = Roughness value Ra in micrometre or grade number

b = Production method, treatment or coating

c = Sampling length

d = Direction of lay

e = Machining allowance

f = Other roughness value than Ra

2.16 Checking Drawings

2.16.1 Drawing Numbering

This will follow the standard laid down by the chief draughtsman.

2.16.2 Format for Checking Drawings

These include the basic checking procedures:

- Check title block
- Check the drawing number
- Revisions and description
- Scale

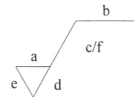

FIGURE 2.71
Complete description of surface finish symbol.

2.16.3 Read Notes

- Check spelling
- Special instructions (heat treatment, test pressures)
- Torque values (check callouts are correct)
- If engineering notes are referenced check that they are called out correctly

2.16.4 Detailed Drawings

- Material, specification and sizes
- All views are orthogonal and placed correctly
- Check overall sizes, length, width and thicknesses
- Check that British Standards are correctly interpreted
- Check that all dimensions on all parts correspond to dimensions on all mating parts
- Undertake a tolerance stack up and ensure it is within the tolerance limit

2.16.5 Assembly Drawings

- Check title block and notes
- Check each item in the parts list (BOM) and make sure that the quantities and item numbers correspond
- All views should be orthogonal and correctly positioned
- Follow assembly instructions to see that all the information is correct and understandable
- Check all referenced dimensions
- Check that all views have corresponding scales unless specified differently
- Make sure all mating parts dimensions are correct
- Carry out a tolerance stack up and ensure it stays within the tolerance limit

2.16.6 General Draughting Rules

- Do not overcrowd a drawing, use additional sheets if required
- Unless it is not possible, all sections shall be in line with their parent view
- Do not dimension to a hidden line
- Do not place a dimension inside geometry
- All circle and cylinders shall have centre lines
- Maintain consistency, e.g., note call outs, dimension size, features, etc.
- Confirm if all company and British Standards have been adhered to
- Confirm if all assembly drawings to have the weight have been called out

3

The Engineering Design Process

3.1 Introduction

Designing a mechanical artefact is a complex process and will require a significant financial and resource commitment to achieve a successful marketable product.

The following text will give the engineering designer a better understanding of the design process to achieve this. It is specifically aimed for the mechanical engineering designer although the principles will be applicable to a number of activities including electrical and electronic design.

In this chapter, the design activities have been laid out in a sequence (see Figure 3.1). It is not proposed that this procedure should be slavishly followed; some parts can be amended as the reader gains experience with the method.

As with any design activity it has to be started with a 'need'. It is said that 'necessity is the mother of invention'; examples range from a device required by an old lady with arthritic fingers to allow her to open a tight bottle top to a facility for processing nuclear waste. This need is generally identified from a market requirement.

A brief description of the basic sequence is discussed next and will be amplified in the following sections.

3.1.2 Design Specification

On receipt of the marketing report requesting a design study, the project engineer will raise a product design specification (PDS) in which every part of the proposed design will be carefully reviewed. The PDS will be incomplete to begin with and will be completed as the design progresses.

3.1.3 Concept Development

The design engineer allocated to the project will prepare sketches of the concepts that will fulfil the design requirements.

These concepts will be studied by the management and all risks will be considered before making a final decision on which concept to adopt.

3.1.4 Feasibility Assessment

A feasibility study will also be undertaken to establish the proposed design requirements.

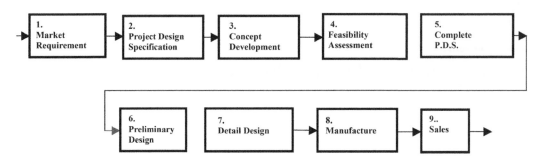

FIGURE 3.1
A basic design sequence.

3.1.5 Complete PDS

At this stage there will be sufficient information available to complete the PDS.

3.1.6 Preliminary Design

The preliminary design will now be completed and will be carefully reviewed in the first of the scheduled design reviews.

3.1.7 Detail Design

Detailed drawings will now be started, taking into account all the statements within the PDS.

3.1.8 Manufacture

All the component and assembly drawings will be studied by the production engineers and they will comment on all aspects of the design. All 'marked up' drawings will be returned to the drawing office for these comments to be incorporated.

3.1.9 Marketing and Sales

The sales department will have sight of the completed design to allow them to begin their development of the marketing strategy and sales literature.

3.2 Classification of Design

Engineering design may be classified in the following areas:

3.2.1 Adaptive Design

This is a design based upon an existing design using a basic product or system that is being adapted for a new application. As an example, a lathe manufacturer extends the centre distance of the lathe to satisfy a prospective customer.

3.2.2 Development Design

In this case, the design starts with an existing design, but a modified design emerges. For example, when Ford owned Jaguar Land Rover, a new design of body was developed and it was merged with a current Ford Mondeo design using the existing transmission and running gear.

3.2.3 New Design

In this case, the design is entirely new without any reference to any previous design, but it is based on existing scientific concepts. No scientific invention is involved; it only requires a creative thought to solve a problem. For example, an engine manufacturer designs a small low-cost engine to serve an emerging market of new garden machinery.

3.2.4 Rational Design

This is based on determining the stresses and strains and determining the shape of the component that can contain these stresses and displacements without any failure occurring. An example would be an engine connecting rod having to transmit the loads and forces generated by the burning of fuel in the combustion chamber and transmitting this force to the crankshaft.

3.2.5 Empirical Design

This type of design is based on using empirical formula which in turn is developed from experiments and experience. A typical example is the torque required to tighten a large nut on a bolt,

$$T = K D F$$

where T = Torque (N.m)

  K = Nut factor (ranges from 0.03 to 0.35)
  D = Nominal diameter (mm)
  F = Force (N)

The design office will have conducted experiments on a wide range of bolt sizes and degrees of lubrication.

3.2.6 Industrial Design

This is a design specifically aimed at the consumer market such as white goods, i.e., washing machines and similar products where style is paramount to attract the customer. The engineering is dictated by the shape and has its own problems for the engineering designer.

3.2.7 Product Design

There is very little difference between engineering and product design, as they both follow the same principles of methodology. Where engineering design concentrates on industrial aspects, product design considers the human aspects of the product.

3.2.8 Optimum Design

This type of design is more mathematical and is based on differential equations to find the most optimal design in terms of a wide range of criteria. Examples would be the design of a racing cycle frame to minimise weight and maximise strength.

3.2.9 System Design

Systems design is the process of defining the architecture, modules, interfaces and data for a system to satisfy a specific requirement. Systems design could be seen as the application of systems theory to product development.

3.2.10 Tooling Design

This is a specialised area of manufacturing engineering which comprises the analysis, planning, design, construction and application of tools, and methods and procedures necessary to improve manufacturing productivity. An example would be the design of 'preset' tooling for use on a Multi-Axis Machining Centre.

3.3 New Design Requirements

3.3.1 Update an Existing Product

There may be a number of compelling reasons to update an existing design or product:

1. An existing material used in the construction of the product has become obsolete; therefore, requiring a material change or update in which case the company decides if it is an ideal opportunity to revisit the design to see if there are any further improvements to be made.
2. An unpredictable failure of a product has occurred requiring an immediate redesign.
3. The service department has identified an area of the design or product that is in need of improvement to minimise any future problems or potential failures.
4. The product is losing its share of the market and is being overtaken by more innovative designs.
5. The company has invested or is investing in new up-to-date machinery including 3-, 4- or 5-axis machinery, this enables more complex shapes to be produced easily thereby reducing the need to fabricate certain complex-shaped components leading to reduced production costs.

3.3.2 New Product

The company wishes to expand its range of products to capture a wider share of the market. Initial market research has identified a potential market for a product not currently being manufactured or marketed.

A good example is a small company that manufactures a range of garden irrigation products. Its marketing department has identified a further range of products that is complementary to the current range and it sees an opportunity to capture a greater share of the garden supplies market. Over a period of time with careful control, the company sees a gradual growth in its market share.

3.3.3 Market Research

In this chapter the basic preliminary research needed to determine the potential market for a new product will be considered.

3.3.3.1 Preliminary Market Research

Consider that the management has conceived a new product and wishes to establish if there is a marketing opportunity for the new product.

3.3.3.2 Review Current Competitors and Products

The initial step is to determine the current competition and their position within the marketplace. If the subsequent report is favourable, the company has the options of taking the market research further. This work can be supported by either an internal marketing department, or the work can be outsourced to a specialised market research company.

3.3.3.3 Is There a Marketing Opportunity?

Following this initial examination of the market, the company will have to consider a few hard facts:

1. Does the new product have any significant advantages over any other product currently in the marketplace?
2. How financially strong are the competitors? As these companies already established their strategy may be to reduce the purchase price of their product to undermine your new product entry into the market to try and maintain their market share.
3. Does the company have the resources and finances to sustain a long-term fight to capture the market lead?

If the answers to these questions are positive, then the engineering design office will be involved in preparing the initial designs for evaluation.

3.3.4 Initial Design Review

Prior to the initial design review, the design office will have prepared a number of potential design solutions based upon the initial specification generated by the marketing department.

The initial design review will normally be chaired by a senior member of the company, notably its design/engineering director; the remainder of the review panel will be represented by managers of the engineering, financial, marketing and production departments.

The purpose of this design review is to acquaint all departments of the potential of the new product or design and allow them to voice any potential problems that are likely to arise in introducing the new product into the manufacturing schedule. As an example, the production department may be operating at near-full capacity to maintain the current production schedule and will require either an additional production plant or floor area to accommodate the new product. The choice will be to either negotiate the purchase of additional land or purchase a separate production facility.

At this stage, it is not the purpose of this design review to determine which design will be selected; this selection process will be considered in the next stage, the preliminary design review.

3.3.5 Preliminary Design Review

The purpose of this design review is to establish the design requirements and objectives. The main intention is to begin completing the preliminary 'Product Design Specification' (PDS). This can be considered as a 'wish list', i.e., objectives, and what specific design features are thought to be constrained. Generally, performance-related criteria are considered constraints, i.e., must be sustained; for example, a new hydraulic press must be able to generate a force of 100 tonnes to produce items at the rate of 20 parts per minute.

The 'wish list' would contain statements such as 'it would be desirable if the construction would be modular', etc. and these would be considered objectives.

Table 3.1 shows an initial requirement list for a handheld electric drill.

In Table 3.1, items 4 to 7 are considered constraints in the design and it would be expected that these will be incorporated as standard in the product. Items 1 to 3 and 8 are objectives that the customer would like to see in the product; although important in the customer's eyes these could be omitted if the design or price was compromised.

Some requirements can be considered a 'wish' on the part of the customer such as item 8 (built-in charger); if this was not attainable without significantly affecting the price, then this objective would not be considered.

A requirements tree is a means of 'thought ordering'. It is also a means of providing a means of communication to other designers working within the same group. Figure 3.2 shows a restricted requirements tree used to consider Figure 3.4.

The objective of a requirements tree is to clarify the prime requirements and sub-requirements together with the relationship between them.

The starting point for constructing a requirements tree is to define the prime requirement, as shown in Figure 3.2, 'An efficient keyless chuck'. This statement will be the top-level requirement and this will then be broken down to show the two sub-requirements. Note: At this point, no solutions to the problem have been sought. Just the requirements of the product have been identified. In some cases the reader will see a requirement tree referred to as an 'Objective Tree', which is much the same thing.

Figure 3.4 is an example of applying the requirements or the objective tree to an engineering design problem.

It is required to design and build a test machine for measuring the fracture toughness of 'Charpy' test specimens when subject to an impact load resulting from a swinging hammer striking the specimen. The test specimens are cooled to the test temperature in a cold chamber, and then they are quickly moved to the specimen support blocks with a minimum increase in temperature.

TABLE 3.1

An Initial Requirement List for a Handheld Electric Drill

	Requirement	Type
1	Comfortable to hold	Objective
2	Aesthetically pleasing	Objective
3	Ergonomic design	Objective
4	Two-speed gearbox	Constraint
5	Be capable of drilling 12 mm diameter in wood	Constraint
6	Battery powered	Constraint
7	Keyless chuck	Constraint
8	Built-in battery charger	Objective

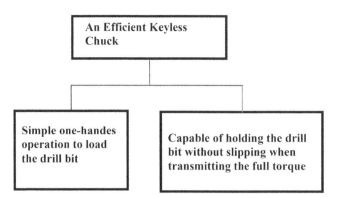

FIGURE 3.2
A requirement tree for a keyless chuck.

Figure 3.5 shows a typical Charpy test machine, and Figure 3.3 shows a typical Charpy test piece set-up. This test piece arrangement is specified by international standards and cannot be veered away from.

The machine is to be as simple and reliable as possible using as many standard parts to minimise manufacturing costs.

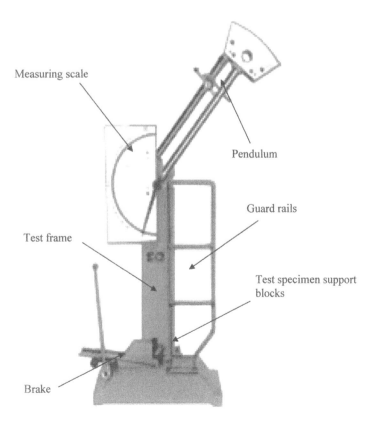

FIGURE 3.3
Charpy test piece set-up.

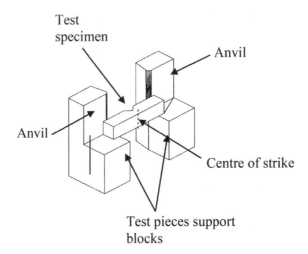

FIGURE 3.4
A requirement tree for a Charpy impact test machine.

It is important not to be too restrictive in describing both the prime and sub-prime requirements; the object is to develop as many low-level requirements as possible. In this case the top-level prime requirement will be described as 'a simple reliable test machine'.

As seen in Figure 3.5, a vague requirement can be expanded into a much more detailed set of requirements. In a first attempt at expanding, a list of requirements would produce general statements where 'simple' would likely to produce statements such as 'easy maintenance' and 'simple assembly'; providing the statements are not too restrictive it will be possible to expand the sub-requirements to a further level of sub-sub-requirements. It will be shown later in Section 1.6 (Concept Evaluation and Selection) that how important it is to generate as many levels as possible.

3.3.6 Product Design Specification

The PDS is the most singularly important document in the engineering design documentation. The object of the PDS is to list all the critical parameters the design is required to meet and to identify all the realistic constraints the design is required to achieve without pre-supposing the final outcome of the design.

Every department in the company's organisation will have an input into the document and it will specify all the elements the product will have to meet.

If the product is destined for the consumer market, the customer will have a voice in the PDS content usually through 'focus groups'.

The PDS should be as comprehensive and unambiguous as possible. It is a constantly evolving document and is therefore subject to change as the project progresses and further information is gathered of the product's needs.

The following is intended as a checklist of elements that might appear in a PDS. It is not intended to be all inclusive. Specific products will require their own additional items.

Some companies will have their own standard forms and procedures for completing the PDS so that they are consistent with each other.

The following subjects to be covered by the PDS.

When preparing a PDS, most engineers consider performance as the major element of the design activity; therefore, in this instance the discussion will start with that subject.

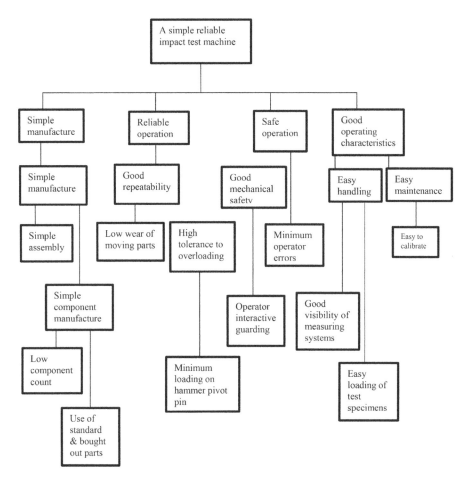

FIGURE 3.5
A typical Charpy impact text machine.

3.3.6.1 Performance

Great care is needed to ensure that performance figures quoted are realistically attainable within the project cost constraints.

Examples include:

What speed must it operate at?

How often is it expected to operate – is it continuous or discontinuous?

What is the expected lifespan of the product?

3.3.6.2 Environment

Every aspect of the product's possible environment should be considered including for example:

- Operating temperature range
- Storage temperature range

- Humidity
- Shock loading.
- Atmosphere – corrosive?
- Vibration

3.3.6.3 Target Production Cost

This manufacturing cost should be established at an early stage in the design process. Initial costing will need to be developed from the design schemes before any production drawings are produced and then checked against similar products the company may manufacture.

The production cost will have an influence on the selling price of the product; therefore, sale costs of competitor's products will need to be analysed to ensure that the new product will be competitive in the marketplace.

3.3.6.4 Competition

A thorough analysis of the competition needs to be carried out related to the product under consideration. This information should be available from the marketing report or from the marketing department if this work was undertaken internally. This should include details of a comprehensive product literature search to establish if there are any similar products on the market and if our specification differs from that of the competition. What do we have to do to establish a competitive edge over the existing competition?

A detailed search of all patents covering similar products should be instigated quickly before any further design work is undertaken to minimise the chances of future litigation or hindrance in future development.

3.3.6.5 Standards

Most products have to meet national/international standards covering a wide range of features. An example includes the humble electric plug where the shape and size has to conform to the national standard, including the position of the electrical contacts so they fit in existing sockets.

The standards that the product is designed against need to be identified and copies of the standards obtained from the national standards office. Correlation of these standards will need to be carried out prior to the commencement of any design activity to minimise any disruption to the design process if there is any retrospective redesign needed if the product is found not to comply with a particular standard. Generally all National Standard organisations conform to the International Standards Organisation (ISO), but in some cases National Standards may not comply with the ISO recommendations, and here special care will be required if the product is to be distributed to the international market; a case in point will be electrical voltages, etc.

3.3.6.6 Packing

Although initially packing may not be a priority in the designers mind, it is a very important element within the PDS and needs to be addressed as soon as possible such that packing is available when the product is ready for distribution. A well-designed packing will protect the product from a wide range of environmental issues such as high and low temperatures, salt water atmospheres and accidental damage if the package is dropped or is subject to rough handling. Companies also design attractive graphics for the visible outer packing if the product is destined for the consumer market.

3.3.6.7 Shipping

It is necessary to determine the manner in which the product will be delivered.

- Are there any restrictions on size, i.e., can the product pass through the normal openings in buildings without major disruption to the fabric of the building?
- Are there any lifting points needed to enable the product to be easily moved around?
- Will the product be fastened to a standard-size pallet?
- Does the assembly require breaking down into sub-assemblies such that they pass through specific accesses?

3.3.6.8 Size

Are there any restrictions on the size of the product? Is it being designed to fit into a specific place, or in the case of 'white goods' such as a refrigerator or washing machine fit into a standard type of opening used by fitted kitchen designers? Consideration should be given to the sizes of the openings in buildings so that easy access is possible. In the author's experience, it will not be the first time that part of the roof of a factory has had to be removed so that a particular machine could be installed. Other examples include the road connecting the factory to the canal modified by removing lamp posts and traffic bollards so that the Airbus A380 wing sections could be moved easily.

3.3.6.9 Materials

The materials used in the manufacture of the product will need careful consideration to ensure that where possible the material selected is readily available (ex-stock). If the material is of a special nature, purchasing will need time to source and procure the material before the manufacture begins.

3.3.6.10 Proprietary Items (Bought Out Parts)

To try and reduce costs, try and use as many 'standard' parts as possible that are not manufactured on site. There are a number of companies that specialise in the manufacture of these standard parts including hydraulic pumps and fittings, electric motors, pneumatic cylinders and accessories, etc.

It is possible for some products to be manufactured with a high percentage of these proprietary items and only a small number of in-house designed and manufactured parts.

However, there are some disadvantages of using these bought out parts other than fittings that are designed against specific standards, such as pipe unions. It is not unknown for a supplier to amend the design so that when a replacement part is fitted, the manufacturer finds that the redesigned part will not fit the original assembly, resulting in long delays to the customer if additional parts need to be manufactured to fit the new part.

3.3.6.11 Maintenance

The maintenance strategy will need to be considered at the early stages of design. Is it intended that the product be maintenance free for the working life of the product? Or will this have a deleterious effect on the design and have a cost impact and price it out of the market.

   If the product is a machine part, will the customer have the means of carrying out low-level maintenance, or have a pre-planned maintenance schedule for the machine?

- Are the parts that require regular servicing or maintenance easily accessible?
- Will any special tooling be required to carry out the servicing?
- Will sufficient spares be available, and who will be responsible for holding these spares?

If any special equipment or tooling be required for the maintenance or servicing of the product, these will need to be addressed at some point in the planning stage?

3.3.6.12 Product Lifespan

The answer to this question will be dictated by the nature of the market for which the product is destined. If the product is made for the consumer electronic market, the expected lifespan could be measured in months, whereas if the product is for the industrial markets such as machine tools or even sewage farms, then the product life could be 25 years or even longer. Some machine tools have been in service for over 75 years and are still operating efficiently.

3.3.6.13 Reliability

Reliability of the product will be a key issue regardless of whether the product is destined for the consumer or the industrial market. If the product is intended for the defence or offshore industry the reliability will be more stringent and values shown with guarantees on the life of the component.

   In the PDS the reliability may be specified in a number of formats:

- Failure rate
- Mean time between failures
- Mean time to repair

Electronic systems are well protected from the elements compared with mechanical components which are in general exposed to the environments and as such it is very difficult to give quantitative data in respect to their reliability.

   There are a number of organisations that will give guidance and undertake the analysis of a design, giving quantitative data if the resource is not available 'in-house'.

3.3.6.14 Finishing

Finishing may be applied to make a product for the consumer market attractive or aesthetically pleasing and will be dictated by the customer to match a particular brand style such as handheld hairdryers, refrigerators, etc. Where the product is destined for the industrial market, different criteria will apply and finishing may be required to give a degree of corrosion protection particularly if the product is for the offshore or the petrochemical industry. Certain colours may also be specified where the product will be installed in a particular hazard area for easy identification.

4

Product Design Specification

4.0 Introduction

A critical document in the design process that is usually overlooked is the *Product Design Specification* or PDS. When it is used correctly, it will save a lot of embarrassment in reducing items overlooked and could cost the company a heavy financial cost to correct the problem.

The PDS is essentially a contract between the manufacturer and the customer. The manufacturer knows what he is going to produce and the customer knows what they are going to receive.

The problem of converting the frequently non-technical, non-quantifiable customer requirements to a set of product characteristics expressed in engineering terms leads to the PDS.

The PDS defines the customer requirements as completely as possible. When the document is completed, the design team can then commence to undertake the design activity of proposing product arrangements to meet the customer's needs. It is inevitable that a number of alternative designs will be generated in this exercise. It is more than likely that one of the designs will be able to offer the best options when assessed against the requirements as stated in the PDS. This is the concept generation phase as identified at stage 3 in Figure 4.1. Those concepts that do not meet the design specification will either be rejected or after a degree of rework will be reconsidered.

A number of techniques will be discussed in the next conceptualisation stage in which other attributes identified such as reliability, cost, ease of manufacture, etc., will be discussed.

A typical PDS covers the following details.

4.1 Description of the Product

This provides an overview of the proposed product being specified. This is NOT intended to be a requirement section.

The starting point of any PDS is the brief that is put together by the marketing department and describes what the customer is requiring. If the product is specific to one customer, it will describe in detail exactly what the product is expected to fulfil. In case the product is more generally commercially orientated, the data would usually have been

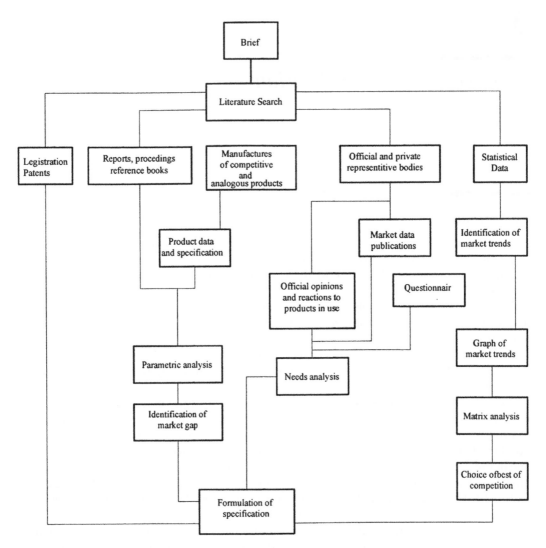

FIGURE 4.1
Information flow for the compilation of a PDS.

obtained from 'focus groups' or other marketing techniques. In this case, the brief will be couched in more general terms giving the designer a little more latitude to how he will approach the design.

The designer has a number of tools available to him, the most important one is the QFD (Quality Function Deployment) that is described in more detail in Chapter 12 (Quality in the Design Function).

4.1.1 Product Brief (Description and Justification)

Product brief provides a brief description of the products purpose and the reasoning for developing the product including any technical factors that call for a new product.

Operational requirements:

Product speed (how fast? How slow? How often?)
Continuous or discontinuous
Stresses and loadings likely to be encountered
Power requirements
Product expected shelf life
Product expected service life

4.1.2 The Environment the Product Will Be Expected to Operate in

What is the expected operating temperature range for the product?
What is the operating humidity range?
What levels of shock loading will the product be exposed to?
Will the product be exposed to contamination such as corrosive fluids?
How will the product be treated in service?
What impact will the product have on the environment?

4.1.3 Product Safety Requirements

Potential sources of product liability litigation
Potential operator hazards
Potential manufacturing and assembly hazards
Potential for misuse and abuse

4.1.4 Expected Product Reliability Standards and Requirements

What level of reliability can be expected from this product?

4.1.5 Expected Product Ergonomic Requirements – Customer Requirement

Which user/operator features are desirable in this product?
Are there problem areas for user/operators? Can they be designed around?

4.1.6 Expected Product Aesthetics – Customer Requirement

Discuss with the customer any special requirements they would prefer to see in the design of the product.

4.1.7 Expected Product Maintenance Requirements

Can product be maintenance free?
If routine maintenance is required can it be undertaken by the operator?
Will a professional maintenance engineer be required?
Will any special tools/tooling be required?

4.1.8 Possible 'Off-the-Shelf' Proprietary Parts Are Used?

Which parts can be can be purchased instead of being manufactured in house?
Will the quality and reliability of the proprietary parts be adequate?

4.1.9 Material Requirements

Are there any strength issues requiring special materials?
What are the strength/compliance requirements?
Is the product weight important?

4.1.10 Product End-of-Life Requirements

Does any part of this product constitute an environmental hazard?
Can any part of the product be recycled by existing processes?

4.1.11 Manufacturing Process Requirements and Limitations

Is environmental protection necessary?
Is there a customer requirement for a particular finish?
How can environmental impact be minimised?

4.1.12 Product Packaging Requirements

Can environmentally friendly packaging and packaging materials be used?
What is the minimum amount of packaging and materials that can be used?

4.1.13 Applicable Codes of Practice and Standards to Be Checked

Check for any applicable national and international codes of practice and standards that should be followed.

4.1.14 Check for Any Patent Infringement

Check for any patent infringements that may have been inadvertently broken.

4.1.15 Processes to Be Researched and Benchmarked: Special Fabrication Techniques to Be Researched

Are there any new processes or practices that required to be studied and benchmarked as being good practices. Any new fabrication techniques that need to be investigated.

4.1.16 Any Special Product or Part Testing Requirements

Any special product testing that requires further study before the product is fit for sale.

4.2 Marketing Issues

Any marketing issues that need to be investigated further to help build a better picture of the future sales of the product.

4.2.1 Potential Customer Base

Who will purchase this product? And why?
  Have all the potential classes of customers been listed?
  Is it possible to tap into a new segment of the market? How can this be done?

4.2.2 Market Constraints on Products

Who is purchasing this type of product (customer base)?
  What is currently selling?
  What is not currently selling?

4.2.3 Expected Product Competition (These Will Be Benchmarked)

What are the strengths of the competitors' products? Can they be incorporated?
  What are the weaknesses of each competitors' products? Can they be improved?
  What is the market share of the competing products?

4.2.4 Product Target Price – OEM^Y and MSRP*

^{Y}Original Equipment Manufacture.
  *Manufacturer's Suggested Retail Price.

4.2.5 Target Production Volume and Potential Market Share

Is it possible to determine the market for this product?
  Is the potential market sufficiently large to justify any investment in a new product?
  Is the new product sufficiently better than the competition?

4.2.6 Expected Product Distribution Environment

How will the packaged product be treated in shipping, storage and on the shelf?
  Are adequate shipping facilities available?
  Will installation require a professional installation engineer?

4.3 Capability Issues

4.3.1 Company Constraints on Product Design, Manufacture and Distribution

What is the company's manufacturing capability?
  Can the manufacture be carried out 'in house' or will it have to be 'outsourced'?

4.3.2 Schedule Requirements – Time to Market

What are the times scales to bring this product to market to capture maximum market share?
  How much time should be allocated to design?
  What time scales needed to implement a manufacturing process?

5

Conceptual Design

5.1 Creativity Methods

In this chapter, a number of procedures will be discussed in brief that will aid the design team to develop a wide range of solutions to the design problem being considered.

One of the biggest problem faced by a designer is that of 'Mindset', where a preconceived idea predominates his/her thinking and is unable to get round to it. Creativity techniques help designers to change their thinking and generate new ideas.

5.2 Breaking the Mindset

There are a number of proven techniques that help the designer to 'think outside the box' and come up with some inspiring and surprising ideas. These include the following:

- Inversion
- Analogy
- Empathy
- Fantasy
- Brainstorming
- Mindmaps
- SCAMPER
- TRIZ

5.2.1 Inversion

The viewpoint changes with this method. It simply calls for a conscious breaking of the set, the old way of looking at the problem. In this method, if the usual way of looking at the problem is from the outside, then this technique helps the designer to change the viewpoint and try looking at things from inside. If one part of the system moves and another is stationary, then invert them so that the moving part is stationary and the previous stationary part now moves.

Inversion means switching them around, upside down, inside out, reversed, etc.

5.2.2 Analogy

In trying to solve a problem, the analogy may help to look around and find if there is a solution in other areas, especially in nature and literature.

If the objective of the new design is to develop an industrial gripper, then a number of possible areas come to mind that use something similar.

- Human hand
- Plants
- Insects

5.2.3 Empathy

Empathy means personal identification and feeling for another. In human terms it roughly means 'putting oneself in the other man's shoes'. From a designer's point of view, it will be helpful in identifying the part and 'seeing' from its point of view.

5.2.4 Fantasy

Fantasy is make-believe and involves dreaming of some fanciful solutions. The hope is that it may bring up a new idea or perspective to the problem. There are many examples including personal communications that owe their existence to science fiction comics and films.

The first technique to be discussed is that of 'Brainstorming'. In recent years this has become a popular method of generating ideas and solutions to specific problems in a group environment.

5.2.5 Brainstorming

Brainstorming was originally developed by Madison Avenue advertising executive Alex Osborn in his 1953 book 'Applied Imagination'. It has since gone through many developments to his original technique.

It had a lot of attention in the past, but it is not a technique which should be thought of as a panacea. It had some successes and a lot of failures and the effective use of brainstorming requires a knowledge of its limitations, how it works and when is the most appropriate time to apply it.

Used in the right situations and circumstances, it can be a very powerful idea generator.

Contrary to popular belief, brainstorming is quite difficult to apply and requires a lot of practice. It can lead to a lot of frustration if the rules of brainstorming are not followed correctly.

Rule 1: No criticism or judgements are allowed.

Rule 2: The object is to generate as many ideas as possible.

Rule 3: Think wild, the free flow of ideas and as wild is required from the session.

There are four phases in brainstorming:

- Problem definition
- Divergence
- Categorisation
- Convergence

5.2.6 Problem Definition

The presentation of the problem definition will have a big impact on the outcome of the session. If the problem is not clearly defined, the results may be irrelevant for the project. Suitable guide lines for defining the problem include the following:

A. Define the goal of the session in one sentence.
B. Keep a close eye on the progress of the session and be prepared to refocus the session if it is diverging from the central theme.
C. Start the session with 'how' or 'invent'. The pronouns 'how', 'what',' where' and 'when' help to stimulate solution generation.

5.2.7 Divergence

The method depends on generating as many alternative ideas and solutions as possible. This is known as the divergent phase and creates quality of the ideas through quantity as many of the ideas will be discarded in the categorisation phase.

5.2.8 Categorisation

Each of the ideas presented during the session are recorded and given a unique number for later evaluation. It may aid later evaluation if the ideas can be classified into common groups as the session progresses, this will be helpful at the evaluation stage.

5.2.9 Convergence Phase

All the ideas and solutions that have the benefit of the doubt can be kept at one side in this phase. The value of some ideas may not be immediately apparent at first, but the team should make decisions and work towards the required objective.

Brainstorming can be accomplished using either one of two methods, i.e.

- Individual brainstorming
- Group brainstorming

5.2.10 Individual Brainstorming

Group brainstorming can often be most effective in generating ideas when the team works efficiently, but in some cases the group does not always follow the rules of brainstorming and often bad behaviour creeps in particularly as people do not pay attention to what other group members are saying and as a result they do not generate ideas of their own.

Individual sessions may be more productive as the individual does not have to worry about other people's opinions and are free to be more creative and not to hesitate to bring up in the group an idea that develops into something more special. It is most effective when there is a need to solve a simple problem by generating a list of ideas or focusing on a broad issue.

5.2.11 Group Brainstorming

Group brainstorming sessions are more effective for solving complex problems by taking advantage of the wider diversity of experiences from other group members, particularly where the members come from a wider range of disciplines. This wider range of experience can make the sessions more creative. Do not make the group too big, usually a maximum size of five to seven is usually most effective.

5.2.12 Brainwriting

Brainwriting is a similar technique to brainstorming, there are a number of variations but generally the participant writes down their ideas and then passes them onto the next person who uses them to trigger their own ideas. This method for persons who are concerned about voicing their own thoughts in a broader group, but being anominous they do not have to compete with stronger members of the team to be heard.

5.2.13 Mind Mapping

In the 1970s, Tony Buzan proposed a method called 'mind mapping' in which an attempt was made to provide a means of externalising ideas generated in the brain. They tend to be interlinked thoughts following a previous idea radiating out from the original problem.
   The following are the steps that are undertaken to generate a mind map.

1. On a large sheet of paper write a brief description of the problem being considered in the centre of the paper. As with all stages of producing a mind map, it is best to keep the description down to a minimum number of words.

2. Write down around the topic, the sub-problems, consequences, ideas or sub-areas relating to the topic that needs further investigation.

3. Taking each one of the sub-topics in turn, identify the issues that relate to it and represent these on the mind map using either words, short phrases or even little sketches. Occasionally ideas may occur that do not relate to the sub-topic, in this case either add a new sub-topic or construct a new sub-topic unconnected to the main map. There will be time later to consider how the thoughts relate to the central topic.

4. Organise the map by reviewing the connections between the various sub-topics, if there are logical connections between the ideas or groups of ideas in different sub-topics, link them by connecting with lines.

5. Complete the activity by writing a report on the structure with subheadings for each sub-topic. The map and the report will provide a valuable record on which any future decisions are based.

5.2.14 SCAMPER

'SCAMPER' is a checklist that is designed to help in thinking about the changes that could be made to an existing product to create a new one and is an acronym for the following:
   Substitute
   What can be substituted? What can be used instead? Can I replace this part for another? Other materials?
   Combine
   Can this part be combined with another? Can this assembly be combined with another assembly?
   Adapt
   Can I adapt part of that assembly? Can I change that function? Can I use part of another element?

Modify

Can I change the item in some way? Can I increase or reduce in size? Modify attributes?

Put to other uses

How can I put this part to another use? Is there a new way of using it? Are there other uses if it is modified?

Eliminate

What can I eliminate? Can I remove this element? Can it be reduced to its core functionality?

Reverse/Rearrange

Can this element be turned inside out or upside down? Can this part be rearranged in some way? Can the components be interchanged?

SCAMPER works by providing a list of active verbs that can be associated with the problem in question. Continue asking 'How can …?', 'How else …?', 'What if …?' for every idea.

5.2.15 TRIZ

In the 1980s, the Russian engineer Genrich Altshuller developed the TRIZ theory which is an acronym for Teorya Reshenia Izobreatatelskikh Zadatch (the literal translation is the theory of Inventive Problem Solving and known as TIPS in English). TRIZ is a method that will help solve difficult technological problems through the identification and elimination of conflicts that are present in all engineering systems. A further feature of TRIZ is the ability of the method to predict how technical systems evolve over time. In the period of time TRIZ has been practiced in North America and Europe, it has proved to be extremely powerful in generating elegant solutions to complicated paradoxical problems.

This method was originally devised by Genrich Altshuller a patent investigator who was imprisoned in a Gulag under the orders of Stalin. While there he met with other similar scientists and together further developed the method which he called 'the theory of inventive problem solving'. In his study, he developed a set of systematic thinking tools by analysing more than 200 000 patents. He discovered that 98% of patented innovations were based on an already known principles and only 2% of all the patents were really new innovations From his research he developed a database. The essence of this database has been captured into a generic list of 40 inventive principles known as the TRIZ 40 principles. TRIZ is based on the fundamental premise that problems occur due to physical or technical contradictions in the system. The solution resolving these contradictions is inherently a creative or innovative solution. TRIZ provides 40 inventive principles to resolve contradictions in the system. The principles are generic enough to apply across different problems, products and industries to create innovative solutions.

The workflow of the TRIZ method follows what is shown in Figure 5.1. The problem is defined based on the main functions that need to be achieved. Once the problem is identified, the TRIZ expert will try to find the cases that closely match the problem in the TRIZ Contradiction Matrix (Figure 5.2). This results in a number of suggested TRIZ principles that can then be used to solve the problem. Once the suggested solution is chosen, it is then customised based on the current situation.

Nomenclature

1. Specified problem
2. Based on TRIZ 40 principles
3. Customised solution

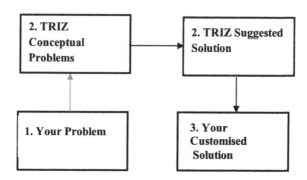

FIGURE 5.1
TRIZ method of solving solution.

Worsening Feature ➡ Improving Feature ⬇	Speed	Shape	Loss of Time	Reliability	Measurement accuracy	Measurement accuracy	Adaptability or versatility	System complexity	Measurement Difficulty	Productivity
Speed	+	35, 15, 18, 34		11, 35, 27, 28	28, 32, 1, 24	32, 28, 13, 12	15, 10, 26	10, 28, 4, 34	3, 34, 27, 16	
Shape	35, 15, 34, 18	+	14, 10, 34, 17	10, 40, 16	28, 32, 1	32, 15, 26	1, 15, 29	16, 29, 1, 28	15, 13, 39	17, 26, 34, 10
Loss of Information	26, 32		24, 26, 28, 32	10, 28, 23		27, 22			35, 33	13, 23, 15
Loss of Time		4, 10, 34, 17	+	10, 30, 4	24, 34, 28, 32	4, 28, 10, 34	35, 28	6, 29	18, 28, 32, 10	
Measurement accuracy	28, 13, 32, 24	6, 28, 32	24, 34, 28, 32	5, 11, 1, 23	+	1, 13, 17, 34	13, 35, 2	27, 35, 10, 34	26, 24, 32, 28	10, 34, 28, 32
Ease of operation	18, 13, 34	15, 34, 29, 28	4, 28, 10, 34	17, 27, 8, 40	25, 13, 2, 34	+	15, 34, 1, 16	32, 26, 12, 17		15, 1, 28
Ease of repair	34, 9	1, 13, 2, 4	32, 1, 10, 25	11, 10, 1, 16	10, 2, 13	1, 12, 26, 15	7, 1, 4, 16	35, 1, 13, 11		1, 32, 10
Adaptability or versatility	35, 10, 14	15, 37, 1, 8	35, 28	35, 13, 8, 24	35, 5, 1, 10	15, 34, 1, 16	+	15, 29, 37, 28	1	35, 28, 6, 37
System complexity	34, 10, 28	29, 13, 28, 15	6, 29	13, 35, 1	2, 26, 10, 34	27, 9, 26, 24	29, 15, 28, 37	+	15, 10, 37, 28	12, 17, 28
Productivity		14, 10, 34, 40		1, 35, 10, 38	1, 10, 34, 28	1, 28, 7, 10	1, 35, 28, 37	12, 17, 28, 24	35, 18, 27, 2	+

FIGURE 5.2
Subset of contradiction matrix.

To improve the method, TRIZ used five basic principles and 40 inventive principles forcing the designer to look at problems differently.

1. **The ideal end result (IFR).**
   The IFR has the following 4 characteristics:

   Eliminates the deficiencies of the original system

   Preserves the advantages of the original system

   Does not make the system more complicated (uses free or available resources)

   Does not introduce new disadvantages

2. **Less is more.**
   There is not always a need to invest large amounts of money to arrive at the best solution. Innovation can be understood with existing materials and sometimes the solution is closer to hand.

3. **Solutions already exist.**
   TRIZ helps the designer to define the problem in terms of frequently used and general principles which enables searching for solutions outside their primary field of expertise.

4. **Search for fundamental contradictions.**
   Innovation equates to problem solving, which mostly exists with contradictions, when these contradictions are defined, the solution usually presents itself.

5. **Lines of evolution.**
   Systems do not evolve randomly. There are fixed patterns that make the evolution of technology predictable.

40 Inventive Principles

Althuller arrived at 40 inventive principles to solve complex problems. Each innovation can be traced back to the application of one or more of these principles.

To arrive with the correct application of the 40 principles, it is important to formulate the right contradiction very closely with respect to what should be improved and what should not get worse.

1. **Segmentation:**
   Divide an object into independent parts.
   - Multi-pin connectors
   - Multiple pistons in an internal combustion engine

2. **Extraction:**
   Extract a disturbing part or property from an object and/or single out the only necessary part or property.
   - Air-conditioning in a room where it is wanted with the noise of the system outside of the room.
   - Non-smoking areas in restaurants or rail carriages.

3. **Local quality:**
   Change of an object's structure from uniform to non-uniform
   - Drink cans shaped to facilitate stable stacking.
   - Moulded grips on hand tools.

4. **Asymmetry:**
Change the shape or properties of an object from symmetrical to asymmetrical:
- Machine a flat spot on a cylindrical shaft to facilitate a locking feature.
- Amend the profile to provide a camming action.

5. **Merging:**
By merging functions, properties or parts of a product in space or time, a new or unique result is created.
- Multicolour pens.
- Double/triple glazing.

6. **Universality:**
Make a product more uniform, universal and multifunctional and eliminate the need for other parts.
- Child's car safety seat converts into a pushchair
- Swiss Army Knife.

7. **Nested doll:**
Place multiple objects inside one another:
- Retractable aircraft undercarriage.
- Telescopic car aerial.

8. **Counterweight:**
Compensate for the weight of an object by combining it with other objects that provide lift.
- Hot air or helium balloon.
- Hydrofoils lift boats out of the water to reduce drag.

9. **Preliminary counteraction:**
When it is necessary to perform an action that has harmful and useful effects, this should be replaced with a counteraction to control harmful effects.
- Manufacture clay pigeons out of ice – they just melt away.
- Predict effects of signal distortion – compensate prior to transmitting.

10. **Preliminary action:**
Place an object before it is needed so that it can be put into service immediately from the most convenient location for their delivery.
- Ambulances placed at strategic positions within the community – ready for immediate action.
- Assemble all tools and materials required for a particular operation before starting.

11. **Cushion in advance:**
Prepare emergency means beforehand to compensate for the relatively low reliability of an object.
- Multichannel control system.
- Airbag in a car, spare wheel, etc.

12. **Equipotentiality:**
Where an object has to be raised or lowered, redesign the objects environment so the need to raise or lower is eliminated or performed by the environment.
- Canal locks.
- Descending cable cars balanced by the weight of the ascending cars.

13. **The other way round:**
    Invert the action to eliminate the problem.
    - Linear walkways to speedily transport passengers at an airport.
    - Reversible rain-ware.

14. **Spheroidality – curvature:**
    Replace linear parts with spherical parts.
    - Use arches or domes to strengthen architectural features.
    - Rotary actuators in hydraulic systems.

15. **Dynamics:**
    Make a product or property temporarily flexible or flexible for a short time while.
    - Car handbrake adjustable for brake pad wear.
    - Telescopic curtain rail – 'one size fits all'.

16. **Partial or excessive actions:**
    If it is not possible to achieve 100% of a desired effect – then go for more or less.
    - 'Roughing' and 'Finish' machining operations.
    - Over-fill holes with plaster and then rub back to smooth.

17. **Transition to another dimension:**
    Move to an additional dimension – from one to two – from two to three
    - CD player using many disks.
    - Stacked or multilayer circuit boards.

18. **Mechanical vibrations:**
    Causing an object to oscillate or vibrate:
    - Hammer drill.
    - Using resonant frequencies – destroys gall stones.

19. **Periodic action:**
    Instead of continuous action use periodic or pulsating actions
    - Electric toothbrush.
    - Pulsed water jet cutting

20. **Continuity:**
    Carry on work continuously and eliminate all idle or intermittent actions
    - Shearing flywheel stores energy during idle stroke providing full energy on the cutting stroke.
    - Auxiliary power unit (APU) on aircraft runs at full power when switched on.

21. **Rushing through:**
    Conduct a process at high speed to prevent errors.
    - Cut plastic faster than heat can propagate in the material to avoid distorting shape.
    - Super critical speed of turbine shaft to prevent severe vibration due to whirling.

22. **Blessing in disguise:**
    Use harmful factors to achieve a positive effect.
    - Use waste heat to generate electric power.
    - Use pressure differences to help rather than hinder seal performance.

23. **Feedback:**
Introduce feedback to improve a process or action.
- Thermostat controls temperature accurately.
- Engine management system using exhaust gas levels to monitor CO.

24. **Intermediary:**
Use an intermediary carrier article or intermediary process.
- Oven bag for cooking chicken.
- Dwell period during a manufacture process operation.

25. **Self-service:**
Make an object serve itself by performing auxiliary helpful functions.
- Self-cleaning ovens.
- Self-aligning bearings/self-adjusting seals.

26. **Copying:**
Replace unavailable, expensive or fragile objects with an inexpensive copy.
- Crash test dummies.
- Imitation jewellery.

27. **Cheap short-living objects:**
Replace inexpensive and/or disposable objects to reduce costs:
- Disposable cutlery.
- Sacrificial coatings/components.

28. **Replace mechanical system:**
Replace a mechanical system with a sensory one.
- Add a bad smell to natural gas to alert users to gas leaks.
- Electrostatic precipitators separate particles for fluid flow.

29. **Pneumatics and hydraulics:**
Replace mechanical solid parts with pneumatics (air) or hydraulics (water) units.
- Lifting systems (Barber chair).
- Hovercraft.

30. **Flexible shells:**
Replace traditional constructions with flexible shells or thin films.
- Tarpaulin car covers.
- Accumulators using flexible bags to store energy in a hydraulic system.

31. **Porous materials:**
Make an object porous or add porous elements.
- Drill holes in a structure to reduce weight.
- Foam metals.

32. **Colour change:**
Change the colour or other optical property of an object.
- Use colour changing thermal paint to measure temperature.
- Plastic spoons that change colour when hot – for baby food.

33. **Homogeneity:**
    Objects interacting with the main object should have identical properties.
    - Containers made from the same material to avoid chemical reactions.
    - Friction welding requires no intermediary material between the two surfaces to be joined.

34. **Discarding and recovering:**
    By removing objects or parts of objects that have fulfilled their useful function and by subsequently restoring them, they can be reused.
    - Dissolving capsules for medication.
    - Investment casting – total lost wax method.

35. **Parametric changes:**
    Change the properties of an object.
    - Transport oxygen or hydrogen as a liquid instead of as a gas – to reduce volume.
    - Liquid soap.

36. **Phase transitions:**
    Use phenomena of phase transitions (volume change, loss of absorption of heat).
    - Latent heat effects in melting/boiling.
    - Superconductivity.

37. **Thermal expansion:**
    Use thermal expansion or contraction of materials.
    - Metal tie bars used to straighten buckling walls on old buildings.
    - Shrink wrapping.

38. **String oxidants:**
    Replace common air with oxygen-enriched air.
    - Place asthmatic patients in an oxygen tent.
    - Nitrous oxide injection to improve the performance of an internal combustion engine.

39. **Inert atmosphere:**
    Replace a normal environment with an inert one.
    - Prevent degradation of a hot metal filament by using argon atmosphere.
    - Electron beam welding conducted in a vacuum chamber.

40. **Composite materials:**
    Change from normal materials to composite (multiple) materials.
    - Aircraft structural components where weight is critical.
    - Fibre-reinforced ceramics.

5.2.16 Concept Evaluation and Selection

Having generated a number of concepts, it now becomes necessary to evaluate them and select the most appropriate ones for further detailed analysis. The objective at this stage is to reduce the number of candidate concepts where possible.

5.2.17 Criteria for Evaluation

When evaluating concepts, a specific requirement is needed to make a comparison against it. It is important not to compare concepts with each other but to use an unchanging criteria and in this case usually the Product Design Specification (PDS). This will ensure that a constant 'yardstick' is used against all concepts.

Concept evaluation can be considered a form of analysis, but it does not take on the highly quantitative analysis as in stress analysis. It is recommended that a procedural approach to the evaluation is followed in order that which concept best meets the design goals.

5.2.18 Feasibility Judgement

The first step in the evaluation is to eliminate those concepts deemed to be considered 'not feasible' under any conditions. Trained engineers use intuition to determine if the concept is workable. A simple tool that can be used is the implications of simple physics with respect to its operation, i.e., which way do the forces act? Where (roughly) do they act? And in which direction do they operate? As a consequence of these forces what effect will they have on the operation of the product?

Occasionally a concept could be considered 'conditionally feasible' if a change to the concept makes it work. This 'change' may be obtaining further information or the development of an associated component. Conditionally feasible concepts will require further evaluation but may fail for reasons such as technological un-readiness.

5.2.19 Technological Readiness

The second major evaluation is based upon the readiness of the technologies that may be used in the concept such as materials, manufacturing techniques, etc.

Each concept is carefully examined with regard to the following questions. Where a single 'no' may not be enough to exclude the concept, it will mean the concept may require re-examining.

1. Are there reasonable and reliable manufacturing processes available?
2. Are appropriate material choices for the concept exist and are they readily available?
3. Does the design team have sufficient technological expertise?
4. Does the solution make use of mature and fully developed technologies?

5.2.20 Go/No-Go Screening

This procedure is relatively easy to implement. The first step is to consider the PDS and transform each step into a yes, no or maybe. If the response is a 'Yes' for the concept, then it is a 'Go' and then proceeds to the next stage of evaluation. If the response is a 'No', then the concept is a 'No-Go'. Before discarding the No-Go concepts, consider if the concept can be modified to a Go? If so, then the modified concept is allowed to proceed to the next stage.

5.2.21 Decision Matrix

A very popular tool for evaluating concepts is a 'decision matrix'. This is discussed in more detail in Chapter 8.

It answers such questions as:

- The development of an appropriate list of criteria.
- Enables the concepts to be rated against each criterion.
- The use of an evaluation scale, i.e. good, adequate, poor.
- To use the overall ratings to determine the best solution.

The decision matrix is the final level of evaluation. In order that the concepts can be evaluated effectively, a form of criteria is used to compare the concepts against in a quantitative manner. Within the decision matrix, the concepts are not compared to one another but to the evaluation criteria. The selection criterion is based on the functional requirements and the objectives of the design problem together with the main product characteristics of the problem. The product characteristics make up the PDS therefore it makes sense to use these as labels for the groups of requirements.

5.2.22 Feasibility Assessment

Once the 'winning' concept(s) has been selected, it will be appropriate for the company to undertake a complete feasibility study before committing any resources to the design and development of the concept(s).

The assessment is carried out at three levels:

1. Technical feasibility
2. Financial feasibility
3. Organisational feasibility

5.2.23 Technical Feasibility

This will cover a complete technical assessment of the chosen design. It will require a full and honest assessment of the design, including a detailed risk analysis of the project.

Bear in mind that just a technical feasibility study conducted does not automatically assume that the product is going to be a success in the market place. Table 5.1 lists a small selection of products that have been successful and those that have been failures.

TABLE 5.1

Examples of Successful and Unsuccessful Designs

Successful Designs	Unsuccessful Designs
Jug kettle	Concorde
Microwave ovens	Ford Edsel
3M stick-on notelets	Sinclair C5
Sony walkman	Advanced passenger train

In Table 5.1 it may seem strange to some that 'Concorde' is considered an unsuccessful design. The design was a technological success but commercially it was a failure. The aircraft had originally been conceived to be sold to a number of private airlines. Twenty aircrafts were originally constructed. In the end, only the two national airlines, 'British Airways', with seven aircraft, and 'Air France', operating five aircrafts, have been very heavily subsidised by both the UK and French governments before being withdrawn following an awful crash in Charles de Gaulle Airport in Paris on February 2, 2010.

5.2.24 Financial and Market Feasibility

The impact of the financial status of the company depends on how much start-up capital will be needed, sources of capital, returns on investment, etc. Sufficient funds to be provided in sustaining the development of the new product, this will be throughout the development and manufacturing phase.

The marketing section of the study will require a description of the current market, the anticipated future market potential, the competition and sales projections and potential buyers, etc.

5.2.25 Organisational Feasibility

This covers all the commercial aspects of introducing the new product into the market place, including distribution, warehousing and storage, servicing, etc.

6

Design for 'X'

6.1 Introduction

In the mid-1970s considerable efforts were being applied in the field of automated machining. Different ways to minimise the labour content in manufactured parts were investigated, every aspect of the component part was carefully reviewed including its shape, surface finish and tolerances and their impact on the component cost.

In the early 1980s, proposals were put forward to automate the assembly process which led to further investigations into other improvements that could be obtained during the early stages of the design process. This included improvements in life, reliability and maintainability.

This initiative is known as 'Design for "X"' (DfX) and has now become an important feature of design during the conceptual stages of the project and covers the disciplines shown in Table 6.1.

6.2 Design for Manufacture

The purpose of Design for Manufacture (DfM) is to ensure that the most economical practice has been applied to the design of the part. The following subheadings cover the issues that need to be considered.

6.2.1 Machinability

Machinability is a measure of the relative ease of a machining operation and is given a machinability rating. Basic steel is given a rating of 1.0 due to the ease of machining and a rating of 0.2 is given for cutting titanium alloys. Table 6.2 lists some of the machinability ratings for a range of commonly used materials.

6.2.1.1 Machinability Rating

The machinability rating of a material attempts to quantify the machinability of various materials. It is expressed as a percentage or a normalized value. The American Iron and Steel Institute (AISI) determined machinability ratings for a wide variety of materials by running turning tests at 180 surface feet per minute (sfpm). It then arbitrarily assigned 160 Brinell B1112 steel a machinability rating of 1.00. The machinability rating is determined by measuring the weighted averages of the normal cutting speed, surface finish, and tool life for

TABLE 6.1

Index for Design for 'X'

Ident No.	Description
6.1	Design for Manufacture
6.2	Design for Quality
6.4	Design for Reliability
6.4.1	Failure Modes and Effects Analysis
6.4.2	Fault Tree Analysis
6.5	Design for Robustness
6.6	Design for Maintainability
6.7	Design for the Environment
6.8	Design for Life Cycle Cost

each material. Note that a material with a machinability rating less than 1.00 would be more difficult to machine than B1112 and a material with a value more than 1.00 would be easier.

Machinability rating = (Speed of machining the workpiece giving 60-min tool life)/ (Speed of machining the standard metal).

Machinability ratings can be used in conjunction with the Taylor tool life equation, in order to determine cutting speeds or tool life.

$$V_c T^n = C$$

where V_c = cutting speed,

   T = tool life and n and C are constants found by experimentation or published data; they are properties of tool material, workpiece and feed rate.

It is known that B1112 has a tool life of 60 minutes at a cutting speed of 100 sfpm. If a material has a machinability rating of 0.70, it can be determined, with the above values, that in order to maintain the same tool life (60 minutes) the cutting speed must be 70 sfpm (assuming the same tooling is used).

The carbon content of steel greatly influences its machinability. High-carbon steels are found to be more difficult to machine because they are strong and may contain carbides that abrade the cutting tool. At the other end of the range, low-carbon steels are difficult to machine because they are generally too soft. Low-carbon steels are 'gummy' and stick to the cutting tool, resulting in a built up edge that shortens the life of the cutting tool. Steel has the best machinability with medium amounts of carbon of approximately 0.20%.

TABLE 6.2

Machinability Index

Material	Machinability Index
C-20 Steel	65
C-45 Steel	60
Stainless Steel	25
Copper	70
Brass	180
Al Alloys	30 - 1500
Mg Alloys	600 - 2000

Chromium, molybdenum and other alloying metals are often added to steel to improve its strength. However, most of these additives also decrease machinability.

Inclusions in steel, especially of oxides, may abrade the cutting tool. Machinable steel should be free of these oxides.

It can be shown that a longer tool life will result in better machinability and that greater cutting forces and machine power will give lower machinability ratings.

6.2.2 Shape

The shape of a component will dictate to a large measure the method of manufacture.

- Rotational parts will be achieved by turning and boring.
- Internal rotational features will be achieved by drilling.
- Non-rotational features will be produced by milling.
- Other features include:
  - Slotting – broaching
  - Generating polygon shapes – multi-axis milling machine.

By careful attention at the preliminary design stage, expensive features, such as undercuts and recesses, and other features that do not add value to the part can be eliminated before the detailed design phase is reached. This will reduce the time to manufacture the part and the range of tooling required such as special-shaped cutting tools and inspection fixtures.

6.2.3 Tolerances and Surface Finish

6.2.3.1 Tolerances

Can the general tolerance be relaxed? Geometric features for the fitting of bearings, contact features for sliding and press fits will be dictated by company standard fits and tolerances.

Reducing tolerances where possible can give substantial cost savings. Increasing tolerances will increase the cost of the part significantly. Table 6.3 tabulates the costs expected with increased part tolerances.

6.2.3.2 Surface Finishes

To a certain extent surface finish is related to the part tolerance grade. As an example it would be completely impracticable to specify a turned surface finish of 12.5 μm for a feature designed for a close-running fit say 25g6.

Figure 6.4 relates the cost of achieving a surface finish against a base value of zero for a flamecut or as-cast blank. It is readily seen that the cost of producing an improved surface finish is not proportional. To produce a surface finish of 32, Centre Line Average (CLA) is 140% more expensive compared to a finish turned of 63 CLA.

6.2.4 Product Design Guidelines 1

6.2.4.1 Design Parts to Minimise Machining

- Using a *net shape* process such as precision casting, closed die forging or plastic moulding
- A *near net shape* process including impression die forging.

TABLE 6.3

Approx Relative Cost of Tighter Tolerances

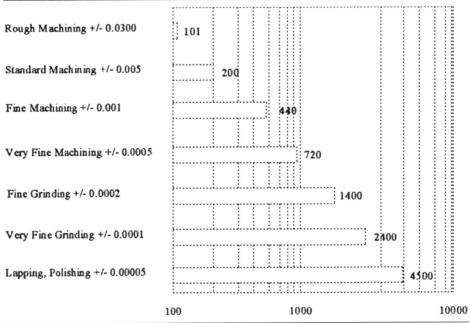

	100	1000	10000
Rough Machining +/- 0.0300	101		
Standard Machining +/- 0.005	200		
Fine Machining +/- 0.001	430		
Very Fine Machining +/- 0.0005	720		
Fine Grinding +/- 0.0002	1400		
Very Fine Grinding +/- 0.0001	2400		
Lapping, Polishing +/- 0.00005	4500		

6.2.4.2 Essential Reasons for Machining

- Close tolerances
- Good surface finish
- Special features such as threads, precision holes, cylindrical features with a high degree of roundness
- Specify the minimum tolerance grade to satisfy the functional requirements and process capability – unnecessary cost created from additional processes
- Specify the surface finish to meet functional and/or aesthetic requirements – add processing cost by requiring additional operations including grinding or lapping

6.2.5 Product Design Guidelines II

- Avoid features such as sharp corners, edges and points as these are difficult to machine; these features also tend to be stress raisers and will have a limiting effect on the life of the components.
- Try to machine parts from standard stock sizes as this reduces some machining.
- Use standard cutting tools where possible. Special form of cutting tools can add to the cost of machining unless costed for.
- Minimise the number of individual cutting tools used if possible.
- Where possible select materials that have a good machinability rating. Materials with low ratings take longer to machine and also cost more.
- Minimise the number of set-ups.

6.3 Design for Quality

6.3.1 Defining Quality

The definition of quality can be summarised as follows:

> "The standard of something as measured against other things of a similar kind; the degree of excellence of something."

In this section, the term quality is considered when used to describe a design or a product.

The term quality of a part (or products or components) according to Joseph M. Juran (1904–2008) should refer to the product features that meet customers' needs and satisfaction, and to avoid from deficiencies that would minimise the chance of failure of the part.

In 1987, David Garvin from the Harvard Business School proposed a definition of quality in the form of eight basic dimensions. Garvin's eight dimensions can be summarized as follows:

1. **Performance:** Performance refers to a product's primary operating characteristics. This dimension of quality involves measurable attributes; brands can usually be ranked objectively on individual aspects of performance.
2. **Features:** Features are additional characteristics that enhance the appeal of the product or service to the user.
3. **Reliability:** Reliability is the likelihood that a product will not fail within a specific time period. This is a key element for users who need the product to work without fail.
4. **Conformance:** Conformance is the precision with which the product or service meets the specified standards.
5. **Durability:** Durability measures the length of a product's life. When the product can be repaired, estimating durability is more complicated. The item will be used until it is no longer economical to operate it. This happens when the repair rate and the associated costs increase significantly.
6. **Serviceability:** Serviceability is the speed with which the product can be put into service when it breaks down, as well as the competence and the behaviour of the service person.
7. **Aesthetics:** Aesthetics is the subjective dimension indicating the kind of response a user has to a product. It represents the individual's personal preference.
8. **Perceived Quality:** Perceived quality is the quality attributed to a good or a service based on indirect measures.

6.3.2 The Importance of Design for Quality

Engineering designers are more responsible for specifying the level of quality of a product more than anyone else within the manufacturing organisation. The materials of manufacture are specified by them together with the method of manufacture and assembly. Proprietary parts purchased from outside the organisation are also specified by the design office. Both design and manufacturing are collectively responsible for the final quality of the part or components and this can be inherent in the companies' design procedures.

6.3.3 Design for Quality

Quality is the most effective factor a company can use in the battle for customers.

For a company to be competitive, the customer must be satisfied with the product or service. It follows that in order to be more competitive, the customer needs to be totally satisfied or even delighted with the product or service from the company. To ensure total customer satisfaction, quality must be designed into the product.

The Japanese term Kaizen (which means 'change for better') is used to define the philosophy and the driving force for designing for quality. Total Quality Control provides the implementation. The concepts are simple and elegant. If quality is made the driving force, then customers will obtain the best value possible and will use the product in preference to any other product. Profits will be maximised by focussing on increased revenue. If design for minimum cost is implemented then profits will be increased further.

After World War II, Japanese discovered quality as a philosophy for economic revival. To accomplish this recovery, a number of tools were developed that gave the company a competitive edge in designing for quality and cost.

These tools included:

1. Histograms
2. Cause and Effect Diagrams
3. Check Sheets
4. Pareto Diagrams
5. Graphs
6. Control Charts
7. Scatter Diagrams

These tools were largely developed as aids within the process of statistical quality control.

6.3.4 Benefits of Design for Quality

- The design for quality (DfQ) process allows the designer to identify, plan and manage factors that will have an impact on the reliability and robustness of the products in the design process.
- Having a robust attitude to DfQ within an organisation actually reduces the cost of quality considering the cost incurred in inspection and rework and the procurement of replacement materials.
- Improved and consistent quality of parts and components provide better appeal to the customer that leads to greater stability within the manufacturing department and can create greater amount of opportunities.

6.3.5 Design Reviews

Design review is an important feature in ensuring that the quality in the design process is maintained. The design review provides a forum where all stakeholders can come together and discuss aspects of the design that will have an impact on their respective activity. The review allows any question to be raised and answered and assumptions clarified and even advise sought. There is no restriction on the size of the project, ranging from, say, a domestic product such as a hair dryer to very large projects covering say, mooring systems for an offshore oil or gas platform. Although in the latter case the project will be broken down to individual units each having its own individual design review and is then coordinated at the top level to ensure consistency and compatibility across the project.

Typically a number of formal and informal reviews will be conducted during the duration of the design project, some only lasting a few hours or lasting several days depending upon the complexity, scope and the phase of the project.

6.3.6 The Importance of Formal Design Reviews

An important step in ensuring full quality in the design process is the inclusion of formal design reviews.

During the period of the design activity there should be a number of reviews chaired by a senior representative of management having an engineering degree. This is to ensure that the full weight of management is put behind the design review.

Some companies do not carry out a structured design review. In one case, many months of design work was wasted due to a misunderstanding between the team dealing with marketing requirements for a new product and the design office interpretation of these requirements. Needles to add, this company now adheres to a full formal design review for each project.

In another example, an insurance company estimated the cost of not correcting a design fault at the design review stage to be approximately £25.00. The cost would have increased to £177.00 if the defect had been corrected following the design review but before any part procurement. The cost would have increased to £368.00 to correct the defect after procurement but before assembly. This figure would have increased significantly to £17 000.00 for correction following assembly but before dispatch. Once the product was in the market place, it was estimated that the cost to correct the design fault would have been approximately £400 000.00. The field correction ended up being 16 000 times the price of the correction at the design review stage.

Reports are often seen in newspapers and on TV where products have been recalled for repair or replacement, and this represents considerable cost to the company in terms of financial loss and loss of face in the market place.

6.3.7 Types of Design Reviews

A design review is a means of controlling the quality of the design and ensuring that all aspects of the design process fully meet the design requirements.

- Design requirements review
- Conceptual design review
- Preliminary design review
- Critical design review
- Qualification readiness review
- Final design review

6.3.7.1 Design Requirements Review

This first review is to establish that the design requirements can be met and that it reflects the needs of the customer before the start of the conceptual design. The initial *Product Design Specification* is reviewed before the conceptual design phase is started.

6.3.7.2 Conceptual Design Review

The conceptual design review is held to establish that the final design concept selected will fulfil the requirements before any project definition begins. There may be a number of conceptual designs generated, and it is the purpose of this review to select the most appropriate design to proceed with.

6.3.7.3 Preliminary Design Review

This review establishes that all the known risks have been addressed and resolved and that design specifications for each sub-element of the project have been satisfactorily completed.

6.3.7.4 Critical Design Review

The critical design review establishes that the detailed design for each sub-element complies with its development specification and that production specifications have been produced prior to the manufacture of any prototype models.

6.3.7.5 Qualification Readiness Review

This review creates the baseline of the design and shows that the qualification of the product is in hand before the commencement of proving trials.

6.3.7.6 Final Design Review

The final design review establishes that the design addresses all the issues raised in the preceding design reviews and fulfils the requirements of the development specification before releasing the design for production.

6.3.8 The Design Review Team

For a design review to be effective it should be conducted by someone other than the designer. The team should comprise representatives from marketing, purchasing, manufacturing, servicing, inspection, test, reliability and QA authorities. This will ensure that all aspects of the design have sufficient practical experience available and provide ample advance warning of any potential problems in implementing the design.

The chairman of the review team should have the authority to make any decisions as to whether the design should proceed to the next phase based on the evidence substantiated by the review team.

6.3.9 Design Review Input Data

Input data relevant to the review should be distributed and examined by all active partners within the team in advance of the time of the individual review meeting. However, a sub-meeting may need to be held to examine and analyse the input data prior to the main meeting so that the proposed design solution is the most practical and cost-effective way of meeting the design requirements.

6.3.10 Design Review Reports

The results of the design reviews should be documented in a report rather than taking minutes of the meeting, as it represents an objective evidence that may later be required to justify a products compliance with the requirements. The report should also show the investigation of design problems and compare similar designs. The reports should also have the agreement of the entire review team.

6.3.11 Design Review Follow-Up

Any corrective actions arising from the design reviews should be tracked to confirm that they have been implemented as agreed and that any reported problems have been fully resolved.

6.3.12 Failure Modes and Effects Analysis

6.3.12.1 A Brief History

In 1949, the US Armed Forces introduced MIL-P 1629, a *procedure for performing a failure mode and effect and criticality analysis*. This enabled failures to be classified according to the impact on mission's success and personnel/equipment safety. NASA also implemented it in the Apollo space program to mitigate the risk due to small sample sizes.

In the 1970s, the Ford Motor Company introduced Failure Modes and Effects Analysis (FMEA) into the company following the problems in the Pinto model. Although originally developed for the military, the FMEA method is now used extensively in a wide range of industries covering mechanical, electronic, food-production and healthcare to name a few.

6.3.12.2 Purpose of FMEA

FMEA is designed to identify and fully understand potential failure modes in a design and assess the risk that is associated with the potential failure and prioritise issues for corrective action and address the most serious concerns.

An FMEA can be implemented and carried out at any point during the design phase.

It is most effective if the method is carried out in the early stages of the design phase as this will reduce the risk of having to amend the design and incur additional cost of having to change the design when moving into the pre-production phase.

6.3.12.3 Steps to Carry Out an FMEA

In carrying out an FMEA exercise the following steps are undertaken:

Step 1: Review the design

The purpose for reviewing the design is to identify all the components making up the design at a given level of the design hierarchy and determine the function or functions of each part. In some cases, components may have more than one function.

Step 2: Identify potential failure modes

Each part is carefully studied to identify a potential failure site. There are several ways in which a part may fail: insufficient lubrication causing a bearing to seize or fail, a potential overload causing excessive deformation of the part reducing its dimensional accuracy, etc.

TABLE 6.4

Severity and Corresponding Ranks of Failure

Rank	Effect	Rank	Effect
1	None	6	Severe
2	Very slight	7	High Severity
3	Slight	8	Very High Severity
4	Minor	9	Extreme Severity
5	Moderate	10	Maximum Severity

Step 3: List the potential failure effects

Ascertain the effects (both locally and globally) associated with each failure mode on the system. An effect is the impact of a failure if it occurred. The effect is directly related to the ability of that specific part to perform its intended function.

Step 4: Assign a severity rating

A severity ranking is applied to each identified effect. The severity ranking is an estimate of how serious an effect would be if it occurred. See Table 6.4 for a list of rankings. To determine the severity of the effect, consider the impact it would have on the system, on downstream operations, on the customer or an employee if failure occurred.

Step 5: Assign occurrence rating

The next step is to determine the failure's probability of occurring. An occurrence ranking is assigned to each of the potential causes or failure mechanisms. The ranking is based on the possibility that the failure will occur. The occurrence ranking scale like the severity ranking is on a relative scale from 1 to 10, as shown in Table 6.5.

Step 6: Assign detection rating

When assigning detection rating, the product is first identified that is related to controls in place for each failure mode, a detection ranking is assigned to each control. Detection rankings evaluate the current process controls in place. The detection ranking scale, like the severity and occurrences, is on a relative scale from 1 to 10, as shown in Table 6.6.

Step 7: Calculate risk priority number

The Risk Priority Number (RPN) gives a relative risk ranking. The RPN is arrived at by multiplying the three rankings together, i.e., multiply the severity ranking by the occurrence ranking and multiplying the result by the detection ranking:

Risk Priority Number (RPN) = (Severity) × (Occurrence) × (Detection)

TABLE 6.5

Likely Occurence of Failure

Rank	Occurrence	Rank	Occurrence
1	Extremely Unlikely	6	Medium Likelihood
2	Remote Likelihood	7	Moderately High Likelihood
3	Very Low Likelihood	8	Very High Likelihood
4	low Likelihood	9	Extreme Likelihood
5	Moderately Low Likelihood	10	Maximum Likelihood

TABLE 6.6

Likely Detection of Failure

Rank	Occurrence	Rank	Occurrence
1	Very Likely	6	Moderately Low Likelihood
2	Very High Likelihood	7	Low Likelihood
3	High Likelihood	8	Very Low Likelihood
4	Moderately High Likelihood	9	Remote Likelihood
5	Medium Likelihood	10	Extremely Unlikelihood

The RPN is calculated for each failure mode and its corresponding effect. The RPN will always be between 1 and 1000. A high RPN indicates that the relative risk will also be high. The RPN is an excellent method to prioritise improvement efforts.

Step 8: Reducing high RPNs

An action plan will be required to reduce high RPNs. It can be reduced by lowering any of the three rankings either individually or in combination with one another.

Step 9: Action plan

The action plan will outline the steps needed to:

- Implement a solution
- Identify who will undertake the implementation
- Identify time scales

Responsibility and target completion dates for the specified actions should be identified together with the individual assigned to that task. A completion date must accompany each recommended action.

Step 10: Re-evaluate the RPN after the actions have been completed

This final step is to confirm if the action plan has had the desired results. The RPN is recalculated to reassess the Severity, Occurrence and Detection Rankings for the failure modes after the action plan has been completed.

Table 6.7 show a typical worksheet together with an example of an FMEA for a typical failure of an engineering component.

TABLE 6.7

FMEA Typical work sheet

Function	Potential Failure Mode	Potential Effects of Failure	Severity No.	Potential Causes of Failure
Provide adequate support according to specification.	Excessive structural deflection.	Frame deflection can result in stability during impact loads.	9	Structure not stiff enough to withstand impact loads.
	Complete structural failure	Structure may fail and cause an accident	10	Structure cross-section insufficient for severe loading.
Provide correct dimensional support for entire structure sub-assembly.	Incorrect structure length.	Design may not perform in terms of stability and handling as intended	6	Correct analysis of the contribution of the upper structure in-correctly undertaken.

6.3.13 Summary

The FMEA procedure is a tool that has been adapted in numerous ways for a number of different purposes.

It is able to contribute to improved designs for products resulting in improved reliability, better quality control, increased safety, enhanced customer satisfaction and reduced manufacturing costs.

The procedure can also be used to establish and optimise maintenance plans for repairable units. Contribute to control plans and other quality assurance procedures.

A knowledge base of failure modes will be generated together with the corrective action information that can be used as a resource for future problems.

6.4 Design for Reliability

A definition of reliability is the probability that a physical entity delivers it functional requirements for an intended period of time under specified operating conditions with low overall life cycle costs.

The old adage *'a chain is only as strong as its weakest link'* is equally true when considering the design of an artefact such as a mechanism or structural item. A 'weak' component in a system will compromise the entire system and possibly lead to a catastrophic failure with the potential of loss of life.

The assessment of reliability usually involves testing and analysis of stress, strength and environmental factors and should include an appraisal for the improper usage by the end user. A reliable design should anticipate all that can go wrong with the product during its operational life.

6.4.1 Reliability and the Bathtub Curve

For a sufficiently large population of a particular product, it will be found that failures will be distributed over time, as shown in Figure 6.1. Failure rates will occur at different times depending on the item, although the basic shape will be found to be similar in all cases. This type of graph is known as a 'bathtub curve' due to its characteristic shape. It will be seen from the figure that the highest failures occur within the premature failure (also known as 'infant mortality' and the end-of-life wear out periods. Following the premature period which will generally correspond to a running-in period to bed the assembly down, failure rates will reduce significantly for the expected life of the system.

During the life of a mechanical product following the running-in period, there will be random failures occurring due to a number of reasons such as unpredicted overloading or misuse. Figure 6.1 depicts the type of failure curve to be expected for this type of product with the failure rate rising slightly during its working life.

Failures will be expected to increase when the system reaches its predicted life largely due to mechanical wear within the components comprising the system.

6.4.1.1 Causes of Component Failure

A product is generally a system of interconnected components, ranging from a very simple product consisting of a single component such as a spanner to a complex product such as

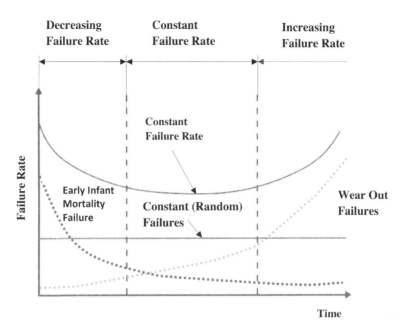

FIGURE 6.1
Bathtub curve.

an automotive engine. A component failure will usually lead to a failure of the whole product. There can be many reasons why a component might fail, and these may be collected categorized into broad groups, as shown in Table 6.8.

It is usual for the design office and service department to keep a detailed record of all service failures to identify a potential problem in the design. These failures where possible should be logged together with a serial number of the product (if it is known).

6.4.2 Safety Critical Design

Product reliability and safety are related; if the product is performing a safety-critical role, then the failure of a key component can have disastrous consequences. Some of the approaches to minimise the risk of a catastrophic failure are as follows:

- **Over-specification:** For material test rigs and fatigue testing machines, it is usual practice to include an 'x6' safety factor in all material strength calculations. As an example, an attachment bracket subject to a 600 kg loading will be designed to carry a 3600 kg load.

  This type of equipment will be subject to the loads and forces the rig is subjecting the test part to, hence it should not fail during operation.

- **Redundancy (parallel):** Numerous identical parts are used each having independent load paths simultaneously, where any one part alone will be capable of carrying the full load without failure. An example is the humble passenger lift which has four cables carrying the lift and a full load of passengers and sharing the load between them. Should any one cable fail the remaining three cables will be more than adequate in carrying the load.

TABLE 6.8

Probable Causes of Component Failure

Life Phase	Cause of Failure	Prevention/Remedy
Premature failure	Component is good but incorrectly installed	Assembly procedure is part of the design responsibility
Premature failure	Component is damaged during assembly	Liaison with production Change component design or assembly method
Premature failure	Component is damages during scheduled maintenance	Adjust design according to field data. Redesign for maintainability
Premature failure	Component incorrectly designed and fails due to high stress levels	Review design
Normal service phase (random failures)	Careless handling. Accidents.	Re-design product with respect to shock and vibration
	Severe natural phenomena (lightning, freak weather). Acts of War.	Ruggedisation, otherwise no economic remedy.
	Random failure of components. Fatigue life dependent upon the duty cycle.	Careful inspection, no surface scratches or cracks. Eliminate sharp corners and other stress raisers.
	Natural aging – component material degraded exposure to air, light, salt-water. Galvanic corrosion.	Revise material specification if extended life is required. Planned inspection schedule.
Wear-out failures	Mechanical wear. Component wears out at the end of its declared life (through abrasion or material depletion).	Consider product maintenance or disposal e.g. bushes, seals, bearings etc.
	Component wears out before reaching its declared life.	Increase specification, ruggedize, reduce stress environment, revise target life.

- **Redundancy (standby):** A backup system is held in reserve and becomes operative when the main system fails. An example of this is the use of standby generators in hospitals.

  Flight controls and instrument systems in aircraft rely on a similar strategy. Triple wiring on military systems is used in case one signal goes down or becomes wild, an inbuilt computer system will analyse the received signal and disregard the incorrect one.

- **Fail-safe design:** This strategy assumes that there is an inherent risk of failure for which the cost of any of the above approaches would be prohibitively high or uneconomical. In this case, the product or system is designed to drop into a safe condition in the event of a partial or total failure. Examples include:

  1. Articulated trailer brakes are released using vacuum. In the event of a brake line failure, the admitted air will automatically apply the trailer brakes. A similar arrangement is used in railway trains.

  2. The gas supply to a domestic central heating boiler or cooker will be shut off in the absence of a 'healthy' signal from gas pressure sensor, flame sensor or water pressure sensor.

- **Safe life:** In this strategy, the part or assembly is designed for a finite life, and when a percentage of that life is reached, the part or assembly is immediately withdrawn from the service. This approach is extensively used in military aircraft and equipment.

FIGURE 6.2
RBD for two events in series.

6.4.3 Fault Tree Analysis (FTA)

Fault Tree Analysis (FTA) is another technique for reliability and safety analysis. The concept was developed by Bell Telephone Laboratories in 1962 for the US Air force Minuteman guided weapon system and later extensively applied by the Boeing Company.

Fault tree diagrams (or negative analysis trees) are logic block diagrams that are most often used as a system-level risk assessment technique. It is able to model the possible combinations of equipment failures, human errors and external conditions that can lead to a specific type of accident.

It follows a top-down structure and is represented by a graphical model of the pathways within a system between the basic events that can lead to a foreseeable loss event (or failure) which is referred to as the top event.

6.4.3.1 Drawing Fault Trees: Gates and Events

Fault trees are built up using gates and events (blocks). The two most common used gates are the **AND** and **OR** gates. For example, consider two events (called input events) that can lead to a further event (called the output event). If the occurrence of either of the input events causes the output event to occur, then they are connected by an **AND** gate. As an example, consider the simple case of a system comprising of two components, **A** and **B**, where a failure of either component results in a system failure. The system reliability block diagram (RBD) is made up of two blocks in series, as shown in Figure 6.2.

The fault tree diagram for this system includes two input events connected to an **OR** gate (see Figure 6.3) which is the output event or (the 'top event'). If the top event is a system failure and the two input events are component failures, then this fault tree indicates that the failure of either **A** or **B** will cause the system to fail.

If the **OR** gate was replaced by an **AND** gate, as in Figure 6.4, a fault in either **A** or **B** would result in a system failure.

Table 6.9 lists the most common fault tree symbols used in the construction of a fault tree.

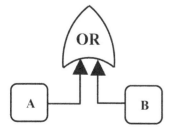

FIGURE 6.3
Two input events connected to an OR gate.

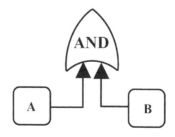

FIGURE 6.4
Two input events connected to an AND gate.

TABLE 6.9

Fault Tree Symbols

Symbols	Definitions
	Resultant event: represents the fault event above the gates, which is a result of the combination of other fault events.
	Basic fault event: represents a fault where the failure probability can be driven from empirical data. It is the limit of resolution of the fault tree.
	House event: Represents a basic event that is expected to occur during the system operation.
IN / OUT	Transfer Symbol: transfer-in and transfer-out triangles used to transfer fault tree from one part to another.
	And Gate: Output fault event occurs only when all inputs occur simultaneously
	OR Gate: Output fault event occur when one or more input faults occur.

6.4.4 General Procedure for Fault Tree Analysis

The following procedure is taken from the US Coast Guard Risk-based Decision-Making Guidelines Vol. 3 – Risk Assessment Tools Reference, Chapter 9 – Fault Tree Analysis.

Step 1: Define the system of interest

Specify and clearly define the boundaries and initial conditions of the system for which the failure analysis is required.

Step 2: Define the top event for the analysis

Specify the problem of interest that the analysis will address (e.g. a specific quality problem, shutdown, safety issues, etc.).

Step 3: Define the treetop structure

Determine the events and conditions (i.e. intermediate events) that most directly lead to the top event.

Step 4: Explore each branch in successive level of detail

Determine the events and conditions that most directly lead to each intermediate event. Repeat the process at each successive level of the tree until the fault tree model is complete.

Step 5: Solve the fault tree for the combinations of events and conditions that can cause the top event of interest. A combination of events and conditions *sufficient* and *necessary* to cause the top event is called a minimal cut set

Step 6: Identify important failure potentials and adjust the model appropriately (qualitative common cause failure analysis)

Study the fault tree model and the list of minimal cut sets to identify potentially important dependencies among the events. Dependencies are single occurrences that may cause multiple events or conditions to occur at the same time.

Step 7: Perform quantitative analysis (if necessary)

Use statistical characterisations regarding the failure and repair of specific events and conditions in the fault tree model to predict future performance for the system.

Step 8: Use results in decision-making

Use results of the analysis to identify the most significant vulnerabilities in the system and to make effective recommendations for reducing the risks associated with those vulnerabilities.

6.4.5 Rules to Fault Tree Construction

- A fault tree should only be constructed once the functioning of the entire system is fully understood.
- Objective to identify all the component failures or combinations thereof that could lead to the top event (Steps 2–4 above).

Rule 1

State the fault event as a fault, including the description and timing of a fault condition at some particular time.

Include:

a. What the fault state of that system or components is

b. When that system or component is in the fault state

Test the fault event by asking:

c. Is it a fault?

d. Is the what and when portion included in the fault statement?

Rule 2

There are two basic types of fault statements:

a. State-of-system

b. State-of-component

To continue the tree,

c. If the state-of-system fault statement, use Rule 3

d. If the state-of-component statement, use Rule 4

Rule 3

A state-of-system fault may use an **AND, OR,** or **INHIBIT** gate or no gate at all.
To determine which gate to use, the faults must be then:

a. Minimum necessary and sufficient fault events

b. Immediate fault events

Rule 4

A state-of-component fault always uses an **OR** gate.
To continue, look for the primary, secondary and command failure fault events. Then state those fault events.

a. Primary failures are failures of that component within the design envelope or environment.

b. Secondary failures are failures of the component due to excessive environments exceeding the design environment.

c. Command faults are inadvertent operation of the component because of a failure of a control element.

Rule 5

Put an event statement between two gates.

Rule 6

Expect no miracles.
Those things that normally occur as a result of a fault will occur and only those things.
Also normal system operation may be expected to occur when faults occur.

Rule 7

In an **OR** gate, the input does not cause output.
If an input exists, the output exists. Fault events under the gate may be a restatement of the output events.

Rule 8

An **AND** gate defines a causal relationship.
If the output events coexist, the output is produced.

Rule 9

An **INHIBIT** gate describes a causal relationship between one fault and another, but the indicated condition must be present.
The fault is the direct and sole cause of the output when that specified condition is present. Inhibit conditions may be the faults or situations, which is why **AND** and **INHIBIT** gates differ.

6.4.5.1 Example

Construct a fault tree for the simple solenoid circuit shown in Figure 6.5.
Solution:

Step 1: Define the system of interest
Need to identify,

- Intended functions.
- Physical boundaries (avoid overlooking key elements of a system at interfaces and penalising a system by associating other equipment with the subject of study).

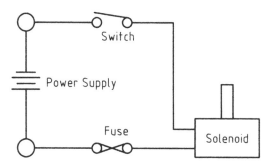

FIGURE 6.5
A Simple Solenoid Circuit.

- Analytical boundaries (to limit the level of analysis resolution, to explicitly exclude certain types of events and conditions, such as sabotage, from the analysis).
- Initial conditions (including equipment that is assumed to be out of service initially, which affect the combinations of additional events necessary to produce a specific system problem).

For this particular problem:
Intended function – The solenoid is used for an unknown purpose.
Physical boundaries – Power supply.
Analytical boundaries – Include all contributors in Figure 6.5.
Initial Conditions – Switch closed, solenoid operative.

Step 2: Define the top event
The top event is defined as the event of interest that the solenoid fails to operate.

Step 3: Construct the fault tree, starting from the top, i.e., define the treetop structure. Identify the main contributing events, including all events and scenarios that may cause the top event.

Step 4: Explore each branch in successive levels of detail, following the rules of fault tree construction.

6.4.6 Fault Tree Construction

Gate 1
One primary failure event is the failure of the solenoid itself (for example, there is a wiring failure within the solenoid or a loss of lubrication to the bearings). This event is considered as no details have been supplied; therefore, the event cannot be developed further. The other possibility is the consequence that there no current is being supplied the solenoid.

Gate 2
The event 'No current to solenoid' is the result of other events and is therefore developed further. The lack of current to the solenoid may result from a broken connection in any of the four components in the circuit, including failure of the variable resistance, the switch being open, failure of the fuse (open circuit) or failure of power supply (basic event).

Gate 3

The open switch may be due to a basic failure of the switch, or the event was opened incorrectly. The erroneous opening of the switch is due to human error, which could be developed further into more basic events (i.e. inexperienced operator under stress, etc.) However, due to insufficient information, the event cannot be developed any further.

This deliberately undeveloped event is therefore denoted by a diamond symbol.

Gate 4

The fuse failure event may be caused by failure under normal conditions (primary failure) or due to an overload from the circuit.

Gate 5

The secondary fuse failure can occur if the fuse does not open every time an overload is present in the circuit. (All conditions of an overload do not necessarily result in sufficient overcurrent to open the fuse.) Therefore, a conditional gate denoted by a hexagon is used in this situation. The condition, i.e., 'Fuse fails to open' is placed in the connecting oval, and the conditional gate is treated similarly to an **AND** gate in the subsequent tree analysis.

Gate 6

The overload in the circuit may be caused by either a short or a power surge, both of which are primary (i.e. basic) events.

Considerations:

- The construction of a fault tree is subjective.
- The engineer needs to take into account:
  - Level of detail – the number of basic events should be defined such that the size of the tree is a reasonable size with respect to the scope of the analysis.
  - Probability assignment – need to stop development at the level where probability or failure data is available.
  - Meaningfulness – the level of detail should be such that the basic and undeveloped events correspond to the design aspects being analysed.

6.5 Fault Tree Evaluation

- Identify the critical events and event combinations that lead to the top event.
- Calculate the probability of the top event based on the probabilities of the basic and undeveloped events in the fault tree.
- There are two types of analysis:
  - Qualitative
  - Quantitative
- The analysis is based on Boolean logic

Boolean Algebra

- Fault trees describe the relationships between events using Boolean logic.
- The fault tree can be translated into an equivalent set of Boolean equations.

6.5.1 The 'OR' Gate

This gate represents the union of events. For event 'Q' with two input events 'A' and 'B' attached to the **OR** gate, the probability is obtained as follows:

$$P(Q) = P(A) + P(B) - P(A \cap B)$$
$$\text{or } P(Q) = P(A) + P(B) - P(A)P(B|A)$$

If A and B are mutually exclusive events then:

$$P(A \cap B) = 0$$
$$\text{and } P(Q) = P(A) + P(B)$$

If A and B are independent events then:

$$P(B|A) = P(B)$$
$$\text{and } P(Q) = P(A) + P(B) - P(A)P(B)$$

If event 'B' is completely dependent upon event 'A' then:

$$P(B|A) = 1$$
$$\text{and } P(Q) = P(A) + P(B) - P(A)(1) = P(B)$$

Therefore, the approximation of:

$$P(Q) = P(A) + P(B)$$

and is always a conservative estimate for the probability of event 'Q' (because $P(A \cap B)$ is small compared with $P(A) + P(B)$ for very low probability events.

6.6 Robust Design

6.6.1 Introduction

Robust design is a concept developed by Dr. Genichi Taguchi, a Japanese quality guru in the early 1950s while working for the Electrical Communications Laboratory (ECL) of the Nippon Telegraph and Telephone Corporation. It is defined as reducing variation in a product without eliminating the causes of the variation. Essentially, the product becomes insensitive to variations. This variation (sometimes called noise) comes from a variety of factors and can be classified into three main areas, namely:

- Internal variation
- External variation
- Unit-to-unit variation

Internal variation is due to deterioration in the product such as wear and aging of materials. External variation is due to factors relating to environmental conditions such as temperature and humidity. Unit-to-unit variations are variations occurring between parts due to variations in material, processes and equipment.

Examples of robust design include:

a. Composite products that have long curing lives (internal variations)
b. High tensile steels that will not corrode and deteriorate when exposed to varying environments (external variation),
c. Replacement parts that will interchange correctly (unit-to-unit variation).

The object of robust design is to achieve ways of making the final product insensitive when the process is subjected to a wide variety of variations or 'noise'.

The procedure is to find design solutions that are robust against the variation they are likely to experience during use, rather than tightening tolerances when faced with a sensitive design, the system should be redesigned to find an alternative solution that is insensitive.

Robust design has now become an established methodology in most serious engineering companies and this has resulted in a major contribution being made to product quality within these companies.

6.6.2 Sources of Variation

The uncontrollable operating influences originally defined by Taguchi can also be called sources of variation.

6.6.2.1 Material Properties

Selecting materials is a fundamental part of design in the component meeting its design specification. Inputs from marketing, production, quality and other departments have an impact on the final material of choice. Each material will react differently to external forces. Some materials also react differently to internal forces (residual forces or stresses); if these are too high it can have a major impact on the life of the component. Mould cooling times can impact the integrity of pressure injected plastics, where increased density will impact flexibility.

6.6.2.2 Applied Forces

Almost all products are subject to some external force. At a minimum they will be subject to the force of gravity. Most products will be exposed to some form of dynamic forces, either from the end user, interaction from other systems, environmental forces, etc. Designs are analysed using the expected 'worst-case' applied forces with engineering factors of safety being applied to ensure that the product will perform as designed. Random dynamic loading over a period of time creates fatigue which is more difficult to predict.

6.6.2.3 Temperature

Temperature fluctuations influence almost all material properties. Fluctuations in the operating temperature not only cause dimensional changes, but also lead to changes in properties including brittleness, thermal conductance, electrical conductivity, pressure of a gas, chemical reaction time, etc. Design nominal at ambient temperature must take into account these changes particularly if the standard operating temperature is higher or lower.

6.6.2.4 Environmental Factors

Water, wind and other environmental elements alter the physical properties of materials. Furthermore, the impact the environment has on the applied forces and temperatures, can lead to varying rates of corrosion that influence the material properties and often lead to premature failure. Managing this variation is necessary as this variation can have a negative impact on the robustness of the product. An example includes material selection to evade galvanic corrosion of a part immersed in a seawater environment.

6.6.2.5 Assembly Methods

Variations in the method or sequence of assembly can have an impact on the part variation in its position and orientation between other adjacent parts. Problems occur when different fitters use alternate techniques in assembling the parts, and trying to troubleshoot the root cause of any problem can be difficult. It is important to ensure that parts are not assembled incorrectly, such as angular contact bearings being inserted the wrong way round, and also to ensure that such mistakes do not lead to safety issues or equipment failures.

6.6.2.6 Kinematic Effects

Kinematic variations occur due to motion between parts resulting from clearances that are required for either running or assembly. Products having moving parts will need to be examined at multiple positions throughout the range of movement to ensure the part will perform as designed.

6.6.2.7 Manufacturing Processes

For a given assembly there are numerous manufacturing options. Increased accuracy and precision incur higher costs; therefore, the challenge for the engineering designer is to select the most accurate and precise method using the least restrictive tolerances possible.

6.6.2.8 Classify the Variables

Figure 6.6 shows the relationships between the four classes of variables.

Signal factors are the process inputs and the responses are the results of the process.

Control factors are those factors that can be controlled. In the tile example, they include limestone content of the in the clay mixture, fineness of the additives, amalgamate content, type of amalgamate, raw material quantity, waste return content and type of feldspar.

Noise factors are those factors that cannot be controlled. In Dr. Taguchi's application of robustness experiments, he treated temperature as a noise factor since it is difficult to control and its variation is a necessary evil. He investigated varying other factors that were much less expensive to control than temperature in order to make more robust products. Robust design is called minimum sensitivity design.

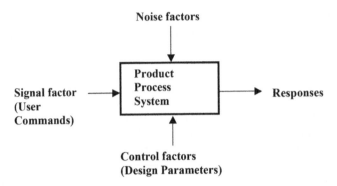

FIGURE 6.6
The four classes of variables in the Taguchi method.

6.6.3 Taguchi's Loss Function

Traditionally, companies measure quality by the number of defects or defect rate. In this system, defects are identified through inspections in which upper and lower quality limits are established. Everything that does not fall within the limits is considered a defect. This view of quality is referred to as a goal post philosophy (Figure 6.7). This philosophy considers the quality of the product offgrade if suddenly the product dimension is out of the upper or lower tolerance limit.

Taguchi explained that from a customer's point of view this drop of quality is not sudden. The customer experiences a loss of quality the moment the product specification deviates from the 'target value'. This 'loss' is represented by a quality loss function, and it follows a parabolic curve given by:

$$L = k(y-m)^2$$

where 'm' is the theoretical 'target value' or 'mean value'
'y' is the actual size of the product

$$k = \left(\frac{A_o}{\Delta_o{}^2}\right)$$

'L' is the loss

If the difference between 'actual size' and 'target value, i.e. (y – m) is large, loss would be more, irrespective of tolerance specifications.

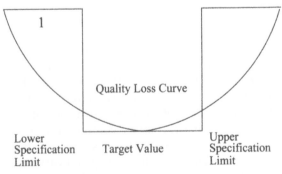

FIGURE 6.7
Goalpost philosophy (Tagushi's loss function).

6.6.4 P-Diagram (Parametric Diagram)

The first step in Robust Design is to establish all the design parameters, including, noise factors and signal factors that relate to the system output that is under investigation. Figure 6.9 shows the basic parameter diagram for a product or process.

Taguchi argued that there are three types of factors that determine the output of a system:

1. **Signal factors** (or user commands) are parameters set by the user to set or command the intended value for the output of the system.
2. **Control factors** (or design parameters) are parameters that are freely set by the designer. In fact it is the responsibility of the designer to determine the best values for these parameters.
3. **Noise factors** are parameters that are outside the control of the designer, such as temperature. They cause the output to deviate from the target values specified by the signal factors.

A P-diagram can help the designer (or design team) identify all the possible factors that could have a role to play in delivering a good performance. Figure 6.10 shows a P-diagram for a catalytic converter used in an automotive exhaust system. It shows the overall nature of the design problem. It is not uncommon to have around 50 to 100 noise factors and 20 to 50 design parameters.

6.6.5 Taguchi Concepts

Dr. Genichi Taguchi developed a means of dramatically improving processes in the 1980s. Since then his methods have been widely used in achieving 'robustness of design'.

'Robust' here means strong, healthy, enduring, not easily broken and not fragile. When we refer to a robust design we are describing a product design that is sturdy and intrinsically avoids defects. The concept of 'designing quality into the product or process' is another expression of a robust design.

Taguchi's approach for making product design robust involved the application of five practices:

1. Classify the variables associated with the product into signal (input), response (result), control, and noise factors.
2. Mathematically specify the ideal form of the signal-to-response process that will produce a product that will make the system, in which it is used, work perfectly.
3. Compute the loss experienced when the output response deviates from the ideal (this practice is also known as the Taguchi loss function).
4. Predict the field quality through laboratory experiments given a measured signal-to-noise ratio.
5. Employ design-of-experiments (DOE) to determine in a small number of experiments the control factors that create the best performance for the process.

To illustrate how this Taguchi method reduces variations and produces higher quality products, examples of the Taguchi method are considered.

6.6.5.1 An Example of Robust design via the Taguchi Method

In 1953, the Ina Seito tile manufacturing company experienced non-linear heat distribution in its brick baking kiln causing the tiles nearest the walls of the kiln to warp and break. Replacing the kiln would be expensive, so Taguchi proposed the less costly option of reformulating the clay recipe so the tiles were less sensitive to temperature variations. Taguchi was able to show via laboratory experiments that if 5% more lime were added to the clay mix they would be more robust, that is, less likely to break and warp. The Ina Seito plant did not need to purchase a new expensive kiln but was rather able to solve the problem in a much less expensive fashion. This experiment has become the showcase example of how intelligent use of DOE can produce products that are robust process noise.

6.6.6 The Taguchi Loss Function

The Taguchi loss function is a conception of quality that is more demanding than most. Genichi Taguchi contended that as product characteristics deviate from the design aim, the losses increase parabolically. The diagram on the left in Figure 6.8 illustrates the traditional concept, in which the product is considered good if its characteristics fall within the lower to upper specification limits, and it is considered bad if it falls outside the specification limits. The diagram on the right in Figure 6.8 shows the Taguchi concept where the loss that society suffers increases parabolically as the product's characteristics deviate from the design target.

The formula expressing the Taguchi loss function is:

$$L = K(Y - T)^2$$

where

L = loss in dollars

K = cost coefficient

T = design target or aim

Y = actual quality value

The point of this equation is that merely attempting to produce a product within specifications doesn't prevent loss. Loss occurs even if the product passes final inspection

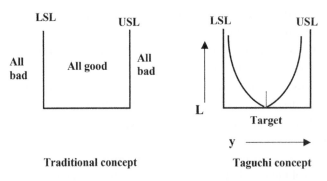

FIGURE 6.8
Comparison between the traditional and Taguchi concepts.

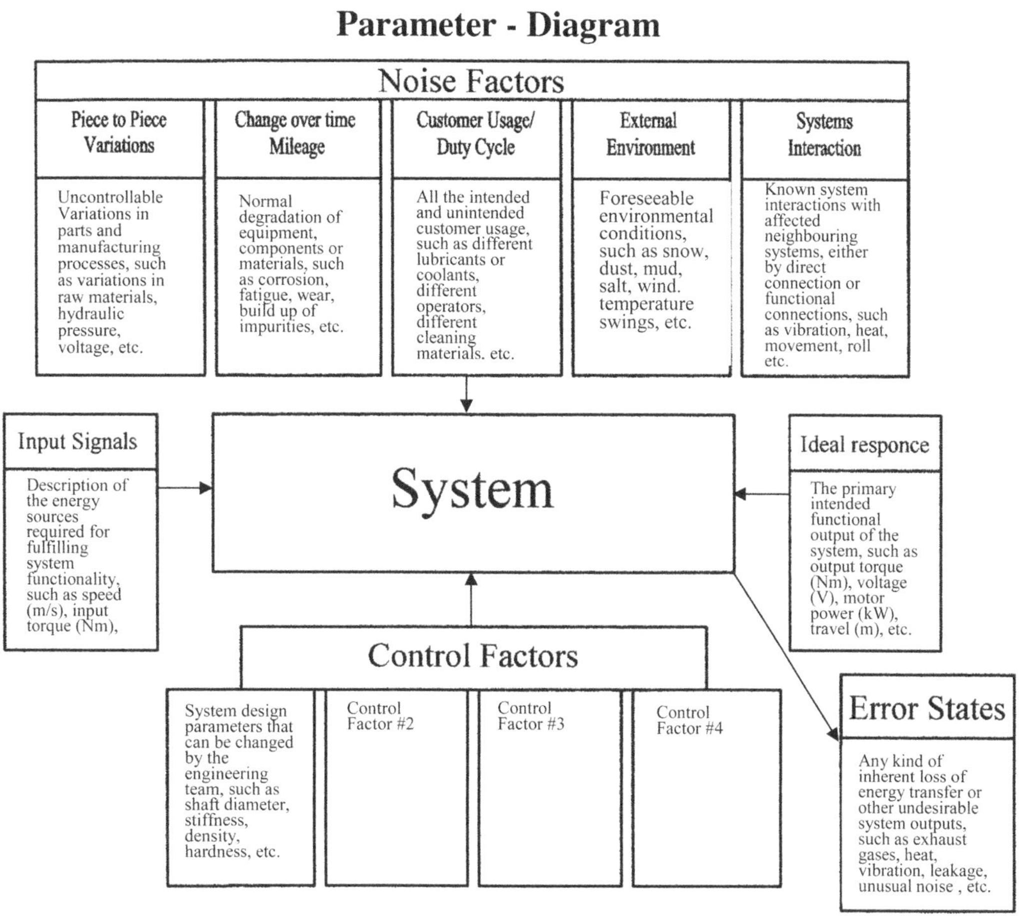

Parameter - Diagram

FIGURE 6.9
Parametric diagram.

by falling within the specification limits but doesn't exactly meet the design target. Consider an automobile driveshaft. Suppose its target design diameter is 3.3 ± 0.1 cm. If the housing that contains the driveshaft is built extremely close to its tolerances (i.e. to accommodate a driveshaft exactly 3.3 cm), and the driveshaft is slightly larger or smaller, even though it is within the specification limits, over time it will wear out faster than it would if it were exactly 3.3 cm. If it is 3.26 cm, it will pass final inspection and will power the automobile for a long time. But after hundreds of thousands of revolutions it will wear out faster. The automobile owner will have his/her car repaired earlier than he/she would if the drive shaft were exactly 3.3 cm. The loss function for this driveshaft would be:

$$L = K(3.3 - 3.26)^2$$
$$= K(0.04)^2$$
$$= 0.0016K$$

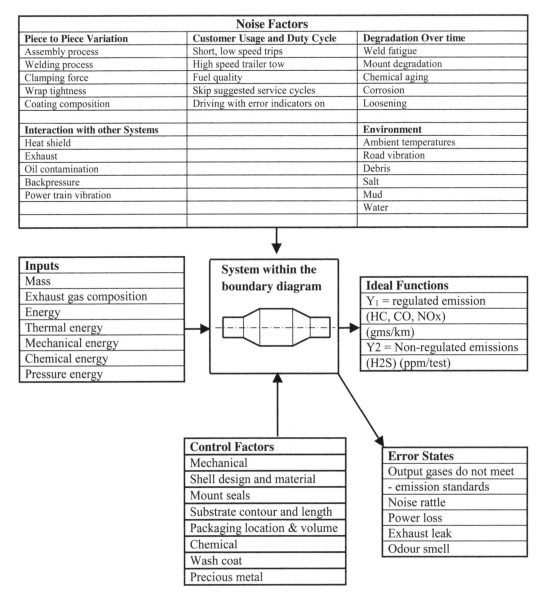

Noise Factors		
Piece to Piece Variation	**Customer Usage and Duty Cycle**	**Degradation Over time**
Assembly process	Short, low speed trips	Weld fatigue
Welding process	High speed trailer tow	Mount degradation
Clamping force	Fuel quality	Chemical aging
Wrap tightness	Skip suggested service cycles	Corrosion
Coating composition	Driving with error indicators on	Loosening
Interaction with other Systems		**Environment**
Heat shield		Ambient temperatures
Exhaust		Road vibration
Oil contamination		Debris
Backpressure		Salt
Power train vibration		Mud
		Water

Inputs
Mass
Exhaust gas composition
Energy
Thermal energy
Mechanical energy
Chemical energy
Pressure energy

System within the boundary diagram

Ideal Functions
Y_1 = regulated emission
(HC, CO, NOx)
(gms/km)
Y2 = Non-regulated emissions
(H2S) (ppm/test)

Control Factors
Mechanical
Shell design and material
Mount seals
Substrate contour and length
Packaging location & volume
Chemical
Wash coat
Precious metal

Error States
Output gases do not meet
- emission standards
Noise rattle
Power loss
Exhaust leak
Odour smell

FIGURE 6.10
Example diagram for catalytic converter.

6.6.7 Signal-to-Noise Ratio

The signal-to-noise (S/N) ratio is used to evaluate system performances.

$$\eta = \frac{S}{N} = +10\log_{10}\frac{1}{r}\left[\frac{S_\beta - V_e}{V_N}\right]$$

where:

   r = magnitude of the input signal

   S_b = sum of squares of the ideal function (useful part)

V_e = mean square of non-linearity

V_N = an error term of non-linearity and linearity

In assessing the results of experiments, the S/N ratio is calculated at each design point. The combinations of the design variables that maximise the S/N ratio are selected for consideration as product or process parameter settings. There are three cases of S/N ratios:

Case 1: S/N ratio for 'smaller is better'
Where S/N ratio = 110 log10 (mean-squared response).
This value should be used for minimising the wear, shrinkage, deterioration and so on of a product or process.

Case 2: S/N ratio for 'bigger is better'

$$\eta = \frac{S}{N} = -10\log_{10} \frac{1}{r}\left[\frac{\Sigma \frac{1}{y_i^2}}{n}\right]$$

Where S/N ratio = $-10\log_{10}$(mean square of the reciprocal response).
This value would be used for maximising values such as strength, life, fuel efficiency and so on of a product or process.

Case 3: S/N ratio for 'normal is best'

$$\eta = \frac{S}{N} = +10\log_{10} \frac{\text{mean}^2}{\text{variance}}$$

$$= +10\log_{10} \frac{y^2}{S^2}$$

This S/N ratio is applicable for dimensions, clearances, viscosities and so on.

6.7 Design for Maintenance

When designing for maintenance, there are eight factors needed to be considered to ensure that the cost of maintenance is minimised.

The factors that need to be considered have been discussed in the next sections.

6.7.1 Standardisation

Standardisation has important ramifications not only in maintenance but also in general cost reduction. One example will be to reduce the size of fasteners to say one size of screw thread instead of a number of different thread sizes and lengths. This also helps as the fitter has to carry only one size of the ring spanner or Allan key. This in turn helps in managing the parts inventory and reduces shelf space for storage.

6.7.1.1 Authors Note

The author was involved in a variety reduction exercise for an automatic machine tool. It was found that reducing the number of fasteners to one size reduces the cost of the machine by £5000. The number of fasteners used in the design was a surprise, which then led to explore how some components could be combined to further reduce the cost.

6.7.2 Modularisation

Designs are created based on modular features allowing the unit to be changed quickly. These parts can be interchanged easily between different models of products carrying out the same function.

6.7.3 Functional Packaging

Prior to carrying out a maintenance task the fitter has to ensure they have all the correct fittings such as 'o' rings and washers. If all the parts are contained in a 'Kit' it will minimise the time spent in obtaining the individual parts and help reduce the breakdown time. This approach will also help in reducing assembly times on the shop floor.

6.7.4 Interchangeability

In the 'variety reduction exercise' mentioned earlier, it was surprising to find the wide variation of parts that benefited from being designed with the intention of being made interchangeable.

By having different design teams involved across a range of products and making a determined effort to minimise the component count within the product, significant savings can be made. From the maintenance fitter's point of view, he/she knows that only three sizes need to be carried in the transport, i.e. small, medium and large.

6.7.5 Accessibility

When a part requires removal or replacement (planned or unplanned), the design should provide sufficient space so that access through the panel is easy for the use of tools and for extracting the part from the assembly without any harm to the maintenance personnel or damage to the machinery.

6.7.6 Malfunction Annunciation

Time can be saved when performing a maintenance task if it is known what caused the problem or which parts have suffered damage and requires replacement.

In modern complex systems, it is not always feasible to identify the problem without a detailed investigation. With the high levels of computerisation in modern machinery and vehicles, it sometimes becomes difficult to identify the individual part when an electronic component fails, and hence the interchangeability rule applies in such cases where the entire module is replaced thereby reducing the breakdown time.

6.7.7 Fault isolation

Fault identification in computerised systems can be improved by the narrowing down the fault through error signals to identify the failure mode. Usually, a failure in one part of the system can result in failure of other adjacent elements.

Where possible ensure that the damage caused by the failure of one element is minimised by containing the damage.

6.7.8 Identification

Ensure every part has a unique serial or part number. This saves a significant amount of time in the field if the failed item has a clear identifier, so that a correct replacement part is shipped to the site. It does not help the integrity of the company if the incorrect part arrives after a long breakdown.

6.7.9 Summary

If the designers work considering that they will be the ones who will have to carry out the maintenance, it would help in sorting out the problems experienced by the maintenance fitters to a great extent.

Many automotive companies now allow the service fitters full access to the prototype of a new automobile so that they can work out their strategies for undertaking replacement and repair work.

6.8 Design for the Environment

6.8.1 Introduction

During the Industrial Revolution fossil fuels were in abundance and material ores were also plentiful. Man was extremely wasteful and paid no heed to the long-term damage he was causing. Today, we are paying the price for this damage with increasing levels of carbon dioxide in the atmosphere creating a 'glass house' environment leading to global warming and rising sea levels, etc. Mankind is now trying to redress most of the excesses by being careful with the levels of energy and materials he is using.

Victor Papanek wrote in *Design for the Real World* in 1971:

> Design. If it is to be ecologically responsible and socially responsive, must be revolutionary and radical in the truest sence.
>
> It must dedicate itself to natures principle of least effort.
>
> That means consuming less, using things longer, recycling materials and probably not wasting paper printing books.

To a large extent, the world is slowly moving in this direction. Even today with all the evidence that is around us, some countries are in denial of global warming.

6.8.2 The Importance of Design for the Environment

Over 70% of costs of product development, manufacture and use are decided early in the design stages as discussed in the chapters relating to conceptual design. Likewise, decisions regarding choices that affect future environmental issues are also made at the design stage.

Designers need to bear in mind the following:

- Functionality and performance
- Manufacturability, logistics
- Reliability, safety, quality
- Cost, market penetration

It is during this phase that material selection has an important part to play in setting the levels of material performance to meet the product requirements.

6.8.2.1 Non-Toxic Processes and Production Methods

Many workshop processes use very toxic materials including sulphuric acid and cyanide. Early fridges used Freon as the thermodynamic fluid till it was discovered to have a deleterious effect on the ozone layer and legislation was passed to replace it with a less damaging fluid.

6.8.2.2 Minimum Energy Utilisation

An MEPS (Minimum Energy Performance Standard) is a specification, containing a number of performance requirements for an *energy*-using device, that effectively limits the maximum amount of energy that may be consumed by a product in performing a specified task.

A MEPS is usually made mandatory by a government energy efficiency body. It may include requirements not directly related to energy; this is to ensure that general performance and user satisfaction are not adversely affected by increasing energy efficiency.

This standard has been adopted by California in the United States, Australia and New Zealand.

6.8.2.3 Minimum Emissions

Emission standards are the legal requirements governing air pollutants released into the atmosphere. Emission standards set quantitative limits on the permissible amount of specific air pollutants that may be released from specific sources over specific timeframes.

6.8.2.4 Minimum Waste, Scrap and By-Products

Waste minimisation involves a set of processes and practices intended to reduce the amount of *waste* produced. By reducing or eliminating the generation of harmful and persistent wastes, waste processes and/or changing societal patterns of *consumption* and production, minimisation supports efforts to promote a more *sustainable* society. Waste minimisation involves redesigning products and production and/or changing societal patterns of *consumption* and production.

The use of waste exchanges encourages the waste product of one process to become the raw material for a second process. Waste exchanges represent another way of reducing waste disposal volumes for waste that cannot be eliminated.

6.8.3 Design for Environmental Packaging Involving the Following Considerations

6.8.3.1 Minimum of Packaging Materials

All packaging material to be minimal and using the minimum types of material.

6.8.3.2 Reusable Pallets, Totes and Packaging

Pallets or tugs used in the transport of products designed to withstand a high degree of abuse and if damaged do not detract from their use.

Containerisation for transport has spurred the use of pallets because shipping containers have the smooth, level surfaces needed for easy pallet movement. Many pallets can handle a load of up to 1000 kg (2205 lb). Today, over half a billion pallets are made each year and about two billion pallets are in use across the *United States* alone.

6.8.3.3 Recyclable Packaging Materials

Environmentally friendly packaging causes less damage to the environment. Reusable packaging can be cleaned and reused. For example, glass milk bottles are reused. Recyclable packaging is made of materials that can be used again, usually after processing. Recyclable materials include glass, metal, card and paper.

Plastic milk containers are also recycled to provide loft insulation to retain heat in buildings and homes.

6.8.3.4 Bio-Degradable Packaging Materials

Types of biodegradable and recyclable packaging material include:

Paper and cardboard – paper and cardboard are reusable, recyclable and biodegradable.

Corn starch – items made from corn starch are biodegradable and are ideal for items which have a limited use, such as takeaway food.

Bagasse is the fibrous, dry and pulpy residue produced during extraction of juice from sugar cane. Bagasse is used as a biofuel and in the manufacture of pulp and building materials.

A number of commercial bioplastic films are totally biodegradable within 18 days and can also be used as home compost.

6.8.4 Design for Disposable and Recyclability Involving the Following Considerations

- Reuse/refurbishment of components and assemblies
- Material selection to enable reuse (e.g. thermostatic plastics vs. thermoplastics) and minimise toxicity).
- Avoid filler material in plastics such as fibreglass and graphite.
- Minimum number of materials/colours to facilitate separating materials and reuse.
- Material identification to facilitate reuse.
- Design to enable materials to be easily separated.
- Design for disassembly (e.g. fracture points, fastenings vs. bonding).
- Avoid the use of adhesives.
- Limit contaminants – additives, coatings, metal plating of plastics, etc.
- Maximise the use of recycled or ground material with virgin material.
- Design for serviceability to minimise disposal of non-working products.

6.8.5 Design for Disassembly

- Provide ready access to parts, fasteners, etc., to support disassembly.
- Design modular products to enable modules to be disassembled for service reuse.
- Minimise weight of individual parts and modules to facilitate disassembly.
- Use joining and fastening techniques to facilitate disassembly (i.e. fasteners instead of adhesives).
- Minimise fragile parts to enable re-use and re-assembly.
- Use connectors instead of hard-wired connections.
- Design to enable use of common hand tools for disassembly.

6.9 Design for Life Cycle Costs

Essentially, 'Life Cycle Costing' considers the costs incurred during the life of a product from initial production, through operation to the end of the product's life.

The life cycle cost of a product is includes the costs incurred by the manufacturer, user and society. The total cost of any product from its earliest concept through its retirement is borne by the user and has a direct bearing on the marketability of that product.

Consider the life cycle of a product from initial design to final decommissioning (see Figure 6.11). This depicts a comparison of product sales and profits generated over its life. The profit line shows an expenditure trough during the initial development phase

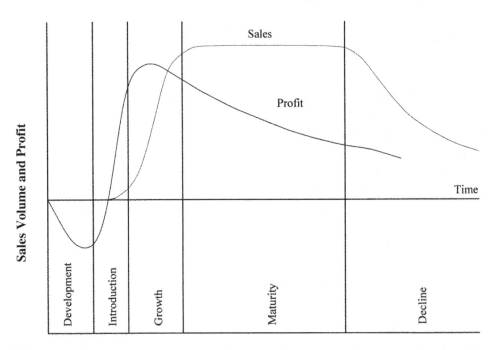

FIGURE 6.11
Life cycle curve for sales and profit.

which is recovered shortly after the product goes on sale, depending on the pricing schedule. It reaches a peak and then there is a gentle decline in profits, although the sales figures continue to rise before plateauing out during the maturity phase. The reason for the decline in profit is the expenditure on marketing and advertising, which will increase as the product matures to keep it in the public eye. At the end of the maturity phase, the company (hopefully) would have introduced a new replacement product and that will be entering its maturity phase; a good example of this is 'toothpaste'. Some products have a product life of nearly 30 years requiring a constant marketing effort to maintain sales.

Another example is the humble plant pot: its life starts when the raw material is delivered to the factory. It is processed through manufacturing, packaging, storage, and subsequent transport. At this point, the distribution chain divides and the pots are either distributed to retail outlets for sale as empty pots or supplied to the horticulture centres to be potted up with plants. The potted plants are then sold through garden centres to either the general public or alternatively supplied to offices. In private houses they are either stored in garden glass houses or kept inside the house as decorative pieces. At the end of the plant's life, the pot is either reused or discarded as refuse. In each case, there is a cost incurred by the pot as it progresses through its life. This is balanced by the profit margin from the sale of the pot when it enters the distribution chain from the point of manufacture to the point of sale at the garden centre or the horticulture centre. A choice is made whether to manufacture a very cheap plant pot that is easily discarded or a more upmarket pot that will be retained after the original plant has died, allowing the pot to be reused.

As purchasers, we pay for the resources required to bring the product to the market, and as owners of the product, we pay for the resources required to deploy, operate and dispose of the product. While the life cycle cost is the aggregate of all the costs incurred in the product's life, it must be pointed out that the developed approach focuses on the cost that can be influenced by the designer. Some of the costs incurred in the life of the product are not a result of the design. These costs are related to the way the product is manufactured.

The life cycle costing originally found strong advocates in military procurement, where it is used for comparison of comparison for competing weapon systems, particularly when decisions regarding the replacement of aging equipment are to be made.

Life cycle costing deals, to a large extent, with future costs, there is considerable uncertainty of putting an accurate cost during the life of the product. The predicted service life is a critical parameter where estimation is very uncertain. It is possible that its life may be unexpectedly foreshortened due to an unrecognised design defect occurring leading to early failures. Alternatively a superior product being marketed or the introduction of a new technology making all existing technology obsolete.

The reliability of the product will have a significant effect on the life of the product in the event that the operating life is much less than the design life. The "Mean Time Between Failures" and the "Mean time to Repair" become key factors from reliability theory that have an important influence on the life cycle cost.

6.9.1 Manufacturing Costs

The cost of manufacture is usually the easiest cost to evaluate. Modern estimation techniques have improved significantly over the last few years with research into machining methods. Now it is possible to arrive at a very accurate cost to manufacture a wide range of products and to arrive at a cost/piece in terms of part handling, tool changing, machining and overheads; included in this is the cost of special tool grinding if required.

6.9.2 Life Cycle Costing

These costs comprise the following costs:

- Raw material
- Manufacturing
- Testing
- Design and development
- Packaging
- Distribution
- End of life

The life cycle costs will be the addition of all the previous costs.

7

Feasibility Assessment

Once the 'winning' concept(s) has been selected, it will be appropriate for the company to undertake a complete feasibility study before committing any resources to the design and development of the concept(s).

The assessment is carried out at the following three levels:

1. Technical feasibility
2. Financial feasibility
3. Organisational feasibility

7.1 Strategic Management

Strategic management is the process in which an organization develops and implements plans that espouse the goals and objectives of that organization. The process of strategic management is a continuous one that changes as the organizational goals and objectives evolve.

There are according to Professor Michael Porter three main types of corporate strategies are growth, stability and renewal. (a) Growth – A growth strategy is when an organization expands the number of markets served or products offered, either through its current business(es) or through new business(es). (b) Stability Strategy – A strategy that seeks to maintain the status with the uncertainty of the environment, when the industry is experiencing slow- or no-growth conditions. (c) Renewal Strategy – Developing strategies to counter organization weaknesses that are leading to performance declines.

7.2 Technical Feasibility

This will cover a complete technical assessment of the chosen design. It will require a full and honest assessment of the design, including a detailed risk analysis of the project.

It should be remembered that just a technical feasibility study conducted should not automatically lead to the assumption that the product is going to be a success in the marketplace.

7.3 Financial and Market Feasibility

To launch a new product in the market it is required to know how much start-up capital will be needed, sources of capital, returns on investment, etc. The impact on the financial status of the company could be enormous. Sufficient funds are required to sustain the development of the new product, this should be throughout the development and manufacturing phase.

The marketing section of the study will require a description of the current market, the anticipated future market potential, the competition and sales projections and potential buyers, etc.

7.4 Organisational Feasibility

This covers all the commercial aspects of introducing the new product into the marketplace, including distribution, warehousing and storage.

7.5 Marketing Feasibility

A market feasibility study determines the depth and condition of a particular market and its ability to support a particular development. The key concern of a market feasibility study for development is a project's ultimate marketability.

7.5.1 Potential Market Size

The first objective in a marketing study is to ascertain the size of the market and to determine the extent to which the goods/services generated by the project are needed and to design the appropriate marketing strategies and plans that will ensure that the projects outputs will be accepted and reach the intended target users.

7.5.2 Market Trends

The most difficult task is to determine the way a market is going to develop. It will either create a market for a product or destroy it as potential users may prefer a particular preference. This can be better described by the revolution in mobile phones, where the preference is now for new 'smart' mobile phones to standard phones without any frills.

Market growth
Target market
Competition

7.6 Critical Issues

Critical issues are those issues that will have impact on a company's efforts to become and remain competitive within a market and depend on the following.

7.6.1 SWOT (Strength, Weaknesses, Opportunities, Threats)

SWOT analysis is a strategic planning technique used to help a person or an organisation to identify the strengths and weaknesses within the organisation.

Opportunities and Threats are related to business competition or project planning. It is intended to specify the objectives of the business venture or project and identify the internal and external factors that are favourable and unfavourable in achieving these objectives. The users of a SWOT analysis ask and answer questions to generate meaningful information for each category and identify their competitive advantage.

Strengths and Weaknesses are internally related, while Opportunities and Threats are focused on environmental placement.

Strength: characteristics of the business or project and gives it an advantage over others.

Weaknesses: characteristics of the business that place or project disadvantage relative to others.

Opportunities: elements in the environment that a project exploits for its advantage.

Threats: elements in the environment that could cause trouble for the business or project.

The degree to which the internal environment of the firm matches with the external environment is expressed by the concept of strategic fit. Identification of SWOTs is important because they can provide later steps in planning to achieve the objectives. First, decision-makers should consider whether the objective is attainable, and if not, then they must select a different objective and repeat the process.

7.6.2 Pest (Political, Economic, Social, Technological)

Pest analysis (political, economic, social and technological) describes a framework of macro-environmental factors used in the environmental scanning component of strategic management. It is part of an external analysis when conducting a strategic analysis or market research and gives an overview of the different macro-environmental factors to be taken into consideration. It is a strategic tool for understanding market growth or decline, business position, potential, and direction for operations.

Political factors are basically when the government intervenes in the economy. These specifically cover areas including tax policies, labour laws, environmental law, trade restrictions and tariffs on imported goods.

Economic factors cover growth, interest rates, exchange rates and inflation rates. These factors greatly affect how a business operates and decisions made. For example, interest rates impact on the company's cost of capital and therefore to what extent a business grows and expands. Exchange rates can also affect the costs of exporting goods and the supply and price of imported goods in an economy.

Social factors include the cultural aspects and health consciousness, population growth, age distribution, career attitudes. High trends in social factor affect the demand for a company's products. Demographic factors include gender, age, knowledge of languages, disabilities amongst other issues.

Technological factors include technological aspects of the business, including the R&D activity, automation, technology incentives and the rate of technological change in the marketplace. These can determine barriers to entry, minimum efficient production levels and the influence on any outsourcing decisions. Furthermore, technological shifts would affect costs, quality and could lead to innovation.

These factors will vary in importance depending on the market the company is operating in and based on the industry and the goods it produces. As an example, consumer and business to business (B2B) companies tend to be more affected by social factors, whereas a company working in the defence industry will be more affected by political factors. Companies who have borrowed more heavily will be more influenced by economic factors (particularly any change in interest rates). In addition, a company may wish to divide factors into geographical relevance, such as local, national or global.

7.7 Technical Feasibility

A technical feasibility study assesses the details of how it is intended to deliver a product or services to customers. Consider materials, labour and transportation, where the business is located followed by the technology necessary to bring it all together. It is the logistical or tactical plan of how the business will produce, store, deliver, and track its products or services.

A technical feasibility study is a good tool for both short- and long-term planning. It can serve as a flowchart of how the products and services evolve and move through the business to physically reach the market.

7.7.1 Summary

The summary highlights the key points in each section and is usually finalised when the study is completed. The summary should appear at the beginning of the technical feasibility study.

7.7.2 Prepare an Outline

Preparing an outline of the proposed contents of the study will enable the writer to marshal their thoughts on the issues to be discussed. Areas for discussion will include materials, labour, transportation or shipping, physical location and technology. Ensure a full description of the services or products being offered and how they will benefit consumers?

7.7.3 Calculate Material Requirements

Prepare a list of all the material being used in the product or services. This section will include details such as volume discounts would be available as the business grows.

It also includes parts and supplies needed to produce a product no matter how trivial.

Financial data does not need to be included in this section of the study. Financial data that supports in this part of the study should be included as an attachment in a separate spread sheet.

7.7.4 Calculate Labour Requirements

Labour will be one of the biggest expense a small business will have (if not the biggest). List the number and types of employees that will be needed to run the business and the numbers required to employ as the business expands.

The labour can be broken down into categories, if necessary, such as senior-level management, office and clerical support, production and distribution staff, professional staff to include accountants, engineers and marketing.

7.7.5 Transportation and Shipping Requirements

How is it intended to transport items? Smaller items can be distributed using a local courier service such as DHL, but heavier items will need to be transported as freight or a local delivery service.

7.7.6 Calculate Marketing Requirements

Identify the type of consumer being targeted? Show how it is proposed to reach out to them? What type of marketing campaign is planned, will this be by telephone, emails, advertising on the Internet? Running advertisements in local newspapers, etc., explain why they should wish to purchase your product in preference to other competitors.

7.7.7 The Physical Location of the Business

The position of the business will have an effect on the success of the business. If it is a start-up business operating out of a home-based office, determine when and if a 'bricks and mortar' office will be some time in the future. Will warehousing facilities require manufacturing facilities or retail premises?

Discuss the pros and cons of where these facilities would be located. Do they need to be near other facilities such as a rail station, airport, a commercial centre or shopping facility.

7.7.8 Technology Requirements

Every business needs some level of technology to operate. The technology section of the study should include a discussion concerning telephone systems, computer hardware and software and inventory management. Also include in the discussion any security systems that may be required.

7.7.9 Target Dates

Be sure to include all planned target dates.

7.7.10 Financial Information

This is essentially a business plan where all proposed financial information will be detailed in chronological order.

8

Decision-Making

8.1 What Is Decision-Making

In its simplest terms, a decision is making a choice between two or more courses of action.

In the process of 'problem solving', a decision may have to be made that involves making a choice between possible solutions to a problem. Decisions are made by an intuitive or reasoned process or a combination of the two.

8.1.1 Intuition

Intuition is making a choice on an emotional level about possible courses of action.

Intuition is sometimes considered a 'magical sense', it is actually a combination of previous experience and the decision-makers' personal values. It is often worth taking into account personal intuition as it reflects learning about life. It is not always based on reality, only on the individual perceptions.

8.1.2 Reasoning

Reasoning is making use of the facts and figures to make a decision.

Intuition is a perfectly acceptable method of arriving at a decision, though the decision is best kept simple or needs to be made urgently.

More complex decisions require a more formal structured approach, usually involving a combination of intuition and reasoning in arriving at a solution.

8.1.3 Applying Both Intuition and Reasoning

The most effective way is to apply both aspects in turn, it is usual to start with reasoning and have a view of the facts and figures to enable decision to be made on reasoning alone and review the decision using intuition and satisfy oneself if the decision feels right.

If the decision does not seems to be correct, try and understand the emotion behind it. It is possible to revisit the process and review the manner in which the decisions was made.

8.1.4 What Can Prevent Effective Decision-Making?

There are a number of issues that can prevent ineffective decision-making.

There is insufficient information.

Take some time to ensure all the information is available to take the decision, even if the time scales are tight. If necessary, priorities the information gathering by identifying which appropriate information is important.

8.1.4.1 Too Much Information

This problem is the opposite to the previous paragraph in which there is far too much information available leading to 'analysis paralysis' not being able to make a satisfactory decision due to confusion over which information is appropriate to use.

   This problem can be resolved by involving the team to try and establish which information is really important and why. Setting a clear timescale can help focus the team's mind.

8.1.4.2 Too Many People

Trying to make decisions by committee is always difficult; everyone has their own views and agendas and while it is important to know what these views are and why, it is far better that the decision is made by one responsible person and the team accepts the result.

8.1.4.3 Emotional Attachments

Team members are often attached to the status quo. Decisions are often associated with change which many people often feel difficult to accept.

8.1.4.4 No Emotional Attachment

In some instances it is difficult to come to terms in making a decision as the decision-maker doesn't care one way or the other. In this case a more structured approach is called for to help identify the pros and cons of particular actions that perhaps haven't been considered before.

8.1.4.5 Identifying Possible Solutions/Options

The team leader may come up with a list of possible solutions or options and decides to use either brainstorming or other idea-generating process to process a solution. This stage can be important to as a decision will be made from the selection of fixed choices.

8.2 Setting a Time Scale and Deciding Who Is Responsible for the Decision

When deciding the time available to make a decision, it helps to consider the following points:

- How much time is available to spend on the decision?
- Is there a deadline when the decision is to be made and what are the consequences if the deadline is missed?
- Is there any advantage if the decision is made quickly?
- How important is it to make a decision?
- How important is it for that decision to be correct?
- Will spend more time to improve the quality of the decision?

It needs to be set in mind that a quick decision is more important than a correct decision!

8.2.1 Responsibility for the Decision

Before any decision is made, it needs to be clear who is responsible for it.

- Is the individual responsible for their decision or does the organisation hold ulti-mate responsibility?
- Who has to carry out the course of action decided?
- Whom it affects if something goes wrong?
- Are you personally willing to take responsibility for a mistake?

8.2.2 Whenever possible, and if it is not obvious, a better formal agreement is needed to identify who is responsibility for a decision

This idea of responsibility also highlights the need to keep a detailed minuted record of how the decision is reached, what information was available at the time the decision was made and who was involved in making the decision. It needs to be shown that the decision was reasonable in the circumstances and knowledge available at the time.

8.3 Information Gathering

8.3.1 Before Making Any Decision, All Relevant Information Needs to Be Gathered

If there is inadequate or outdated information used in the decision-making process, then it is more than likely an incorrect decision will be made.

However, the amount of time spent on information gathering has to be weighed against the quality of the information being obtained and the risk in making an incorrect deci-sion based on that information. In a team situation, it may be appropriate to delegate team members to research various aspects of the project for the information required.

8.4 Weighing the Risks Involved

One key question needs to be determined in how much risk should be taken in arriving at a decision? Generally the amount of risk a team is willing to take depends upon

- the seriousness of the consequences of taking the wrong decision;
- the benefits of making a correct decision and
- not only how bad the worst outcome might be, but how likely that situation will occur.

It is also useful to consider when the risk of the worst possible outcome occurring might be, but also to decide if the risk is acceptable. There is a choice either to go for a safe option or go "all out" for success.

8.5 Deciding on Values

Everyone has their own unique set of values: Any decision made will be based on your values. That means that any decision that is right for the team leader may not be right for the rest of the team.

It is important for any decision to be shared, in such cases a consensus should be obtained as to which values are to be given the most weight. It is important that the values on which a decision is made is universally understood as they will have a strong influence on the quality of the final decision.

8.6 Weighing Up the Pros and Cons

One good way to carry this out is to use a 'balance sheet approach', weighing up the pros and cons (benefits and costs) associated with that solution. Try to consider each aspect of the situation in turn and identify both good and bad.

As an example; start with costs, then consider staffing problems and the presentation aspects.

Having listed the pros and cons, it may be possible to immediately decide which option is best. However, it may be useful to rate each of the pros and cons on a simple scale based on 1 to 10 with 10 being the most important and 1, the least important.

When scoring each pros and cons, it is helpful to take into account how important each item is in meeting the agreed values. This balance sheet approach allows this to be taken into account and presents in a clear and precise way.

8.7 Making the Decision

The information gathering should now have provided sufficient data on which to base a decision and it is known the advantages and disadvantages of each option.

If possible, it is best to allow a little time to reflect on the decision once it has been reached. It is preferable to sleep on it before announcing it. Once a decision has been announced publically, it is difficult to retract it.

For very important decisions, it is worth keeping a record of the steps undertaken to reach that decision. This way, if you are ever criticised for making what turns out to be a bad decision, you can justify your thoughts based on the information and processes available to you at the time.

8.8 Having Made the Decision ...

Finally and perhaps most importantly once a decision has been made, don't waste any time revisiting it about 'what if'. If something does go wrong and it is required to revise the decision, then do so, but otherwise, accept it and move on.

8.9 Introduction to Constructing Decision Trees

8.9.1 What Is a Decision Tree?

A decision tree is a map of the possible outcomes of a series of related choices. It allows either an individual or organisation to choose possible actions against one another based on either their cost, probabilities or benefits. They can also be used to drive informal or formal discussions or to map out an algorithm that predicts the best choice mathematically.

A decision tree generally starts with a single point that branches out into possible outcomes. Each of these outcomes subsequently leads other additional nodes, which in turn branch into other possibilities, giving a treelike structure.

There are three different types of nodes – chance nodes, decision nodes and endpoint nodes. These can be represented by flowchart symbols.

- A chance node represented by a circle shows the probabilities of certain results.
- A decision node represented by a square, shows a decision is to be made.
- An endpoint node represented by a triangle shows the final outcome of a decision path.

8.9.2 Decision Tree Symbols

Table 8.1 Shows a selection of symbols used in the construction of a decision tree.

TABLE 8.1

Decision Tree Symbols

Shape	Name	Meaning
▨	Decision Mode	Indicates a decision to be made
◉	Chance Mode	Shows multiple uncertain outcomes
<	Alternative Branches	Each branch indicates a possible outcome or action
✕	Rejected Alternative	Shows a choice not selected
◁▨	Endpoint Node	Indicates a final outcome

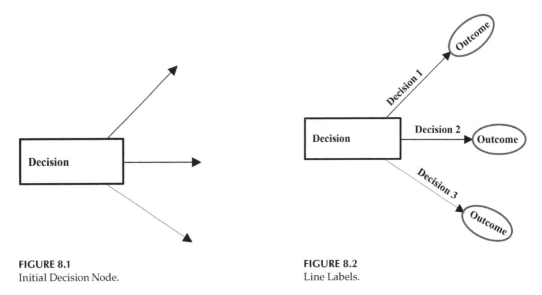

FIGURE 8.1
Initial Decision Node.

FIGURE 8.2
Line Labels.

8.9.3 How to Draw a Decision Tree

Drawing a decision tree is straightforward. First, choose the method to draw the tree. This can either be drawn on paper, or using special decision tree software, in either case the following steps are followed.

8.9.3.1 Start with the Main Decision

Draw a small box to represent the main decision followed by a line from the box to the right for each of the possible solutions as shown in Figure 8.1. Label the lines accordingly as shown in Figure 8.2.

8.9.3.2 Add Chance and Decision Nodes

Chance and decision nodes are added as necessary by drawing another box as depicted in Figure 8.3.

   If the outcome is uncertain draw a circle (circles represent chance nodes).

   In the event the problem is solved, leave it blank (for the time being).

   For each decision node, draw possible solutions. From each chance node, draw lines representing possible outcomes. If it is intended to analyse the options numerically, include the probability of each outcome together with the cost of each action.

8.9.3.3 Continue to Expand the Tree until Every Line Has Reached an Endpoint

This means there are no further choices to be made or chance outcomes to be considered. Assign a value to each possible outcome. This may be an abstract score or a financial value. End node symbols are added to signify the completion of the tree.

8.10 With the Completion of the Decision Tree

The next stage is to begin analysing depending upon the criteria for the decision to be faced.

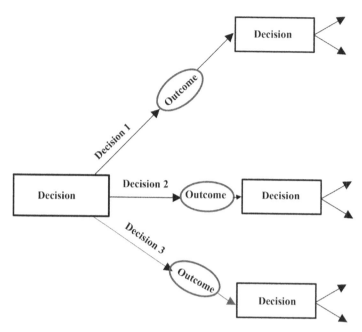

FIGURE 8.3
Additional Nodes.

8.10.1 An Example of a Decision Tree Example

Imagine that you only have time to do four things at weekends:

- Go shopping
- Watch a movie
- Play tennis
- Just stay at home

What you may do, will depend upon the weather (windy. rainy or sunny), your financial situation (rich or poor) and whether your parents have chosen to visit. You may say to yourself: if my parents are visiting, then I will take them to the cinema. If they are not visiting, then if it is sunny I will go and play tennis; but if it is windy and I have the finances, I could go shopping. If they are not visiting and it is windy and I do not have sufficient finances, then in this situation I shall go to the cinema. If they are no vising and it is raining, then I shall stay in.

It becomes more obvious why these diagrams are called decision trees.

To be able to remember these decisions, you construct a flowchart which will enable you to read off your decisions. Such a diagram is called decision tree. A suitable decision tree for the weekend decision choices would be as depicted in Figure 8.1.

It can be seen why these diagrams are referred to as trees, it is due to that they are drawn upside down. They start with a root and have branches that lead to leaves (the tips of the graph at the bottom). Note also that the leaves are always decisions and a particular decision may be at the end of multiple branches (e.g. we may choose to go to the cinema for two very different reasons).

Come Saturday morning armed with our decision tree, the first thing we do is to

a. check the weather,
b. check your finances and
c. is our parent's car parked on the drive?

The decision tree will now enable us to make our next decision. Consider, e.g., that our parent's car hasn't turned up and the sun is shining. This path through our decision tree will advise what to do next. In this case, we run off to play tennis because our decision tree has told us to. Note that the decision tree covers for all eventualities. That is, there are no values that the weather, the parent's turning up or the finance situation could take which was not catered for in the decision tree.

For example, the sun is shining, the parents have not turned up, our decision tree points us to the next step. Hence, we run off to play tennis as the decision tree has told us to do. Note, the decision tree covers for all eventualities. That is, there are no values that the weather, the parents turning up or the money situation could take which are not catered for in this decision tree. Note, in this section we will be looking at how to automatically generate decision trees from examples, not at how to turn thought processes into decision trees.

8.10.2 Reading Decision Trees

There is a link between decision tree representations and logical representations, which can be exploited to make it easier to understand (read) learned decision trees. If we think about it, every decision is actually a disjunction of implications (if ... then statements), and the implications are "Horn" clauses: a conjunction of literals implying a single literal. In the above tree, we can see this by reading from the **root node** to each **leaf node**:

If parents are visiting, then go to the cinema.

or

If parents are not visiting and it is sunny, then play tennis.

or

If the parents are not visiting and it is windy and you are rich, then go shopping.

or

If the parents are not visiting and it is windy and you are poor, then go to the cinema.

or

If the parents are not visiting and it is raining, then stay at home.

It is obvious that this is just a restatement of the original mental decision-making process that has been described. Remember, however, that we will be programming an agent to learn decision trees from examples, so this kind of situation will not occur as we will start with only example situations. It will therefore be important for us to be able to read the decision tree the agent suggests.

Decision trees do not have to be representations of decision-making processes, and they can equally apply to categorisation problems. If we phrase the above questions slightly

TABLE 8.2

Depicts a Decision Data Base for This Problem

Weekend Example	Weather	Parents	Finances	Decision (Category)
W1	Sunny	Yes	Rich	Cinema
W2	Sunny	No	Rich	Tennis
W3	Windy	Yes	Rich	Cinema
W4	Rainy	Yes	Poor	Cinema
W5	Rainy	No	Rich	Stay in
W6	Rainy	Yes	Poor	Cinema
W7	Windy	No	Poor	Cinema
W8	Windy	No	Rich	Shopping
W9	Windy	Yes	Rich	Cinema
W10	Sunny	No	Rich	Tennis

differently, we can see the following: instead of saying that we wish to represent a decision process for what to do on the weekend, we could ask what kind of weekend is this? Is it a weekend where we play tennis, or one where we could go shopping, or one where we see a film, or one where we stay in (see Table 8.2)?

8.11 Learning Decision Trees Using Iterative Dichotomiser 3 (ID3)

8.11.1 Specifying the Problem

At this point, you now need to look at how you mentally constructed your decision tree when deciding what to do at the weekend. One way would be to use some background information as axioms and deduce what to do. For example, you might know that your parents really like going to the cinema, and that your parents are in town, so therefore (using something like *Modus Ponens*) you would decide to go to the cinema.

Another way in which you might have made up your mind was by generating from previous experiences. Imagine that you remembered all the times when you had a really good weekend. A few weeks back, it was sunny and your parents were not visiting, you played tennis and it was good. A month ago, it was raining and you were penniless, but a trip to the cinema cheered you up. And so on. This information could have guided your decision-making, and if that was the case, you would have used an inductive, rather than deductive, method to construct your decision tree. In reality, it is likely that human's reason to take decisions use both inductive and deductive processes combined.

We can state the problem of learning decision trees as follows.

We have a set of examples correctly categorised into categories (decisions). We also have a set of attributes describing the examples and each attribute has a finite set of values which it can possibly take. We want to use the examples to learn the structure of a decision tree which can be used to decide the category of the unseen question.

Assuming that there are no inconstancies in the data (when two examples have exactly the same values for the attributes, but are categorised differently), it is obvious that we can always construct a decision tree to correctly decide for the training cases with 100% accuracy. All we have to do is to make sure every situation is catered for down some branch of the decision tree. Of course, 100% accuracy may indicate over-fitting.

8.11.2 The Basic Idea

In the example of decision tree above, it is significant that the 'parents visiting' node came at the top of the tree. We do not know exactly the reasons for this, as we did not see the example of weekend from which the tree was produced. However, it is likely that the number of weekends the parents visited was relatively high and every weekend they did visit, there was a trip to the cinema. Suppose, e.g., the parents had visited every fortnight for a year, and on each occasion, the family visited the cinema. This means that there is no evidence of doing anything different other than watching a film when the parents visit. Given that we are learning rules from examples, this means that if the parents visit, the decision is already made. Hence, we can put this at the top of the decision tree and disregard all the examples where the parents visited when constructing the rest of the tree. Not having to worry about a set of examples will make the construction job easier.

This kind of thinking underlies the ID3 algorithm (Iterative Dichotomiser) for learning decision trees, which we will describe more formally below. However, the reasoning is a little more subtle, as (in our example) it would also take into account the examples when the parents did not visit.

8.11.3 Entropy

Putting together a decision tree is all a matter of choosing which attributes to test at each node in the tree. We shall define a measure called information gain which will be used to decide which attributes to test at each node. Information gain is itself calculated using a measure called entropy, which we first define for the case of a binary decision problem and then give a definition for the general case.

Given a binary categorisation, 'C', and a set of examples, 'S', for which the proportion of examples categorised as positive by 'C' is 'p' and the proportion of examples categorised as negative by 'C' is 'p', then the entropy of 'S' is:

$$\text{Entropy}(S) = -p_+ \log_2(p_+) - p_- \log_2(p_-)$$

The reason we define entropy first for a binary decision problem is because it is easier to get an impression of what it is we are trying to calculate. Professor Tom Mitchell (Carnegie Mellon University) puts this quite well:

> In order to define information gain precisely, we begin by defining a measure commonly used in information theory, called entropy that characterise the (im) purity of an arbitrary collection of examples.

Imagine having a set of boxes with some balls inside, if all the balls were in a single box then there would be no problem to find a particular ball. If however the balls were distributed amongst the boxes, this would not be so nicely ordered and it may take some time to find a particular ball. If we are going to define a measure based on this notion of purity, we would want to calculate a value for each box based on the number of balls in it, then take the sum of these as the overall measure. We would want to reward two situations: nearly empty boxes (very neat), and boxes with nearly all the balls in (also very neat). This is the basis for the general entropy measure, which we defined as follows:

Given the arbitrary categorisation 'C' into categories $c_i \ldots c_n$, and a set of examples, 'S', for which the proportion of examples in c_i is p_i, then the entropy of 'S' is:

$$\text{Entropy}(S) = \sum_{i=1}^{n} - p_i \log_2(p_i)$$

This measure satisfies our criteria, because of the $-p*\log_2(p)$ construction: when p gets close to zero (i.e. the category has only a few examples in it), then $\log(p)$ becomes a big negative number, but the p part dominates the calculation, so the entropy works out to be nearly zero. Remember that in the disorder of the data, this low score is good, as it reflects our desire to reward categories with few examples in. Similarly, if p gets close to 1 (i.e. the category has most of the examples in), then the $\log(p)$ part gets very close to zero, and it is this which dominates the calculation, so the overall value gets close to zero. Hence, we see that at both conditions, when the category is nearly or completely empty, or when the category nearly contains – or completely contains – all the examples, the score for the category gets close to zero, which models what we wanted it to. Note that $0*\ln(0)$ is taken to be zero by convention.

8.11.4 Information Gain

We now return to the problem of trying to determine the best attribute to choose for a particular node in a tree. The following measure calculates a numerical value for a given attribute, 'A' with respect to a set of examples, 'S'. Note that the values of attribute 'A' will range over a set of possibilities which we call values (A), and that, for a particular value from the set 'v', we write 'S', for the set of examples which have value 'v' for attribute 'A'.

The information gain of attribute 'A', relative to a collection of examples 'S', is calculated as:

$$\text{Gain}(S, A) = \text{Entropy}(S) - \sum_{v \in \text{Values}(A)} \frac{|S_v|}{|S|} \text{Entropy}(S_v)$$

The information gain of an attribute can be seen as the expected reduction in entropy caused by knowing the value of attribute 'A'.

8.11.5 An Example Calculation

As an example, suppose we are working with a set of examples, 'S' = {s1, s2, s3, s4}, categorised into a binary categorisation of positives and negatives, such that s1 is positive and the rest are negative. Suppose further that we want to calculate the information gain of an attribute 'A', and that 'A' can take the values {v1, v2, v3}. Finally, suppose that

s1 takes the value v2 for 'A'

s2 takes the value v2 for A

s3 takes the value v3 for A

s4 takes the value v1 for A

To work out the information gain for 'A' relative to 'S', we first need to calculate the entropy of 'S'. To use our formula for binary categorisations, we need to know the proportion of positives in 'S' and the proportion of negatives. These are given as: $p_+ = 1/4$ and $p_- = 3/4$. So, we can calculate:

$$\text{Entropy}(S) = -(1/4)\log_2(1/4) - (3/4)\log_2(3/4) = -(1/4)(-2) - (3/4)(-0.415)$$
$$= 0.5 + 0.311 = 0.811$$

Note: To do this calculation with your calculator, you may need to remember that $\log(x) = \ln(x)/\ln(2)$, where $\ln(2)$ is the natural log of 2. Next, we need to calculate the weighted entropy (S_v) for each value of $v = v1, v2, v3, v4$, noting that the weighting involves multiplying by $\left(\frac{|S_{v1}|}{|S|}\right)$. Remember also that S_v is the set of examples from 'S' which have value 'v' for attribute 'A'. This means that

$$S_{v1} = \{s_4\}, S_{v2} = \{s_1, s_2\}, S_{v3} = \{s_3\}.$$

We now have need to carry out these calculations:

$$\left(\frac{|S_{v1}|}{|S|}\right) * \text{Entropy}(S_{v1}) = (1/4) * \left(-\left(\frac{0}{1}\right)\log_2\left(\frac{0}{1}\right) - \left(\frac{1}{1}\right)\right) = \left(\frac{1}{4}\right)(-0 - (0)\log_2(1))$$
$$= \left(\frac{1}{4}\right)(-0 - 0) = 0$$

$$\left(\frac{|S_{v2}|}{|S|}\right) * \text{Entropy}(S_{v2}) = \left(\frac{2}{4}\right) * \left(-\left(\frac{1}{2}\right)\log_2\left(\frac{1}{2}\right) - \left(\frac{1}{2}\right)\log_2\left(\frac{1}{2}\right)\right) = \left(\frac{1}{2}\right) * \left(-\left(\frac{1}{2}\right) * (-1)\right)$$
$$= \left(\frac{1}{2}\right) * (-1) - \left(\frac{1}{2}\right) * (1) = \frac{1}{2}$$

$$\left(\frac{|S_{v3}|}{|S|}\right) * \text{Entropy}(S_{v3}) = \left(\frac{1}{4}\right) * \left(-\left(\frac{0}{1}\right)\log_2\left(\frac{0}{1}\right) - \left(\frac{1}{1}\right)\log_2\left(\frac{1}{1}\right)\right)$$
$$= \left(\frac{1}{4}\right)(-0 - (1)\log 2(1)\log 2(1)) = \left(\frac{1}{4}\right)(-0 - 0) = 0$$

Note: We have taken 0 log2(0) to be zero, which is standard. In our calculation, we only required $\log_2(1) = 0$ and $\log_2(1/2) = -1$. We now have to add these values together and take the result from our calculation for Entropy(S) to give us the final result.

$$\text{Gain}(S, A) = 0.811 = (0 + 1/2 + 0) = 0.311$$

We now look at how information gain can be used in practice in an algorithm to construct decision trees.

8.11.6 The ID3 Algorithm

The calculation for information gain is the most difficult part of this algorithm. ID3 performs a search whereby the search states are decision trees and the operator involves adding a node to an existing tree. It uses information gain to measure the attribute to put in each node, and performs a greedy search using this measure of work. The algorithm goes as follows:

Given a set of examples, 'S', categorised in categories 'c_i', then

1. Choose the root node to be the attribute, 'A', which scores the highest for information gain relative to 'S'.
2. For each value 'v' that 'A' can possibly take, draw a branch from the node.
3. For each branch from 'A' corresponding to value 'v', calculate 'S'. Then
   - If 'S' is empty, choose the category '$c_{default}$' which contains the most examples from 'S', and put this as the leaf node category which ends that branch.
   - If 'S' contains only examples from a category 'c', then put 'c' as the leaf node category which ends that branch.
   - Otherwise remove 'A' from the set of attributes which can be put into nodes. Then put a new node in the decision tree, where the new attribute being tested in the node is the one which scores highest for information gain relative to 'S_v' (note not relative to 'S'). This new node starts the cycle again (from 2) with 'S' replaced by 'S_v' in the calculations and the tree gets built iteratively like this.

The algorithm terminates either when all the attributes have been exhausted, or the decision tree perfectly classifies the examples.

The following diagram in Figure 8.4 should explain the ID3 algorithm further.

8.11.7 Worked Example

Returning to the 'weekend' example. Suppose we want to train a decision tree using the following statements.

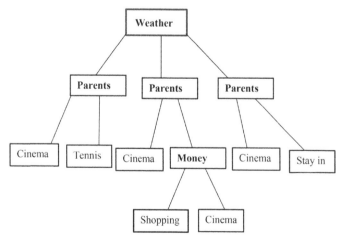

FIGURE 8.4
A Decision Tree for the Weekend Weather.

The first thing we need to do is work out which attribute will be put in the node at the top of our tree: either weather, parents or finance. To do this, we need to calculate:

$$\text{Entropy}(S) = -P_{cinema} \log_2(P_{cinema}) - P_{tennis} \log_2(P_{tennis}) - P_{shopping} \log_2(P_{shopping})$$
$$- P_{stay\_in} \log_2(P_{stay\_in})$$
$$= -(6/10)*\log_2(6/10) - (2/10)*\log_2(2/10) - (1/10)*\log_2(1/10)$$
$$-(1/10)*\log_2(1/10)$$
$$= 0.4422 + 0.4644 + 0.3322 + 0.3322 = 1.571$$

and we need to determine the best of:

$$\text{Gain}(S,_{weather}) = 1.571 - \left(\frac{|S_{sun}|}{10}\right)*\text{Entropy}(S_{Sun}) - \left(\frac{S_{wind}}{10}\right)*\text{Entropy}(S_{wind})$$
$$-\left(\frac{|Srain|}{10}\right)*\text{Entropy}(S_{sun})$$
$$= 1.571 - (0.3)*\text{Entropy}(S_{sun}) - (0.4)*\text{Entropy}(S_{wind}) - (0.3)*\text{Entropy}(S_{rain})$$
$$= 1.571 - (0.3)*(0.918) - (0.4)*(0.81125) - (0.3)*0.918 = 0.70$$

$$\text{Gain}(S, \text{Parents}) = 1.571 - \left(\frac{|S_{yes}|}{10}\right)*\text{Entropy}(S_{yes}) - \left(\frac{|S_{no}|}{10}\right)*\text{Entropy}(S_{no})$$
$$1.571 - (0.5)*0 - (0.5)81.922 = 1.571 - 0.961 = 0.61$$

$$\text{Gain}(\text{finance}) + 1.571 - \left(\frac{|S_{rich}|}{10}\right)*\text{Entropy}(S_{rich}) - \left(\frac{|S_{poor}|}{10}\right)*\text{Entropy}(S_{poor})$$
$$1.571 - (0.7)*(1.842) - (0.3)*0 = 1.571 - 1.2894 = 0.2816$$

From this it is deduced that the first node in the decision tree would be the weather attribute. As an exercise, convince yourself why this scored (slightly) higher than the parents attribute – remember what entropy means and look at the way information gain is calculated.

From the weather node, we draw a branch for the values that the weather can take: sunny, windy and rainy: (see Figure 8.5)

In Figure 8.5, look at the first branch, $S_{sunny} = \{W1, W2, W10\}$. This is not empty, so we do not put a default categorisation leaf mode here. The categorisation of W1, W2 and W10 are Cinema, Tennis and to stay in, respectively. As these are not all the same, we cannot put a categorisation leaf node here. Hence we put an attribute node hear, so we will leave blank for the time being.

Looking at the second branch, $W_{windy} = \{W3, W7, W8, W9\}$. Again, this is not empty, and they do not all belong to the same class, so we put an attribute node here, left blank for now. The same situation happens with the third branch; hence, our amended tree looks as depicted in Figure 8.6.

Now we have to fill in the choice of attribute 'A', which we know cannot be weather, as we have already removed that from the list of attributes to use. So, we need to calculate the

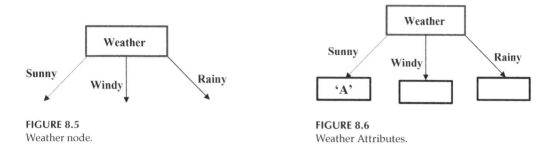

FIGURE 8.5
Weather node.

FIGURE 8.6
Weather Attributes.

values for Gain(S_{sunny}, Parents) and Gain(S_{sunny}, Finance). First, Entropy(S_{sunny}) = 0.918. Next, we set S to be S_{sunny} = {W1, W2, W10} (and for this part of the branch, we will ignore all the other examples). In effect, we are interested only in this part of the Table 8.3.

Hence, we can now calculate:

$$\text{Gain}(S_{sunny}, \text{Parents}) = 0.918 - \left(\frac{|S_{yes}|}{S}\right) * \text{Entropy}(S_{yes}) - \left(\frac{|S_{no}|}{|S|}\right) * \text{Entropy}(S_{no})$$

$$= 0.918 - (1/3)*0 - (2/3)*0 = 0.918$$

$$\text{Gain}(S_{sunny}, \text{Finance}) = 0.918 - \left(\frac{|S_{rich}|}{|S|}\right) * \text{Entropy}(S_{rich}) - \left(\frac{|S_{poor}|}{|S|}\right) * \text{Entropy}(S_{poor})$$

$$= 0.918 - (3/3)*0.918 - (0/3)*0 = 0.918 - 0.918 = 0$$

Notice that Entropy(S_{yes}) and Entropy(S_{no}) were both zero, because S_{yes} contains examples which are all in the same category (cinema), and S_{no} similarly contains examples which are all in the same category (tennis). This should make it more obvious why we use information gain to choose attributes to put in nodes.

Given our calculations, attribute 'A' should be taken as parents. The two values from parents are yes and no, we will draw a branch from the node for each of these. Remembering that we replaced the set 'S' by the set 'S_{sunny}', looking at 'S_{yes}', we see that the only example of this is W1. Hence, the branch for yes stops at a categorisation leaf, with the category being Cinema. Also, 'S_{no}' contains W2 and W10, but they are in the same category (Tennis). Hence, the branch for 'no' ends at a categorisation leaf. Hence, our upgraded tree looks as shown in Figure 8.7. Finishing this tree off is left as student tutorial exercise.

TABLE 8.3

Is a Table of the Weekend Activities

Weekend (Example)	Weather	Parents	Finance	Decision (Category)
W1	Sunny	Yes	Rich	Cinema
W2	Sunny	No	Rich	Tennis
W10	Sunny	No	Rich	Tennis

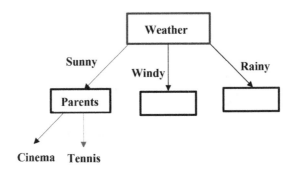

FIGURE 8.7
Weather Upgraded Attributes.

8.12 Avoiding Overfitting

As discussed in the previous section, overfitting is a common problem in machine learning. Decision trees suffer from this, because they are trained to stop when they have perfectly classified all the training data, i.e., each branch is extended just far enough to correctly categorise the examples relevant to that branch. Many examples to overcoming overfitting the decision tree have been attempted. As summarised by Professor Mitchell (Carnegie-Mellon), these examples fit into two types:

- Stop growing the tree before it reaches perfection.
- Allow the tree to fully grow and then **post-prune** some of the branches from it.

The second approach has been found to be more successful in practice. Both approaches boil down to the question of determining the correct tree size.

8.13 Appropriate Problems for Decision Tree Learning

It is a skilled job in Artificial Intelligence (AI) to choose exactly the right learning representation/method for a particular learning task. As elaborated by Professor Mitchell, decision tree learning is best suited to problems with the following characteristics:

- The background concepts describe the examples in terms of **attribute-value** pairs and the values for each attribute range over finitely many fixed possibilities.
- The concept to be learned (Mitchell calls it the **target function) has discrete values.**
- Disjunctive descriptions might be required in the answer.

In addition to this, decision tree learning is robust to errors in the data. In particular, it will function well in the light of (i) errors in the classification instances provided, (ii) errors in the attribute-value pairs provided and (iii) missing values for certain attributes for certain examples.

9

Project Management and Planning

9.1 Introduction

The essentials of a successful business include bringing new products to the marketplace on time and within budget. It is important for the company to focus on its core business and not allow itself to be diverted into areas that will have an impact on its financial and production resources.

The management of projects is to ensure that every aspect of the project plan is recognised and correctly costed in terms of time and finance and any risk to the project is clearly identified.

In the context of engineering design, planning will consist of identifying the key actions within the project and organising them in a logical sequence in which they should be performed. As already discussed in Chapter 1, the design phase can be divided into the following phases:

- Feasibility study
- Preliminary design (also the concept phase)
- Detailed design
- Manufacturing phase
- Operational phase

At the completion of each phase, a detailed design review should be completed before proceeding to the next phase. The consequence of a phase not being completed to the satisfaction of the project manager is to either repeat the phase or even to abandon the project if the risks are seen to be insurmountable.

A good project plan will have clearly defined decision points 'or milestones' that are established through each phase as a means of measuring the progress and thereby having a degree of control over the project.

The next few sections give a description of how the individual activities are developed and controlled.

9.2 Work Breakdown and Coding

It is essential that a detailed plan is developed for the complete project in which the critical activities that are needed to complete the project are identified. These key activities are then broken down into sub-activities and these in turn are subdivided into tasks that are completed by individuals. Generally, this work breakdown proceeds in a hierarchical manner from the total system through the sub-assembly to the component level and down to the individual item.

Consider the breakdown of a metal-cutting centre lathe. The machine consists of a number of major assemblies primarily:

- Lathe bed
- Headstock
- Carriage
- Bed pan
- Tailstock

These in turn are broken down into major assemblies.

Code	Item
100-300	Compound slide
100-301	
100-302	
100-400	Cross slide
100-401	
100-402	
100-500	Top slide
	Micrometre dial
	Screw
	Bearings
	Tool holder
100-400	Carriage
100-500	Headstock
100-600	Headstock spindle
100-700	Countershaft
100-800	Back gear
100-900	Leadscrew
100-1000	Change gears

9.3 Estimating Techniques

Estimating the time to complete activities within the design office can be either straightforward or very difficult and is totally dependent upon the nature of the project. If the activity is to update drawings to incorporate a design modification, it can be accomplished without much difficulty. If it is a new design for an offshore structure, then as expected, it will take several hours to arrive at an estimate time to complete the component drawings and collect bills of materials or parts lists together with all the specifications and reports needed to validate the design.

In general, the principle involved will be similar in both cases and will require an understanding of the methods involved.

Code	Item
100-000	Bed
100-001	Bed casting
100-002	Rack
100-003	Swarf tray
100-004	Coolant tank
100-005	Coolant pump
100-006	Coolant pump piping
100-100	Saddle
100-101	Saddle casting
100-102	Slide seals
100-200	Apron
100-201	Apron casting
100-202	Drive gear box assembly
100-203	Hand wheel
100-204	Half nut assembly
100-205	Threading dial

FIGURE 9.1
Family tree or breakdown diagram.

The raw products from the design office are drawings and parts lists together with specifications for the purchasing and manufacturing departments. It will be these factors that will take a large proportion of the time to complete the project.

To recap from Chapter 1, before the design can proceed, a scheme drawing will need to be prepared from which a work breakdown or family tree can be generated. This will allow a component count to be undertaken and a preliminary parts list to be generated identifying the level 1 assemblies followed by its level 2 assemblies down to its levels 3 and 4 if appropriate (Figure 9.1).

This will allow the designer to estimate the size of the drawing to cover each individual component within the assemblies. Table 9.1 is an approximation of the time to complete each drawing by size. The scheme drawing may be produced by the old pencil and paper method or by using computer-aided design (CAD), developing a solid model. In both these methods, a time has to be allotted to complete either of these activities. The accuracy of the timescales will depend on the skill and experience of the designer. Over time it will be seen that more accurate timescales are developed with experience.

TABLE 9.1

Example of a 'Work Breakdown Statement'

WBS No.	Task	Start Date	Duration (in hours)	End Date
1	Prepare specification	14th April 2014	3	17th April 2014
2	Initial designs	18th April 2014	11	29th April 2014
3	Design reviews	30th April 2014	2	2nd April 2014
4	Final design	3rd April 2014	15	18th April 2014
5	Manufacturing drawing's	19th April 2014	25	14th May 2014
6	Bill of materials	15th May 2014	3	18th May 2014
7	Release for manufacture	19th May 2014	5	24th May 2014

When estimating the time to complete each drawing, a number of factors will also need to be considered:

- In some cases, drawing a solid model of a part may take longer than creating a 2D drawing of the same part. Where CAD scores is in any post-design activity such as creating sections and isometric drawings, etc.

- Is all the information readily available to complete the drawing? Time will have to be allowed for 'information gathering' if the information available is inadequate.

- Is this a new design or is it an amendment of an existing drawing? Time will be affected if a part of an existing drawing is imported.

- Is the scheme drawing to scale? Sometimes this may only be a rough sketch and will require to be drawn accurately to scale.

- At some point the scheme drawing will need to be reviewed by a stress engineer to confirm that sections have an adequate factor of safety. Extra time will be required to cover this unscheduled activity.

The designer may be under severe pressure from the planning team to minimise the design timescales to ensure that specific program milestones are met. It has to be the responsibility of the individual designer to ensure that there is adequate time to undertake the individual design tasks.

When trying to estimate the time to undertake a specific task, the designer should estimate the minimum time and the maximum time needed to complete the task and then select a time that is approximately midpoint. An extra 10% to 15% should be added to this estimate to cover for any contingencies not originally considered. This will give a reasonable starting point for the estimate.

When all the estimates are added together and tabulated, it may be seen that there is room to manoeuvre to reduce the design timescales by cutting back on any slack that might have been included in the estimate.

9.3.1 Gantt Chart

Gantt charts (also known as a 'Bar' chart) were devised by Henry Gantt (an American mechanical engineer and management consultant) between the years 1910 to 1915, Gantt charts were originally used in large construction projects including the construction of the Hoover dam (in the United States) in 1931.

The Gantt chart has become one of the most popular ways of showing activities (tasks or events) displayed against time. The chart illustrates the breakdown structure of the project in the form of cascading horizontal bars giving the start and finish dates together with the relationship between the task activities. This enables the tracking of the various tasks against the scheduled times and project milestones.

The Gantt chart displays a list of activities down the left-hand side and a suitable time scale along the top, as shown in Figure 9.2.

Each task or activity is represented by a bar. The position and length of the bar reflects the start date, duration and end date of the activity.

Its popularity is due to the ability to overview the project at a glance:

- What the activities are.
- When each activity begins and end.

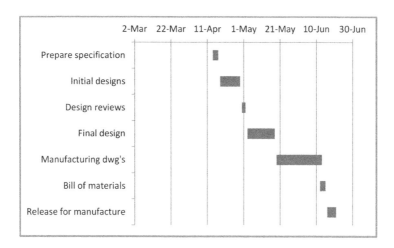

FIGURE 9.2
Example of a Gantt Chart.

- The duration of each activity.
- The interaction between each activity.
- Ability to monitor the project.

9.3.1.1 Creating a Gantt Chart

The first thing is to put together a detailed project plan, which is a series of interdependent tasks or activities that have to be performed in a particular order, and the timescales in which each activity needs to be completed before the next task or activity can begin. This is referred to as a *work breakdown structure*. Complex tasks can also be broken down into sub-tasks.

When the chart is complete, these timescales may need to be adjusted if there is a requirement for the project to be finished in a specific time, as the plan is balanced it will be obvious the knock-on effect adjusting the individual task durations were some tasks may need to be completed in a shorter space of time. This will give an indication of the level of resources needed as the project progresses.

There are a number of programs available to facilitate the creation of the Gantt chart, notably Microsoft Project© and Microsoft Excel©. These programs allow the development of the project at all levels of experience and can used for a wide range of projects including mechanical and civil engineering projects.

Table 9.1 shows a typical example of a work breakdown statement (WBS), and this serves as the task description in the chart and is usually entered in a spreadsheet.

Each task is listed on a separate row and the plan can be structured to include the start date and the duration of the task. The end date can also be entered, but this will normally be deduced from the start date of the activity and its duration.

This is a very simplistic Gantt chart shown as an example only. It does not take into account weekends in which case the respective start and end dates will have to be amended to accommodate this fact.

As the project continues, amendments to the chart will need to be updated to ensure that the timescales reflect the work being undertaken.

9.3.2 Critical Path Method

In 1957, DuPont in conjunction with Remington Rand developed a project management technique which became known as the 'critical path method' (CPM). This consisted of a series of sequential activities from the start to the end of the project.

Many major construction projects have a number of complex interrelated activities or tasks. A number of tasks may need to be completed before the next task can begin. Essentially, the 'critical path method' is a means of identifying the tasks that lie on the critical path and could pose a risk through introducing delays for the project not meeting its time or cost requirements.

Most of the times, if such delays occur, project acceleration or re-sequencing is done in order to meet the original deadlines.

The CPM is based on mathematical calculations that are used to schedule the project activities. The initial method was used for managing plant maintenance projects. In DuPont's case, they wanted to shut down a chemical plant for maintenance and then restart the plant once the maintenance had been completed. This was a very challenging process and was the driving force behind the development of the method.

The method has been refined so that any project that has a number of interdependent activities will benefit from using the method where the critical activities of the program are identified that will have a direct impact on the completion date of the project. Figure 9.3 shows a typical project that has a critical path.

9.3.2.1 Key Steps in the Critical Path Method

There are six steps in producing a critical path diagram:

Step 1: Activity specification

The WBS developed for the Gantt chart that identifies the activities involved in the project is used as the main input for the critical path method.

Step 2: Activity sequence formation

This step establishes the correct activity sequence. There are three questions that require answers for each task in the list.

1. Which tasks need to be completed before this task can begin?
2. Which tasks should be completed at the same time as this task?
3. Which tasks should happen immediately on completion of this task?

Step 3: Network diagram

Once the activity sequence has been correctly defined, the network diagram can be drawn similar to that shown in Figure 9.4.

Step 4: Estimate the duration of each task activity

These values can be derived directly from the WBS estimation sheet. A number of companies use the 'Constructive Cost Model' (COCOMO), which is an algorithm that uses a basic regression formula that has parameters derived from historical project data. The model was developed by Barry W. Boehm and is function points based.

This estimated information can be used for this step of the process.

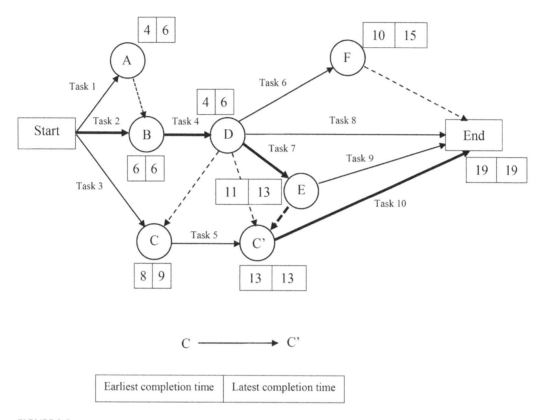

FIGURE 9.3
A typical critical path diagram.

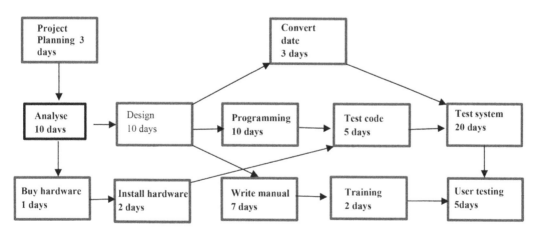

FIGURE 9.4
A typical PERT diagram.

Step 5: Identification of the critical path

For this step, four parameters of each activity on the network needs to be determined.

1. Earliest start time (ES): The earliest time an activity can start once the previous dependent activity has been completed.
2. Earliest finish time (EF): ES + activity duration.
3. Latest finish time (LF): The latest time an activity can finish without delaying the project.
4. Latest start time (LS): LF – activity duration.

The float time for an activity is described as the time between the earliest (ES) and the latest (LS) start times or between the earliest (EF) and latest (LF) finish times.

During the float time, an activity can be delayed without having an effect on the project finish time.

The critical path is the longest path of the network diagram. The activities on the critical path will have an effect on the deadline of the project. If any activity on this path is delayed, the project will be delayed.

The times of those activities that lie on the critical path will need to be reduced if the project management team needs to accelerate the project.

9.3.3 PERT Estimation Technique

9.3.3.1 Introduction

PERT (Program Evaluation and Review Technique) is one of the successful and proven methods for the accurate estimation of a project. Without an accurate estimate, no project can be completed within the allowed budget and target completion date.

PERT was initially created by the US Navy for developing ballistic missiles where there are thousands of contractors involved in the development and construction. Using the PERT methodology the project was completed two years ahead of its initial schedule.

9.3.3.2 The PERT Basics

The critical path method (CPM) and PERT are often confused with each other. Construction of the arrow diagrams is carried out in identical ways for both methods. The main difference only becomes apparent when estimating the activity durations.

When using PERT, three time estimates are required for every activity:

t_o = the most *optimistic* duration.

t_m = the most *likely* duration.

t_p = the most *pessimistic* duration.

A probable duration is calculated using these three quantities based on statistics, assuming that the errors will fall within a normal distribution curve.

$$t_e = \frac{t_o + 4t_m + t_p}{6} \text{ (where } t_e \text{ is the expected time)}$$

This calculation is repeated for every activity on the network and is used for predicting the probability of completing the project within the scheduled time scale.

It is possible to complete this calculation on networks with 'say' less than 100 activities, but if any more than that, it will become necessary to employ a computer to remove the drudgery from the calculations.

Some authorities do not accept that a normal distribution curve is suitable for predicting the spread of estimating errors. Generally speaking, it has been found that estimates are frequently optimistic rather than pessimistic. To allow for this tendency, the use of a skewed distribution curve is often used, using the following equation:

$$t_e = \frac{t_o + 3t_m + 2t_p}{6}$$

Whichever statistical basis is used, PERT will still produce a critical path in the same way as the CPM. Here the emphasis will have changed slightly the cost-time analysis and concentration on the critical path to a more statistical approach.

9.4 Resource Scheduling

In a busy design office there may be a number of important projects being worked on at a time. This will require effective use of the available design office resources when the company decides to implement a new product.

In a large office, personnel will be made available by reallocating them from less prioritised activities. But in a small office this course of action may not be possible if the company is limited by engineers and draughtsmen available.

The option open to the company is to either reallocate some of the less important work or to consider alternative resources by either drafting in contract labour or to outsource some of the activities to trusted contract design offices.

The role of the design manager becomes important to try and maintain the balance of activities within the office without compromising any of the projects.

From the work breakdown used in the development of the project plan, the manager will be able to generate individual work packages that identify a specific task to be undertaken by an individual (as yet to be identified). The work package will state precisely the action to be completed together with the required start date and the date of completion, these to tie in with specific milestones within the project plan.

The availability of personnel free to undertake the work packages is dependent on a number of factors. Parts of the design office staff may not be available at any given time for the following reasons:

- Away on annual leave.
- Attending a training course.
- Absent due to illness.
- Allocated to other urgent projects.
- Working on internal projects including writing engineering standards, design estimates, etc.
- Carrying out modifications on supposedly completed projects.

This will restrict the design manager's options to whom the work packages can be allocated and will require careful attention to the overall project plan.

TABLE 9.2

Part Example of a Project Implementation Plan

1	2	3	4	5	6	7	8	9	10	11	12	13
	Task No.	Task	% Completed	Status	Task Start Date	To Be Completed by	Actual Completion Date	Task Predecessors	Task Assigned to	Priority	Milestone?	Comments
1	1.0	*Project initiation*			1/1/2014	1/1/2014			Owner 1, Owner 2, Owner 3			
2	1.1	*Gather project ideas*	100	Completed	3/1/2014	4/1/2014	4/1/2014		Owner 1			
3	1.2	*Collect business requirements*	100	Completed	5/1/2014	7/1/2014	7/1/2014	1.1	Owner 2		Yes	
4	1.3	*Identify and gather a project team*	100	Completed	8/1/2014	12/1/2014	10/1/2014	1.2	Owner 3	High		
5	1.4	*Assign team members*	20	On schedule	13/1/2014	13/1/2014		1.3	Owner 1, Owner 2, Owner 3	Medium		
6	1.5	*Prepare the requirements document*	30	On schedule	14/1/2014	20/1/2014		1.4	Owner 1, Owner 2, Owner 3	High		
7	2.0	*Brainstorming meeting*			25/1/2014	1/2/2014			Owner 1, Owner 2, Owner 3			
8	2.1	*WBS development*			21/1/2014	12/2/2014			Owner 1, Owner 2, Owner 3		Yes	
9	2.2	*Work breakdown structure meeting*	50	On schedule	21/1/2014	22/1/2014			Owner 1, Owner 2, Owner 3	Medium		

#	WBS	Task	%	Status	Start	End		Owner		
10	2.3	*Build a work breakdown structure*	20	On schedule	23/1/2014	25/1/2014		Owner 1, Owner 2, Owner 3		Started early
11	2.4	*Update WBS in the project plan*	10	On schedule	27/1/2014	1/2/2014		Owner 1, Owner 2, Owner 3		
12	3.0	*Outline the project plan*	100	Completed	30/1/2014	15/2/2014	10/1/2014	Owner 1, Owner 2, Owner 3		
13	3.1	*Assign resources to project tasks*	80	On schedule	1/2/2014	4/2/2104		Owner 1, Owner 2, Owner 3		
14	3.2	*Analysis*			10/2/2014	21/2/2014		Owner 1, Owner 2, Owner 3	Yes	
15	3.3	*Create an entity relationship diagram*	0	Future task	10/2/2014	23/2/2014		Owner 1, Owner 2, Owner 3		
16	3.4	*Create a data flow diagram*	20	On schedule	11/2/2014	15/2/2014		Owner 1, Owner 2, Owner 3		
17								Owner 1, Owner 2, Owner 3		

The option open to the manager is to reallocate some of the less important work or to consider alternative resources by either drafting in contract labour or to outsource some of the activities to trusted contract design companies.

There are a number of project manager software programs available that can operate on a number of programs at the same time. This is known as multi-project resource scheduling. They usually treat all the current projects as a single project and all the individual projects as sub-projects.

Although the individual project leaders are only interested in their own immediate project, the software will print out the resource allocation that is available to that sub-project.

9.5 Project Implementation

This is a document created by the project manager or the team leader and it itemises the project tasks, the responsibility of each task and the associated target dates.

9.5.1 Implementation Plan Structure

The plan is a grid that is made up of columns and rows. Each column represents an area of information and each row lists the tasks (Table 9.2).

For example, the plan may have the following columns:

- Task indent number.
- Task – a list of project tasks.
- Percentage completed – this identifies how much the task has been completed to date.
- Status – the status of the task, 'completed', 'on schedule', 'behind schedule', etc.
- Start date – the date on which the task was started.
- Completion date – estimated date the task is scheduled to be completed.
- Actual completion date – the date the task was completed.
- Task predecessors – tasks that have to be completed prior to this task.
- Task assigned to – name of the individual the task was assigned to.
- Task priority – high, medium or low.
- Milestone – yes or no to indicate that this is a milestone task.
- Notes – any appropriate comments related to the task.

These headings can be altered to suit the style of project management appropriate for the project.

10

Engineering Design Economics

10.1 Project/Design Cost Accounting

10.1.1 Project/Design Cost Estimating

Cost estimating is the practice of forecasting the cost of completing a project with a defined scope. It is the primary element of project cost management, a knowledge area that involves planning, monitoring and controlling a project's monetary costs. (Project cost management has been practiced since the 1950s.) The approximate total project cost, called the cost estimate, is used to authorise a project's budget and manage its costs.

An accurate cost estimate is critical for deciding whether to take on a project for determining a project's eventual scope, and for ensuring that projects remain financially feasible and avoid cost overruns.

Cost estimates are typically revised and updated as the project's scope becomes more precise and as project risks are realised, cost estimating is an iterative process. A cost estimate may also be used to prepare a project cost baseline, which is the milestone-based point of comparison for assessing a project's actual cost performance.

10.1.2 Key Components of a Cost Estimate

A cost estimate is a summation of all the costs involved in successfully finishing a project, from inception to completion (project duration). These project costs can be categorised in a number of ways and levels of detail, but the simplest classification divides costs into two main categories: direct costs and indirect costs.

10.1.2.1 Direct Costs

Direct costs are broadly classified as those directly associated with a single area (such as a department or a project). In project management, direct costs are expenses billed exclusively to a specific project. They can include project team wages, the costs of resources to produce physical products, fuel for equipment, and money spent to address any project-specific risks.

10.1.2.2 Indirect Costs

Indirect costs, on the other hand, cannot be associated with a specific cost centre and are instead incurred by a number of projects simultaneously, sometimes in varying amounts. In project management, quality control, security costs, and utilities are usually classified as indirect costs since they are shared across a number of projects and are not directly billable to any one project.

A cost estimate is more than a simple list of costs, however, it also outlines the assumptions underlying each cost. These assumptions (along with estimates of cost accuracy) are compiled into a report called the basis of estimate, which also details cost exclusions and inclusions. The basis of estimate report allows project stakeholders to interpret project costs and to understand how and where actual costs might differ from approximated costs.

Beyond the broad classifications of direct and indirect costs, project expenses fall into more specific categories. Common types of expenses include:

- **Labour:** The cost of human effort expended towards project objectives.
- **Materials:** The cost of resources needed to create products.
- **Equipment:** The cost of buying and maintaining equipment used in project work.
- **Services:** The cost of external work that a company seeks for any given project (vendors, contractors, etc.).
- **Software:** Non-physical computer resources.
- **Hardware:** Physical computer resources.
- **Facilities:** The cost of renting or using specialised equipment, services, or locations.
- **Contingency costs:** Costs added to the project budget to address specific risks arising during the project.

10.2 Cost Categories

10.2.1 Investment Cost

This is the cost of initiating the product into the workplace and includes the cost of the design and development, prototype testing, the initial procurement and installation of equipment, tooling, training costs, etc. It is considered a one-time cost and is important measure of whether the project is economically viable.

10.2.2 Operations and Maintenance Cost

These costs are incurred in operating and maintain a complete factory, down to items of equipment or individual components. This cost includes:

- Power
- Labour
- Materials
- Spare parts
- Insurances and taxes

An allocated portion of the overhead cost is also included in this cost.

The operations and maintenance costs occur over the lifetime of the item being operated and will usually increase with time as the maintenance costs will begin to dominate as items require to be reconditioned or replaced.

10.2.3 Fixed and Variable Cost

Fixed costs are costs that remain constant over the length of time the item is operating. These include rents, rates, salaries, leasing charges, etc., and is unaffected by the level of output. If there is a significant increase in the output, then additional space may be required resulting in extra rent being required.

Variable costs cover direct materials, labour (especially if paid on piecework) and possibly power. It is assumed that most variable costs vary in direct proportion (linearly) to output. Variations may occur, as an example, if the output was (say) doubled, this may double the purchase of material, there may be quantity discounts available; hence, the cost increase could be less than the increase in output.

There are other terms used include the following:

Semi-variable costs are costs that have a fixed and variable component. An example here is of a telephone charge, where a line rental is applied which is fixed and call charges which are variable. A further example is motor car costs were the tax and insurance is fixed but the cost of fuel is variable.

Stepped fixed costs are costs that remain fixed over specific levels of output but may significantly increase when the output rises above a critical level. An example here would be if a supervisor is able to handle outputs up to 20 000 units without a problem but at higher levels, they cannot handle the production and an additional supervisor may have to be engaged.

10.2.4 Incremental and Marginal Cost

Incremental and marginal costs both refer to increases in cost.

An incremental cost is associated with a choice and only ever includes future costs. Where a previously made purchase or investment has been made this is not included. The incremental cost can include a number of different direct and indirect cost inputs depending upon the situation. Only costs that will change as a result of the decision are included.

As an example, consider a factory production line which is running at full capacity, the incremental cost of adding a further production line may include the cost of the equipment, the labour to staff the line and the electricity to run the line together with any additional recourse.

Marginal cost is a more specific term which refers to the cost to manufacture one more item. This term was used originally to optimise production, products with high marginal costs tend to be exclusive, labour intensive or is usually the first product off a production line. A classic example is the cost to print an encyclopaedia. The cost to produce the first encyclopaedia is considerable as it has to pay for all the research undertaken, entries written and typeset. When the 10 000 encyclopaedia is printed it requires very little additional cost.

Marginal cost may equal the incremental cost when only one additional unit is being considered.

10.2.5 Indirect and Direct Costs

Indirect costs are all costs that include all materials that is not used in the manufacture of the product itself, labour including supervision or management including support operations and indirect expenses covering the cost of utilities, building rentals depreciation insurances, etc. that cannot be traced to specific products and is often referred to as *overheads*. These costs are shared by all the products.

Direct costs include labour, materials and external subcontract work that is used in the manufacture of a particular product. The direct labour costs are only those operators that are hourly paid and exclude staff who are salaried. Direct material costs is determined from the engineering drawing bill of materials (parts list), the cost is obtained from the material suppliers invoices.

In some instances the product may have to leave the manufacturing premises for speciality work to be undertaken by external subcontractors. These are usually companies that have speciality equipment not owned by the parent company and which is an asset the company cannot immediately justify in purchasing as its usage is of a limited nature. This will be classed as a direct cost to the product and will include the transport cost offsite together with the cost of the contract work.

10.2.6 Non-recurring and Recurring Costs

Non-recurring costs are those costs that only occur once in a lifetime of the product and covers testing other than acceptance testing, manufacture of jigs and fixtures, special tooling and equipment. It is considered that initial product research, design and development are a non-recurring cost.

Recurring costs are those that continue to occur through the lifetime of the product and can include tool replacements, continued project management, etc.

10.3 Cost Accounting

Cost accounting is the process of recording, classifying, analysing, summarising and allocating costs associated with a process, and then developing various courses of action to control the costs. Its goal is to advise the *management* on how to optimise business practices and processes based on cost efficiency and capability. Cost accounting provides the detailed cost information that management needs to control current operations and plan for the future.

Since managers are making decisions only for their own organisation, there is no need for the information to be comparable to similar information from other organisations. Instead, information must be relevant for a particular environment. Cost accounting information is commonly used in *financial accounting* information, but its primary function is for use by managers to facilitate making decisions.

10.4 Cost Estimating

A **cost estimate** is the approximation of the cost of a program, *project* or operation. The cost estimate is the product of the cost estimating process. The cost estimate has a single total value and may have identifiable component values. A problem with a *cost overrun* can be avoided with a credible, reliable, and accurate cost estimate. A cost estimator is the professional who prepares cost estimates. There are different types of cost estimators, whose title may be preceded by a modifier, such as *building estimator*, or electrical estimator, or chief estimator. Other professionals such as *quantity surveyors* and *cost engineers* may also prepare cost estimates or contribute to cost estimates. In the United States, according to the *Bureau of Labor Statistics*, there were 185 400 cost estimators in 2010. There are around 75 000 professional quantity surveyors working in the United Kingdom.

10.5 Payback Period

10.5.1 Payback period in *capital budgeting* refers to the period of time required to recoup the funds expended in an investment, or to reach the *break-even point*. For example, a $1000 investment made at the start of Year 1 which returned $500 at the end of Year 1 and Year 2, respectively, would have a two-year payback period. Payback period is usually expressed in years. Starting from investment year by calculating Net Cash Flow for each year: Net Cash Flow Year 1 = Cash Inflow Year 1 − Cash Outflow Year 1. Then, Cumulative Cash Flow = (Net Cash Flow Year 1 + Net Cash Flow Year 2 + Net Cash Flow Year 3, etc.). Accumulate by year until Cumulative Cash Flow is a positive number: that year is the payback year.

The *time value of money* is not taken into account. Payback period intuitively measures how long something takes to 'pay for itself'. *All else being equal*, shorter payback periods are preferable to longer payback periods. Payback period is popular due to its ease of use despite the recognised limitations described below.

The term is also widely used in other types of investment areas, often with respect to *energy efficiency* technologies, maintenance, upgrades or other changes. For example, a *compact fluorescent* light bulb may be described as having a payback period of a certain number of years or operating hours, assuming certain costs. Here, the return to the investment consists of reduced operating costs. Although primarily a financial term, the concept of a payback period is occasionally extended to other uses, such as *energy payback period* (the period of time over which the energy savings of a project equal the amount of energy expended since project inception); these other terms may not be standardised or widely used.

10.6 Interest

Interest is payment from a *borrower* or deposit-taking financial institution to a *lender* or depositor of an amount above repayment of the *principal sum* (i.e. the amount borrowed) at a particular rate. It is distinct from a *fee* which the borrower may pay the lender or some third party. It is also distinct from *dividend* which is paid by a company to its shareholders (owners) from its *profit* or *reserve*, but not at a particular rate decided beforehand, rather on a pro rata basis as a share in the reward gained by *risk*-taking entrepreneurs when the revenue earned exceeds the total costs. For example, a customer would usually pay interest to *borrow* from a bank, so they pay the bank an amount which is more than the amount they borrowed; or a customer may earn interest on their savings, and so they may withdraw more than they originally deposited. In the case of savings, the customer is the lender, and the bank plays the role of the borrower.

Interest differs from *profit*, in that interest is received by a lender, whereas profit is received by the *owner* of an *asset*, *investment* or *enterprise*. (Interest may be part or the whole of the profit on an *investment*, but the two concepts are distinct from each other from an *accounting* perspective.)

The *rate of interest* is equal to the interest amount paid or received over a particular period divided by the *principal sum* borrowed or lent (usually expressed as a percentage).

Compound interest means that interest is earned on prior interest in addition to the principal. Due to compounding, the total amount of debt grows exponentially, and its mathematical study led to the discovery of the number *e*. In practice, interest is most often calculated on a daily, monthly, or yearly basis, and its impact is influenced greatly by its compounding rate.

10.7 Cash Flow

10.7.1 Definition of 'Cash Flow'

10.7.1.1 Definition

The amount of cash or cash-equivalent which the company receives or gives out by the way of payment(s) to creditors is known as cash flow. Cash flow analysis is often used to analyse the liquidity position of the company. It gives a snapshot of the amount of cash coming into the business, from somewhere, and amount flowing out.

10.7.2 Description

As discussed cash flows can either be positive or negative. It is calculated by subtracting the cash balance at the beginning of a period which is also known as opening balance, form the cash balance at the end of the period (could be a month, quarter or a year) or the closing balance.

If the difference is positive, it means you have more cash at the end of a given period. If the difference is negative it means that you have less amount of cash at the end of a given period when compared with the opening balance at the starting of a period.

To analyse where the cash is coming from and going out, cash flow statements are prepared. It has three main categories – operating cash flow which includes day-to-day transactions, investing cash flow which includes transactions which are done for expansion purpose, and financing cash flow which include transactions relating to the amount of dividend paid out to stockholders.

However, the level of cash flow is not an ideal metric to analyse a company when making an investment decision. A company's balance sheet as well as income statements should be studied carefully to come to a conclusion.

Cash level might be increasing for a company because it might have sold some of its assets, but that doesn't mean the liquidity is improving. If the company has sold off some of its assets to pay off debt, then this is a negative sign and should be investigated further for more clarification.

If the company is not reinvesting cash, then this is also a negative sign because in that case it is not using the opportunity to diversify or build business for expansion.

10.8 Depreciation and Taxes

Depreciation is an income **tax** deduction that allows a taxpayer to recover the cost or other basis of certain properties or equipment. It is an annual allowance for the wear and tear, deterioration, or obsolescence of the equipment. … The taxpayer must own the property or equipment.

10.9 Inflation and Deflation

Inflation occurs when the price of goods and services rise, while *deflation* occurs when those prices decrease. The balance between the two *economic conditions*, opposites of the same coin, is delicate, and an *economy* can quickly swing from one condition to the other.

Inflation is caused when goods and services are in high demand, creating a drop in availability. Supplies can decrease for many reasons: A natural disaster can wipe out a food crop; a housing *boom* can exhaust building supplies, etc. Whatever the reason, consumers are willing to pay more for the items they want, causing manufacturers and service providers to charge more.

Deflation occurs when too many goods are available or when there is not enough *money* circulating to purchase those goods. For instance, if a particular type of car becomes highly popular, other manufacturers start to make a similar vehicle to compete. Soon, car companies have more of that vehicle style than they can sell, so they must drop the price to sell the cars. Companies that find themselves stuck with too much *inventory* must cut costs, which often leads to *layoffs*. *Unemployed* individuals do not have enough money available to purchase items; to coax them into buying, prices get lowered, which continues the trend.

When *credit* providers detect a decrease in prices, they often reduce the amount of credit they offer. This creates a *credit crunch* where consumers cannot access *loans* to purchase big-ticket items, leaving companies with overstocked inventory and causing further deflation. Deflation can lead to an economic *recession* or *depression*, and the *central banks* usually work to stop deflation as soon as it starts.

11

Quality in the Design Process

11.1 Introduction

In recent years quality has become a touchstone in the majority of engineering companies, large and small, within the United Kingdom, United States and Europe. Following the example of Japan with the introduction of *kaizen*, this showed that the buying public preferred quality when purchasing a new product.

Recognising the importance of this, the National Standard Organisations such as British standards (BS 5750), the US standards (ANSI/ASQC Q90) and Europe standards (EN29000) were drawn up and adopted. The international standard ISO 9000 has been produced and this has now replaced the individual national standards.

When preparing for ISO 9000 registration, the company needs to show what quality systems it has in place to maintain control, create stability, predictability and capability. The first step in developing a quality system is to document what the company is doing already. Measures can then be built that will enable consistent results to be achieved and then gradually improve the performance. This way the company will obtain lasting improvement by gradual change – in short *kaizen*.

For companies that are always changing, a well-established quality system will enable them to do it under controlled conditions.

In this chapter, quality systems appropriate to the design effort will be considered.

11.2 Design Procedures

Depending on the nature of the company, design can be as simple as replacing an item with another of a different specification to the total new design of an offshore exploration and production platform. Design can also include hardware, software or a combination of both.

The standard requires that the company establishes and maintains procedures that control the design of a product so that the specified requirements are met.

The design activity can be broken down into ten primary steps:

1. Establish the customer's requirements.
2. Develop a definitive specification of the customer's requirements.
3. Undertake a feasibility study to identify if the accomplishment is feasible.
4. Plan for meeting the requirements.

5. Organise resources and materials for meeting these requirements.

6. Prepare a project definition study to determine which of the many solutions are suitable.

7. Develop a specification that details all the features and characteristics of the product.

8. Produce a prototype or model of the proposed design.

9. Undertake extensive trials to evaluate the design if it will meet the design requirements.

10. Assess the data and optimise the design to improve it so that it meets the requirements.

Detailed procedures will ultimately be needed to address each of these stages; however, the control of the design process will require more than procedures. Standards will also need to be considered together with codes of practice and design guides, as design is often a process of adopting solutions from the available technologies.

As an example, if the company is designing heavy lifting equipment in the United Kingdom, the health and safety executive issues a code of practice, 'Lifting Operations and Lifting Equipment Regulations 1998, Approved Code of Practice and Guidance', that needs to be addressed when designing this type of equipment for sale and use in the United Kingdom.

Design guides are important in products where the equipment is modular and uses similar components. An example here would be the design of industrial (fork lift) trucks where the company manufactures a range of trucks in various sizes. The design principles will be similar in each of the designs, but a size factor will apply and will come from a detailed stress analysis of the various designs. When a new design is being proposed and it falls between two current models, it may be possible to interpolate the designs and save valuable design time.

11.2.1 Design Control

11.2.1.1 Design Reviews

A design review is a means of controlling the design and to check that all aspects of the design process fully meet the design requirements.

- Design requirements review.
- Conceptual design review.
- Preliminary design review.
- Critical design review.
- Qualification readiness review.
- Final design review.

11.2.1.2 Design Requirements Review

This first review is to establish that the design requirements are met and that the design reflects the needs of the customer before the start of the conceptual design.

11.2.1.3 Conceptual Design Review

The conceptual design review is held to establish that the final design concept selected will fulfil the requirements before any project definition begins.

11.2.1.4 Preliminary Design Review

This review establishes that all the risks have been completely resolved and that design specifications for each sub-element of the project have been satisfactorily completed.

11.2.1.5 Critical Design Review

The critical design review establishes that the detailed design for each sub-element complies with its development specifications and that production specifications have been produced prior to the manufacture of any prototype models.

11.2.1.6 Qualification Readiness Review

This review establishes the baseline of the design and shows that the qualification of the product is in hand before the commencement of proving trials.

11.2.1.7 Final Design Review

The final design review establishes that the final design fulfils the requirements of the development specifications before releasing the design for production.

11.2.1.8 The Design Review Team

For a design review to be effective it should be conducted by someone other than the designer. The team should comprise representatives from marketing, purchasing, manufacturing, servicing, inspection, test, reliability and QA authorities. This will ensure that all aspects of the design have sufficient practical experience available and provide ample advance warning of any potential problems in implementing the design.

   The chairman of the review team should have the authority to make any decisions as to whether the design should proceed to the next phase based on the evidence substantiated by the review team.

11.2.1.9 Design Review Input Data

Input data relevant to the review should be distributed and examined by all active partners within the team in advance of the time of the individual review meeting. However, a sub-meeting may need to be held to examine and analyse the input data prior to the main meeting in order to confirm that the proposed design solution is the most practical and cost-effective way of meeting the design requirements.

11.2.1.10 Design Review Reports

The results of the design reviews should be documented in a report rather than taking minutes of the meeting, as it represents objective evidence that may later to be required to justify a product's compliance with the requirements. The report should also show the investigation of design problems and compare similar designs. The reports should also have the agreement of the full review team.

11.2.1.11 Design Review Follow-Up

Any corrective actions arising from the design reviews should be tracked to confirm that they have been implemented as agreed and that the reported problems have been resolved.

11.2.1.12 Qualification Tests and Demonstrations

In a new design, many assumptions will have been made and will need to be proven before commitment of any valuable resources is made to the project. Some of the requirements such as reliability, time dependency and other requirements may not be verifiable without subjecting the product beyond its design limits. It may be possible to synthesise the design using modern computer programs such as MatLab©, but it will be at some point necessary to subject a physical element to a series of tests representing actual operating conditions to ensure that they will remain stable.

In some cases, a level of confidence rather than certainty will be acceptable. Such tests are called *qualification tests*. Their difference with other tests is that they are designed to establish the design envelope and prove the capability of the design.

The cost of testing a large amount of products would be uneconomical and take an excessive amount of time. It is more economical in cost and time to perform the tests on a small random sample of products with the test levels taking account of the design assumptions, variations in the manufacturing process and the operating conditions.

When the qualification tests are completed, a customer may request a demonstration of performance in order to accept the product. These tests are called *design acceptance tests*. They usually consist of a combination of functional and environmental tests. These are usually a subset of the qualification test specifications and are supported with the results of the qualification tests. When the design acceptance tests show that the design meets the requirements of the specified requirements, a *Design Certificate* can be issued. This will be the standard that is declared on the certificate against which all subsequent changes will be controlled and from which production versions should be produced.

The procedures for controlling both the qualification and design acceptance tests should provide for:

- Test specifications to be produced that define the features and characteristics that are to be verified for design qualification and acceptance.
- Test plans to be produced that define the sequence of tests, the responsibilities for their conduct and the location of the tests together with the procedures to be used.
- Test procedures to be produced that describe how the tests specified in the test specification together with any tooling and test equipment are to be used within the conduct of the test and how the resultant data is to be recorded.
- The reference to be included that all measuring equipment used is within calibration and is certified during the tests.

- The test samples to have successfully passed all planned in-process and assembly inspections prior to commencing the qualification tests.
- Any deviations or non-conformances of the product and the current design issue to be recorded prior to and subsequent to the tests.
- All test activities to be conducted strictly in accordance with the prescribed specifications, plans and procedures.
- The test results and the conditions under which the test was conducted to be recorded.
- Any deviations to be recorded, any remedial action taken and any re-verification done prior to continuing with the tests.
- Reviews of the tests performed following the qualification tests to confirm that sufficient objective evidence has been obtained, demonstrating that the product fulfils the requirements of the test specification.

11.2.2 Verification Design Calculations

In some cases, the verification of the design may only be possible by analysis rather than by test or demonstration. In this situation, the design calculations should either be checked and confirmed by a third party or by performing the calculations by an alternative method. When this form of verification is used, it should be specified in the verification plan.

11.2.3 Comparing Similar Designs

Verifying a design can be an expensive exercise. It may be possible to avoid these additional costs by comparing the design with a previous similar design that has been proven to meet the same requirements. This tactic is most often used in designs that use a modular manufacture.

If the performance of a module has been verified either as part of a proven design or has been subject to extended use, it is able to demonstrate achievement of the design requirements. Care will need to be exercised using this method of verification to ensure that the operating requirements are the same and are able to show evidence of compliance with the requirements.

11.2.4 Changes and Modifications

It is a requirement of ISO 9000 that the company establishes and maintains procedures.

The following are a selection of procedures the company needs to maintain with respect to design changes:

- Identification of design changes.
- Identification of modifications.
- Documenting design changes.
- Documenting modifications.
- Review and approval of design changes.
- Review and approval of modifications.

- Document control.
  - Requirements.
  - Document control procedures.
- Document review and approval.
- Authorised personnel.
- Indicating approval.
- Issuing documents.
- Availability of controlled documents.
  - Issue notation.
  - Availability of documents.
- Removal of obsolete documents.
- Review and approval of changes to documents.
- Access to relevant background information.
- Identifying the nature of changes.
- Identifying the current revision of documents.
- Reissue of changed documents.

11.3 Quality Assurance and Control

Quality assurance (QA) is a way of preventing mistakes and defects in manufactured products and avoiding problems when delivering solutions or services to customers; the ISO 9000 defines this as 'part of *quality* management focused on providing confidence that *quality* requirements will be fulfilled'.

Quality control (QC) is a procedure or set of procedures intended to ensure that a manufactured product or performed service adheres to a defined set of *quality* criteria or meets the requirements of the client or customer. QC is similar to, but not identical with, QA.

QA is defined as a procedure or set of procedures intended to ensure that a product or service under development (before work is complete, as opposed to afterwards) meets specified requirements. QA is sometimes expressed together with QC as a single expression, quality assurance and control (QA/QC).

Implementing these procedures into the fabric of the company will ensure that customers will have confidence in the products. Over time, quality becomes synonymous with a company.

Take as an example, a manufacturing company manufacturing automotive brake parts. In this situation, quality assurance and quality control go hand in hand, where quality assurance ensures that the quality philosophy is endemic within the psyche of the company and quality control is accepted without question by the operators. All testing procedures are carried out methodically without cutting any corners. Any component failure could result in fatality, which would reflect not only on the operators and engineers but also on the company.

11.4 Design Change Control

This is a systematic approach to managing all *changes* made to a product or system. The purpose is to ensure that no unnecessary *changes* are made, all *changes* are documented, all services are not unnecessarily disrupted and that all the resources are used efficiently.

Changes to the design can be for a number of legitimate reasons including:

- Cost – the original budget is no longer available.
- Change of scope – the client has changed the design brief.
- Changes to design parameters – the original constraining factors have now changed, resulting in the need for an amendment.
- Supply chain issues – restriction on materials or components necessitates a deviation from the original solution.
- Unknowns – previously unavailable information or shortfalls in the supporting design information identify the need for a change.
- Innovation – new technology, lessons learnt or new ideas can all instigate a change.
- Quality – a previously identified defect can drive an improvement.
- Human error – mistakes can be made during design or manufacture/construction.

11.5 Implementing the Change

There are numerous sound reasons why generating and following a documented process is key to protecting employers, employees, clients and members of the public:

- Compliance with ISO 9001 – companies require accreditation in order to meet the requirements of their customers. ISO 9001 accreditation can be a driver for further business from bigger clients who stipulate this as a mandatory requirement.
- Protection – Design liability protects companies from claims of negligence where competence and due diligence can be demonstrated. Failure to follow a process might render this insurance invalid.
- Prosecution – in the event that a change has caused a serious accident, and the change has been authorised or carried out by someone without the required level of competence, that person could then be liable to criminal prosecution.
- Responsibility – the use of a clearly defined process ensures that competent persons are allocated with the required level of competence in order to review and process changes to the original design solution.
- Recovery of costs – where a client is involved, the process of recording the change and getting it approved by the client involved can be a mechanism for highlighting additional costs incurred or indeed act as a means for speedier recovery of these costs incurred.

The following short summary aims to try and ensure that some common pitfalls are avoided, and summarises sound reasoning as to why engineer's should follow the approved procedures to benefit not only their employers but also themselves.

11.6 The Reason for the Change

First the reason for the change needs to be identified; whether the changes are being made on the grounds of cost or on the grounds of safety.

Stage 1:

Once the need for a change has been identified, the supporting information needs to be reviewed, added to and amended where necessary in order to support the amendment. This information could include:

- Drawings – either revised as a *Redline Mark-Up* (RLMU) or a completely new drawing
- Schedules
- Calculations
- Test records
- Confirmation from other parties, where the design affects more than one group, that the amendment suits all involved
- Additional costs
- Impact on the programme

Stage 2:

When processing the change, ensure that the agreed and documented procedures are adhered to. As a minimum, the approval of the Design Change Note (DCN) should include the following items where applicable:

1. Review, comment and acceptance by a competent or chief engineer.
2. Review by the client for acceptance (or a senior engineer, dependent on the process).
3. Further acceptance of the solution before submitting the response where the client is not the end user (i.e. if the client is acting on behalf of the user).
4. Complete the paperwork, and formal record of the outcome on the DCN N.B. If you are responsible for generating/signing off a DCN, ensure that consideration is taken as to whether or not the change is being done as a necessity, as 'Preferential Engineering' or as a Scope Change. This may dictate the need for suitable instruction to carry out the change under the contract, or provide grounds for rejecting the change. Failure to do so may result in your employer incurring unnecessary additional costs.

Stage 3:

Once the change is signed off by all relevant parties, the change needs to be made:

1. Where the change is detailed, and a RLMU will not suffice to accurately communicate the changes, the drawing needs to be transferred to the detailed design drawings.

2. If the design is complex and impacts more than one drawing or document, care needs to be taken to ensure that each document is correctly amended.

3. Checks on all drawings, schedules, calculations, etc. need to be completed and verified by the suitably authorised persons.

4. If required to comply with specific standards or specifications, check that the change has been done in compliance with these to avoid non-conformity.

5. Finally, where required, the change needs to be submitted through any client-specific checks. Ensure that the time required for these checks is considered when making any changes.

Stage 4:

Finally, now that the change is signed off, accepted and designed, it can then be distributed.

All persons on the distribution list should have all their old copies removed, destroyed and replaced by the new copies to ensure that everyone is building to the same design.

Final things to be considered are as follows:

- Ensure that the DCN has all the relevant information included.
- Ensure that the RLMUs are clearly legible and unambiguous.
- Does the change adversely impact any other element of the design or the existing components? This needs to be clearly identified.
- Does the amendment create additional risks for routine maintenance of this or other elements?
- Does the change increase the 'whole-life' costs to the end user which outweigh the cost of making the change in the first place?
- Does the change affect the way other components operate? Consider as a minimum the following:
  - Temperature change
  - Corrosion
  - Abrasion/friction
  - Explosive elements
  - Vibration
  - Noise
  - Friction
  - Efficiency
  - Performance
  - Flow
  - Pressure
  - Waste/recycling
- Is the process of making the change likely to incur costs which are greater than the savings made by implementing the design?
- Maintain channels of communication throughout the design change process in order to minimise the delays in getting the formal sign off for the change.

Despite all these notes, we are firmly advocating the need to initiate and follow a process. Failing to do so creates the opportunity for an organisation to incur significant risks in the form of costs, programme, H&S or environment, all of which are liable not only to damage reputation, but also to undermine businesses, and in the worst cases, destroy lives.

11.7 Quality Function Deployment

11.7.1 Introduction

Quality Function Deployment (QDF) was first developed in Japan by Yoji Akao in the late 1960s when working for Mitsubishi's Shipyards. It was later adopted by other companies including Toyota and its supply chain. In the early 1980s, QFD was introduced in the United States mainly by the big three automotive companies and a few electronics manufacturers. Its acceptance in the United States was rather slow to begin with but has since gained popularity and is currently being used in a number of industries including manufacturing, healthcare and service organisations.

The central core of the method is the *Voice of the Customer* (VOC) in which the design quality and customer-perceived value are actively integrated into the product.

These companies are utilising a structured process to define their customer's wants and needs and transforming them into specific product designs and process plans to produce products that fulfil the customer's requirements.

11.7.2 What is QFD?

QFD is a structured process with a set of tools that is used to effectively define customer requirements and convert them into detailed engineering specifications and plans to produce the products that fulfil those requirements. QFD is used to translate customer requirements into measureable design targets and drive them from the assembly level down through the sub-assembly, component and production process levels. The methodology provides a defined set of matrices utilised to facilitate this progression.

11.7.3 Why Implement QFD?

Effective communication is one of the most important and effective aspects of any organisation's success. The QFD methodology effectively communicates customer needs to multiple business operations throughout the organisation including design, quality, manufacturing, production, marketing and sales. This effective communication of the 'Voice of the Customer' allows the entire organisation to work together and produce products with high levels of customer-perceived value. There are several additional benefits of using QFD:

- **Customer Focused:** QFD methodology places emphasis on the wants and needs of the customer, not on what the company may believe the customer wants. Here the VOC is translated into technical design specifications. During the QFD process, design specifications are driven down from the machine level to system, subsystem and component-level requirements. Finally, the design specifications are controlled throughout the production and assembly processes to assure that the customer needs are met.

- **VOC Competitor Analysis:** The QFD 'House of Quality' tool allows for direct comparison of how your design or product stacks up to the competition in meeting the VOC. This quick analysis can be beneficial in making design decisions that could give the company a commercial advantage.

- It has been shown that shorter development times and lower cost results also reduce the likelihood of late design changes by focusing on product features and improvements that are based on customer's requirements. There is less chance of valuable project time and resources being wasted on the development of non-value added features or functions.

- A strong knowledge database can be developed recording decisions made and any lessons learned during the product development process and can then be used as a historical record for future similar projects.

11.7.4 How to Implement QFD?

The QFD methodology is a 4-phase process that encompasses activities throughout the product development cycle. A series of matrices are utilised at each phase to translate the VOC to design requirements for each system, sub-system and component. The four phases of QFD are:

1. **Product Definition:** The Product Definition phase begins with the collection of VOC and translating the customer wants and needs into product specifications. It may also involve a competitive analysis to evaluate how effectively the competitor's product fulfils the customer's wants and needs. The initial design concept is based on the particular product performance requirements and specifications.

2. **Product Development:** During the Product Development phase, the critical parts and assemblies are identified. The critical product characteristics are cascaded down and translated to critical or key part and assembly characteristics or specifications. The functional requirements or specifications are then defined for each functional level.

3. **Process Development:** During the Process Development phase, the manufacturing and assembly processes are designed based on product and component specifications. The process flow is developed and the critical process characteristics are identified.

4. **Process Quality Control:** Prior to production launch, the QFD process identifies critical part and process characteristics. Process parameters are determined and appropriate process controls are developed and implemented. In addition, any inspection and test specifications are developed. Full production begins upon completion of process capability studies during the pilot build.

These matrices can be cascaded as shown in Figure 11.1, with the output from the preceding QFD exercise becoming the input into the following QFD analysis.

11.7.5 Level 1 QFD

The House of Quality is an effective tool used to translate the customer wants and needs into product or service design characteristics utilizing a relationship matrix. This figure

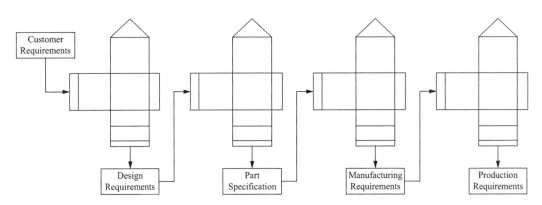

FIGURE 11.1
The four phases of QFD.

clearly illustrates that there are four QFD charts that manage the requirement flow down through the new product introduction process, with each chart being associated with the corresponding phase.

The initial or first matrix (the *Definition phase*) used in the QFD process compares the customer requirements *'whats'* against the design requirements *'hows'*. Figure 11.2 shows the basic structure of the QFD-type matrix diagram.

The matrix is data intensive and allows the team to capture a large amount of information in one place. The matrix earned the name 'House of Quality due to its structure resembling that of a house (see Figure 11.3). A cross-functional team possessing thorough knowledge of the product, the 'Voice of the Customer' and the company's capabilities

	List 2 of Requirements						
Item 1	⊙	⊙		△			
Item 2							
Item 3			○	△			
Item 4		○	△				
...							
...							

List 1 of Requirements (left vertical label)

Column labels (bottom): Items related to Item 'A' | Items related to Item 'B' | Items related to Item 'C' | Items related to Item 'D'

List 3 Many-to-one related with List 2

FIGURE 11.2
The basic structure of the QFD-type matrix diagram.

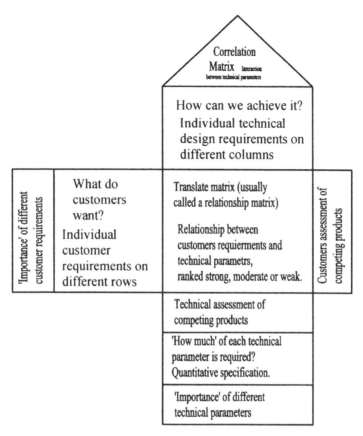

FIGURE 11.3
House of quality.

should complete the matrix. The different sections of the matrix and a brief description of each are listed below:

- **'Whats':** This is usually the first section to be completed. This column is where the VOC, or the wants and needs, of the customer are listed.
- **Importance Factor:** The team should rate each of the functions based on their level of importance to the customer. In many cases, a scale of 1 to 5 is used, with 5 representing the highest level of importance.
- **'Hows' or Ceiling:** Contains the design features and technical requirements the product will need to align with the VOC.
- **Body or Main Room:** Within the main body or room of the house of quality the 'Hows' are ranked according to their correlation or effectiveness of fulfilling each of the 'What's'. The ranking system used is a set of symbols indicating either a strong, moderate or a weak correlation. A blank box would represent no correlation or influence on meeting the 'What', or customer requirement. Each of the symbols represents a numerical value of 0, 1, 3 or 9.
- **Roof:** This matrix is used to indicate how the design requirements interact with each other. The interrelationships are ratings that range from a strong positive interaction (++) to a strong negative interaction (–) with a blank box indicating no interrelationship.

- **Competitor Comparison:** This section visualises a comparison of the competitor's product in regard to fulfilling the 'Whats'. In many cases, a scale of 1 to 5 is used for the ranking, with 5 representing the highest level of customer satisfaction. This section should be completed using direct feedback from customer surveys or other means of data collection.
- **Relative Importance:** This section contains the results of calculating the total of the sums of each column when multiplied by the importance factor. The numerical values are represented as discrete numbers or percentages of the total. The data is useful for ranking each of the 'Hows' and determining where to allocate the most resources.
- **Lower Level/Foundation:** This section lists more specific target values for technical specifications relating to the 'Hows' used to satisfy VOC.

Upon completion of the House of Quality, the technical requirements derived from the VOC can then be deployed to the appropriate teams within the organisation and populated into the Level 2 QFDs for more detailed analysis. This is the first step in driving the VOC throughout the product or process design process. Table 11.1 describes the QFD phase terminology.

11.7.6 Level 2 QFD

The Level 2 QFD matrix is used during the Design Development phase. Using the Level 2 QFD, the team can discover which of the assemblies, systems, sub-systems and components have the most impact on meeting the product design requirements and identify key design characteristics. The information produced from performing a Level 2 QFD is often used as a direct input to the Design Failure Mode and Effects Analysis (DFMEA) process.

Level 2 QFDs may be developed at the following levels:

- **System Level:** The technical specifications and functional requirements or 'Hows' identified and prioritised within the House of Quality become the 'Whats' for the system-level QFD. They are then evaluated according to the systems or assemblies they impact. Any systems deemed critical would then progress to a sub-system QFD.
- **Sub-System Level:** The requirements cascaded down from the system level are re-defined to align with how the sub-system contributes to the system meeting its

TABLE 11.1

QFD Phase Terminology

Phase Name	Phase No.	Brief Description
Definition	1.	The translation of Customer Requirements in to measurable Technical Requirements.
Concept	2.	The translation of Technical Requirements into compliant Design Solution (down to part or component) Requirements
Realisation	3.	Translation of the Design Solution Requirements into Realisation System Requirements
Delivery	4.	Translation of the Realisation System Requirements into a set of Delivery Requirements

functional requirements. This information then becomes the 'Whats' for the QFD and the components and other possible 'Hows' are listed and ranked to determine the critical components. The components deemed critical would then require progression to a component-level QFD.

- **Component Level:** The component-level QFD is extremely helpful in identifying the key and critical characteristics or features that can be detailed on the drawings. The key or critical characteristics then flow down into the Level 3 QFD activities for use in designing the process. For purchased components, this information is valuable for communicating key and critical characteristics to suppliers during sourcing negotiations and as an input to the Production Part Approval Process (PPAP) submission.

11.7.7 Level 3 QFD

The Level 3 QFD is used during the Process Development phase where we examine which of the processes or process steps have any correlation with meeting the component or part specifications. In the Level 3 QFD matrix, the 'Whats' are the component part technical specifications and the 'Hows' are the manufacturing processes or process steps involved in producing the part. The matrix highlights which of the processes or process steps have the most impact on meeting the part specifications. This information allows the production and quality teams to focus on the Critical to Quality (CTQ) processes, which flow down into the Level 4 QFD for further examination.

11.7.8 Level 4 QFD

The Level 4 QFD is not utilised as often as the previous three. Within the Level 4 QFD matrix, the team should list all the critical processes or process characteristics in the 'Whats' column on the left and then determine the 'Hows' for assuring that quality parts are produced and list them across the top of the matrix. Through ranking of the interactions of the 'Whats' and the 'Hows', the team can determine which controls could be most useful and develop quality targets for each. This information may also be used for creating Work Instructions, Inspection Sheets or as an input to Control Plans.

The purpose of QFD is not to replace an organisation's existing design process but rather to support and improve an organisation's design process. The QFD methodology is a systemic, proven means of embedding the voice of the customer into both the design and the production process. QFD is a method of ensuring that customer requirements are accurately translated into relevant technical specifications from product definition to product design, process development and implementation. The fact is that every business, organisation and industry has customers. Meeting the customer's needs is critical to success. Implementing the QFD methodology can enable you to drive the voice of your customers throughout your processes to increase your ability to satisfy or even excite your customers.

12

Design for Optimisation

12.1 Defining Optimum Design

Optimising is the process of maximising a desired property or minimising an undesirable one. An example would be for the engineer to maximise the strength of a component and to minimise its weight. As design is an iterative process, generally starting with a poorly defined problem and gradually refining it and arriving at a solution. In general, there will be a number of solutions to the same problem in which the designer will have to search for the best answer.

Example 12.1

Consider a shaft carrying a concentrated load of 2F as shown in Figure 12.1. The shaft is simply supported between two ball races. Write the equation for the objective function for the minimum volume.

SOLUTION:

In this example the minimum-volume design is required, the objective function is the volume of the shaft that is defined in terms of the four design variables, x_1, x_2, x_3 and x_4.
   Optimisation statement:

   Minimise f(x) the objective function
   Subject to g(x) $\leq$ 0 (inequality constraints)
   h(x) = 0 (equality constraints)
   'x' (design variable)

In this example this is a size optimisation.
   The objective function can be written as:

$$\text{Minimise } f(x) = 2\left[\frac{\pi\left(x_2^2 - x_1^2\right)}{4}\right]x_4 + \frac{\pi\left(x_3^2 - x_1^2\right)}{4}(2L - 2x_4) \qquad (12.1)$$

In this example the shaft is required to withstand a vertical load of 20 000 N at point 'B' with the shaft being supported at points 'A' and 'C'. The equality constraint 'b_1' can be written as:

$$b_1 = 2F = 20\ 000\ \text{N} \qquad (12.2)$$

With the permissible bending stress 'σ_p' of 500 MPa the shaft will be safe from bending failure.

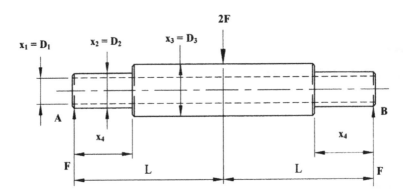

FIGURE 12.1
Simply supported beam.

The inequality constraint (g_x) will be:

$$g_x = \sigma_p = 500 \text{ MPa} \geq \sigma_b \qquad (12.3)$$

Where σb is the bending stress.

The designer can now undertake calculations that will minimise the total volume of the shaft and maintain a minimum value of σ_b and from these calculations establish the minimum diameters of the shaft.

12.2 Tools for Design Optimisation

There is no universal optimisation method available for solving all optimisation problems in a unique and efficient manner. Several methods have been developed for solving different types of optimisation problems and the methods are generally classified under different groups such as:

a. Single variable optimisation
b. Multi-variable optimisation
c. Constrained optimisation
d. Specialised optimisation
e. Nontraditional optimisation

In this section only the first two groups will be studied, i.e., single variable and multi-variable optimisations will be studied. References at the end of the section are added for further studies covering the more advanced optimisation techniques.

12.3 Mathematical Models and Optimisation Methods

The methods used for optimum design can be divided into two groups:

1. Analytical methods
    This method covers differentiation, variational methods and the use of Lagrange multipliers.

2. Numerical methods

This method comprises linear (simplex) and non-linear programming methods.

12.3.1 Differential Calculus Method

This method deals with the optimisation of a single variable. Consider Figure 12.1, this depicts a number of extremes that can occur in an objective function, f(x) curve, where 'x' is the design variable. It is observed from the curve that the points 'A' and 'C' are the mathematical minima. The point 'A' being the larger of the two minima, is called a local minimum, whereas the point 'C' is the global minimum. Point 'D' is referred to a point of inflection.

To find a maximum or minimum using this method, take the first derivative of the objective function f(x) and set it to equal zero; solve for the independent variable 'x',

$$\frac{dU}{dx} = 0 \tag{12.4}$$

Equation (12.4) gives the value of the critical points (optimum points). If the second derivative evaluated at the critical point is less than zero, then this point will be a maximum. The point will also be a minimum if the second derivative is greater than zero.

$$\frac{d^2U}{dx^2} < 0 \text{ implies a local maximum.} \tag{12.5}$$

$$\frac{d^2U}{dx^2} > 0 \text{ Implies a local minimum.} \tag{12.6}$$

As depicted in Figure 12.2, if the slope and the second derivative at a point is zero, as at point 'x_2', this is an inflection point. The function must be continuous to have a maximum or a minimum. Hence point x_6 (in Figure 12.2) is not a maximum.

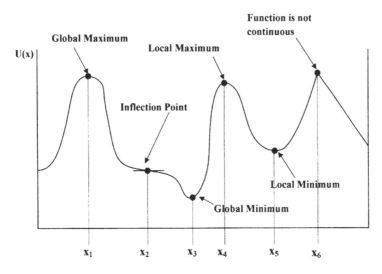

FIGURE 12.2
Global and local optima.

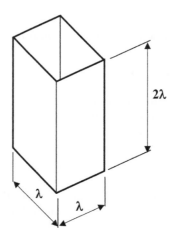

FIGURE 12.3
Design of carton.

Example 12.2

An open tank is to be made from sheet metal; it must have a square base and vertical sides, with a capacity of 8 ft³. Determine its width and depth to use the minimum sheet metal.

SOLUTION:

Let its width and length	= 'w' mm (Figure 12.3)
Let its depth	= 'D' mm
∴ Volume 'V'	= Dw^2 mm³
Area of sheet metal	= $4Dw + w^2$ mm²

$$\therefore A = 4Dw + w^2 \text{ must be a minimum.} \tag{12.7}$$

∴ The differential coefficient of $4Dw + w^2$ must be zero.

As $4Dw + w^2$ contains two variables 'D' and 'w', it cannot be differentiated at this stage.

$$\text{But } V = Dw^2 = 226 \tag{12.8}$$

$$\therefore D = \frac{226}{w^2} \tag{12.9}$$

Substituting this value in Equation (12.3):

$$A = 4. \frac{8}{w^2}. w + w^2, \tag{12.10}$$

$$= \frac{32}{w} + w^2 \tag{12.11}$$

$$= 32w^{-1} + w^2 \tag{12.12}$$

$$\frac{dA}{dw} = -32w^{-2} + 2w \quad (12.13)$$

∴ For a maximum or minimum value of 'A'.

$$-\frac{32}{w^2} + 2w = 0 \quad (12.14)$$

$$\therefore 2w^2 = 32 \quad (12.15)$$

$$\therefore w = \sqrt[3]{16} \quad (12.16)$$

$$\therefore w = 2.52 \quad (12.17)$$

$$\text{But } \frac{d^2A}{dw^2} = \frac{64}{(2.52)^3} + 2 \text{ which is positive} \quad (12.18)$$

∴ w = 2.52 gives a minimum value to 'A'

$$\text{Also, since } D = \frac{8}{w^2} \quad (12.19)$$

$$D = \frac{8}{(2.52)^2} = 1.26 \quad (12.20)$$

∴ For a minimum amount of sheet metal to be used

The width and length = 2.52 ft.
and the depth = 1.26 ft.

12.3.2 The Lagrange Multiplier Method

This method of optimisation is named after its developer, Joseph-Louise Lagrange (1736–1814) an Italian-French mathematician and astronomer. This method has the advantage of dealing with nonlinear optimisation problems. It uses a function called the Lagrange expression, LE, which consists of the objective function bi(x, y, z), multiplied by the Lagrange multiplier, λ_i.

$$LE = U(x,\ y,\ z) + \lambda_1 b_1(x,\ y,\ z) + \ldots, + \lambda_i b_i(x,\ y,\ z) \quad (12.21)$$

The additional unknown, λ_i, is introduced into the Lagrange expression so that in determining the optimum values of x, y, and z, the problem can be treated as though it was constrained. The conditions that must be satisfied for the optimum points are as follows:

$$\frac{\partial LE}{\partial x} = \frac{\partial LE}{\partial y} = \frac{\partial LE}{\partial z} = 0 \quad (12.22)$$

$$\frac{\partial LE}{\partial \lambda_1} = \frac{\partial LE}{\lambda_2} = \ldots = \frac{\partial LE}{\lambda_i} = 0 \quad (12.23)$$

where 'i' is the number of Lagrange multipliers.

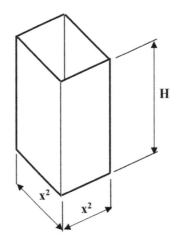

Figure 12.4   Design of Carton #2.

Example 12.3

Consider a carton having dimensions shown in Figure 12.4. It is required that the sum of the dimensions do not exceed 96 ins. Determine the dimensions that will maximise the volume without exceeding the 96 ins. requirement.

SOLUTION:

The objective function is the volume; hence,

$$U = x^2 H$$

The equality constraint is as follows:

$$b(x) = H + 4x - 96 = 0$$

Applying Lagrange expression:

$$LE = x^2 H + \lambda(H + 4x - 96)$$

Differentiating with respect to 'x', 'H' and λ,

$$\frac{\partial LE}{\partial x} = 2xH + 4\lambda = 0 \qquad \text{(a)}$$

$$\frac{\partial LE}{\partial H} = x^2 + \lambda = 0 \qquad \text{(b)}$$

$$\frac{\partial LE}{\partial \lambda} = H + 4x - 96 = 0 \qquad \text{(c)}$$

The solution of equations (a), (b) and (c) gives $x = 16$ ins. and $H = 32$ ins.
   Hence, the optimum volume is:

$$V = x^2 H = (16)^2.(32) = 8192 \text{ ins}^3$$

12.4 Search Methods

There are a number of search methods for examining simultaneous or sequential trial solutions over the entire domain of feasible designs to establish which point is optimal.

These methods include the following:

1. Binary
2. Fibonacci
3. Golden section method
4. Binary search method

In computer science, binary search, also known as half-interval search, logarithmic search or binary chop, is a search algorithm that finds the position of a target value within a sorted array. Binary search compares the target value to the middle element of the array; if they are unequal, the half in which the target cannot lie is eliminated and the search continues on the remaining half until the target value is found. If the search ends with the remaining half being empty, the target is not in the array.

12.5 Fibonacci Search Method

The Fibonacci search technique is a method of searching a *sorted array* using a *divide and conquer algorithm* that narrows down possible locations with the aid of *Fibonacci numbers*. Compared to *binary search* where the sorted array is divided into two equal-sized parts, one of which is examined further, Fibonacci search divides the array into two parts that have sizes that are consecutive Fibonacci numbers. On average, this leads to about 4% more comparisons to be executed, but it has the advantage that one only needs addition and subtraction to calculate the indices of the accessed array elements, while classical binary search needs bit-shift, division or multiplication, operations that were less common at the time Fibonacci search was first published. Fibonacci search has an average- and worst-case complexity of $O(\log n)$ (see *Big O notation*).

12.5.1 What Is the Golden Section Method?

The Golden Section is a technique to find the extremim (maximum or minimum) of a strictly unimodal function by successively narrowing the range of values.

The method maintains the function values for triples of points whose distances form a Golden Ratio and has become known as the Golden Section Method or Golden Ratio Method or Golden Mean Method.

It was developed by Jack Carl Kiefer an American statistician in 1956, who also developed the Fibonacci search method.

12.5.2 Terminology

- **Unimodal function:** A function $f(x)$ is a unimodal function if for some value 'm', it is monotonically increasing for $x \leq m$ and monotonically decreasing for $x \geq m$. In that case, the maximum value $f(x)$ is $f(m)$ and there are no other local maxima.

- Interval of uncertainty: Consider the line search problem to minimise $\theta(\lambda)$ subject to $a \leq \lambda \leq b$. Since the exact location of the minimum of θ over [a.b] is not known, this interval is called the interval of uncertainty.
- Golden ratio: Two quantities are said to be in the Golden Ratio, if their ratio is the same as the rate of their sums to the larger of the two quantities.

For example,

$$a + b / a = a / b = \phi$$

where the Greek letter phi (ϕ) represents the Golden Ratio. Its value is:

$$\varphi = \left(1 + \frac{\sqrt{5}}{2}\right) = 1.6180339887....$$

12.5.3 Working Method

The Golden Section Method for minimising a unimodal function over interval $[a_k, b_k]$:

12.5.3.1 Initialisation Step

Select an allowable final length of uncertainty $1 > 0$.

Let the initial interval of uncertainty be $[a_1, b_1]$ and let $\lambda_1 = a_1 + (1 - \alpha)(b_1 - a_1)$ and $\mu_1 = a_1 + \alpha (b_1 - a_1)$

where $\alpha = 0.618$.

Evaluate $\theta(\lambda_1)$ and $\theta(\mu_1)$. Let $k = 1$ and go to Main Step.

12.5.4 Main Step

1. If $b_k - a_k < 1$, step 1.

   The optimal solution lies in the interval $[a_1.b_1]$.

   Otherwise, if $\theta(\lambda_k) > \theta(\mu_k)$, go to step 2 and

   if $\theta(\lambda_k) \leq \theta(\mu_k)$ go to step 3.

2. Let $a_{k+1} = \lambda_k$ and $b_{k+1} = b_k$. Furthermore, let $\lambda_{k+1} = \mu_k$ and let $\mu_{k+1} = a_{k+1} + \alpha(b_{k+1} - a_{k+1})$ and go to step 4.

3. Let $a_{k+1} = a_k$ and $b_{k+1} + \mu_k$. Furthermore, let $\mu_{k+1} = \lambda_k$ and let $\lambda_{k+1} = a_{k+1} + (1 - \alpha)(b_{k+1} - a_{k+1})$. Evaluate $\theta(_{k+1})$ and go to step 4.

4. Replace k by $k+1$ and go to step 1.

Example 12.4

Consider the following problem:

Minimise	$\lambda 2 + 2\lambda$
Subject to	$-3 \leq \lambda \leq 5$

TABLE 12.1

Results for Example 12.1

Iteration 'k'	a_k	b_k	λ_k	μ_k	$\theta(\lambda_k)$	$\theta(\mu_k)$
1	−3.000	5.000	0.56	1.944	0.115*	7.667*
2	−3.000	1.944	−1.112	0.056	−0.987*	0.115
3	−3.000	0.056	−1.832	−1.112	−0.308*	−0.987
4	−1.832	0.053	−1.112	−0.664	−0.987	−0.887*
5	−1.832	0.664	−1.384	−1.112	−0.853*	−0.987
6	−1.384	0.664	−1.112	−0.936	−0.987	−0.996*
7	−1.112	0.664	−0.936	−0.840	−0.996	−0.974*
8	−1.112	0.840	−1.016	−0.936	−1.000*	−0.996
9	−1.112	0.936				

The value of θ that is computed at every iteration is indicated by an asterisk (*).

Note: After eight iterations involving nine observation, the interval of uncertainty is [−1.112, −0.936], so that the minimum can be estimated to be the midpoint −1.024. The true minimum is in fact −1.000.

SOLUTION:

Clearly, the given function to be minimised and its length of initial interval of uncertainty is 8.

$$\lambda_1 = a_1 + (1 - \alpha)(b_1 - a_1)$$

$$\lambda_1 = -3 + (1 - 0.618)\{5 - (-3)\} = -3 + 0.382(8) = 1.944.$$

Note that $\theta(\lambda_1) < \theta(\mu_1)$

The new interval of uncertainty is [−3.1.944].

The process is repeated and the computations are summarised in Table 12.1.

12.6 Conclusions

The Golden Ratio search is effective in unimodal optimisation as it results in the least number of searches or trials to locate the optimum. Given a unimodal object function defined in a starting range $[a_1.b_1]$ to search step by step, one condenses the range in which the optimal point is located until the width of the range is less than the given accuracy to position the location.

Golden ratio search is the use of the golden section ratio 0.618, or symmetrically $(1 - 0.618) = 0.382$ to condense the width of the range in each step.

13

Probability

13.1 Introduction

Probability is based on the observation of certain events. Probability of an event is the ratio of the number of observations of the event to the total number of observations. An experiment is a situation involving chance or probability that leads to results called outcomes. An outcome is a result of a single trial of an experiment. The probability of an event is the measure of the chance that the event will occur as a result of an experiment.

Probability of an event 'A' is symbolised by P(A). Probability of an event 'A' lies between

$$0 \le P(A) \le 1$$

A simple example is that of tossing a fair coin which has 50% chance of landing with the 'head' facing upwards.

13.2 Probability Formula

Probability is the measure of how likely an event is to occur. And an event is one or more outcomes of an experiment. Probability formula is the ratio of a number of favourable outcomes to the total number of possible outcomes.

Probability formula:

$$\text{Probability of an Event} = \frac{\text{Number of Favourable Outcomes}}{\text{Total Number of Possible Outcomes}}$$

Measures the likelihood of an event in the following way.

If P(A) > P(B), then event 'A' is more likely to occur than event 'B'.

If P(A) = P(B), then events 'A' and 'B' are equally likely to occur.

13.2.1 What is the Formula for Probability?

The probability of an event tells that how likely the event will happen. Situations in which each outcome is equally likely, the probability will be found using the probability formula.

Probability is a chance of prediction. If the probability that an event will occur is 'x', then the probability that an event will not occur is '1–x'. If the probability that one event will occur is 'a' and the independent probability that another event will occur is 'b', then the probability that both events will occur is 'ab'.

The probability of an event 'A' can be written as:

$$P(A) = \frac{\text{Number of Favourable Outcomes}}{\text{Total Number of Possible Outcomes}}$$

13.3 Solving Probability Problems

A probability is determined from an experiment, which is any activity that has an observable outcome such as tossing a coin and recording whether it lands heads up or tails up. The possible outcomes of an experiment are called sample space of the experiment.

Steps to find probability:

1. List the outcomes of the experiment.
2. Count the number of possible outcomes of the experiment.
3. Count the number of favourable outcomes.
4. Use the probability formula.

Example 13.1

What is the probability of getting a 'head' when tossing a fair coin?

SOLUTION:

Sample space – {H, T}
  Number of possible outcomes = 2
  Number of favourable outcomes = 1
  (for there is only one head).

$$\Rightarrow \text{Probability of getting head} = \frac{\text{Number of Favourable Outcomes}}{\text{Total Number of Possible Outcomes}}$$

$$\Rightarrow \text{Probability of getting head is } \frac{1}{2}$$

13.4 Numerical Value of Probability

Probability is expressed on a scale between 0 for an impossible event to occur and 1 for an event that is certain to occur. Other events have probabilities within this range, i.e., when the coin discussed in the introduction is tossed, the probability that the 'head' landing face up will occur is 0.5.

If a horse has a 5 to 4 odds, its chance of winning the race is 5/6 or 0.556; the probability it will lose will, therefore, be 4/5 or 0.444.

In another example, the probability of attaining a six in a throw of an unbiased dice or die will be 1/6 or 0.167. There are six possible outcomes of throwing the dice, all of which are equally likely; hence, the chance of throwing a particular number is 1/6.

13.5 Calculation of Probability

It is important to understand some of the terms that are used in discussing probability before proceeding further.

Events are *equally likely or equally probable* when considering all the relevant evidence that one event cannot be expected to occur more often than any another. For example, when throwing an unbiased dice, the chance of throwing a 'three' is as likely to occur as throwing a 'six'.

Events are *mutually exclusive* if any two of them cannot occur simultaneously, i.e., the occurrence of one event precludes the simultaneous occurrence of any of the other events. For example, it is impossible for a dice to simultaneously show two numbers at the same time.

A set of events is an *exhaustive set* when all the possible events that can occur in an experiment are included. Going back to the example of the dice, the six possible outcomes are 1, 2, 3, 4, 5 and 6, and this forms the exhaustive set.

13.5.1 Proportion of Cases Favourable in an Exhaustive Set

Consider an exhaustive set containing 'n' number of equally and likely and mutually exclusive events, and in 'm' number of these the event 'A' occurs. The probability that the event 'A' will occur is the ratio m/n which is the ratio of:

$$\frac{\text{number of cases favourable to A}}{\text{number of cases in exhaustive set}}$$

This can best be explained by considering some examples:

Example 13.2

Find the probability of scoring an even number in a throw of one dice.
  There are three ways of throwing an even number, i.e., by throwing either a 2, 4 or 6.
  The total number of ways of throwing the dice is 6, i.e., the number of events in the exhaustive set is 6.
  Thus, the probability of throwing an even number is:

$$P = \frac{m}{n} = \frac{\text{number of favourable cases}}{\text{number in exhausted set}} = \frac{3}{6} = 0.5$$

Example 13.3

In a normal pack of 52 playing cards, determine the probability of picking a 'club' at random.
  There are 13 clubs in the pack (i.e. 10 normal cards plus 3 picture cards), and therefore m = number of favourable ways = 13

The pack contains 52 possible cards that can be chosen; therefore, 'n' = the number of ways of choosing a card = 52.

$$\text{Thus } P = \frac{m}{n} = \frac{13}{52} = \frac{1}{4} = 0.25$$

Example 13.4

What is the probability of picking at random a red card with a value greater than nine from a normal pack of playing cards?

There are 10 cards (5 diamonds and 5 hearts) that satisfy this requirement.

$$\text{Thus } P = \frac{m}{n} = \frac{10}{52} = 0.192$$

Example 13.5

A box contains a selection of balls consisting of 4 black, 5 yellow and 3 white balls. Find the probability of choosing at random:

(13.5.1) A yellow ball
(13.5.2) A non-white ball
(13.5.3) A white ball

(13.5.1) The number of yellow balls is 5 and there are 5 ways of choosing a yellow ball. The total number of balls is 12, and therefore the exhaustive set contains 12 possible events, hence the probability of choosing a yellow ball is:

$$P_y = \frac{4}{12} = 0.333$$

(13.5.2) The total number of non-white balls is 9, therefore the probability of picking a non-white ball will be:

$$P_{nw} = \frac{9}{12} = 0.75$$

(13.5.3) The probability of choosing a white ball is:

$$P_w = \frac{3}{12} = 0.25$$

From the above examples it will be deduced that the probability of choosing a non-white ball is 1 – probability of choosing a white ball. This simple relationship, that the probability of an event occurring is 1 – the probability of the event not happening, often enters into probability and statistical calculations, and therefore should be remembered.

13.5.2 Addition of Probabilities

The probability of any one of the mutually exclusive events A_1, A_2, A_3 ... A_n occurring is the sum of the probabilities of these events.

Where the probability of A_1 occurring is p_1
Where the probability of A_2 occurring is p_2
Where the probability of A_3 occurring is p_3

Where the probability of A_n occurring is p_n

The probability that A_1 or A_2 or A_3 or A_n will occur is $P = p_1 + p_2 + p_3 + \ldots + p_n$.

This can be seen by considering 'N' to be the total number of all possible equally likely and mutually exclusive events that can occur, and m_1 to be the number of cases favourable to A_1, m_2 the number favourable to A_2, etc.

Hence, there are $m_1 + m_2 + m_3 + \ldots + m_n$ cases favourable to the occurrence of A_1 or A_2 or A_3 or ......A_n and the probability that A_1 or A_2 or A_3 or ... A_n will occur is:

$$P = \frac{m_1 + m_2 + m_3 + \ldots m_n}{N} = \frac{m_1}{N} + \frac{m_2}{N} + \frac{m_3}{N} + \ldots + \frac{m_n}{N}$$
$$= p_1 + p_2 + p_3 + \ldots + p_n$$

Two examples follow to demonstrate this principle:

Example 13.6

Determine the probability of choosing a yellow or a black ball as in Example 13.5.

Probability of choosing a yellow ball is $P_y = 0.333$

Probability of choosing a black ball is $P_b = 5/12 = 0.417$

Therefore, the probability of choosing a yellow or a black ball will be:

$$P = P_y + P_b = 0.333 + 0.417 = 0.75$$

This is confirmed with the answer in Example (13.5.2).

Example 13.7

Determine the probability of obtaining a number '7' or '11' at a throw of two dice.

(13.7.1) a '7' can be 'thrown' in the following ways:

$(1 + 6), (2 + 5), (3 + 4), (5 + 2), (6 + 1)$.

Hence, there are six ways of 'throwing' a '7'.

As there are six possible ways of 'throwing' the first dice and for each of these six ways of 'throwing' the second, the total number of ways of 'throwing' the two dice is 36; therefore, the probability of a '7' is:

$$\frac{6}{36} = \frac{1}{6}$$

(13.7.2) the number '11' can be 'thrown' in only two ways:

$$(5 + 6) \text{ and } (6 + 5)$$

and the probability of obtaining '11' is:

$$\frac{2}{36} = \frac{1}{18}$$

(13.7.3) the probability of obtaining a '7' or '11' is:

$$\frac{1}{6} + \frac{1}{18} = \frac{4}{18} = 0.2\dot{2}\dot{2}$$

This is slightly more than once in every five attempts.

13.6 Permutations and Combinations

13.6.1 Permutations

Consider a number of items that are arranged among themselves in different orders, then each order or arrangement is a permutation of the objects, then the total number of permutations possible for 'n' items is:

$$^n P_n$$

$$\text{where } ^n P_n = n(n-1)(n-2)$$

This is seen by considering that for the first place in each arrangement there is a choice of n items, for each of those, once the first place has been allocated, there is a choice of $(n-1)$ items for the second place, and so on.

n(n − 1)(n − 2).......... is known as Factorial 'n' and is usually written n! or n.

If a number '*m*' of the items are alike, then the number of possible arrangements of the items is reduced by the number of permutations of the '*m*' items amongst themselves, as each of these permutations will be identical.

Hence, the number of permutations or arrangements of '*n*' items, '*m*' of which are alike is $\frac{n!}{m!}$

The number of permutations of '*n*' different items taken '*r*' at a time is:

$$^n P_r = \frac{n!}{(n-r)!}$$

It can be seen that the first place can be filled in '*n*' ways, the second place filled in $(n-1)$ ways, until the '*r*' places is filled in $(n-r+1)$ ways.

$$\therefore {}^n P_r = n(n-1)(n-2)........(n-r-1)$$

$$= \frac{n(n-1)(n-2).......(n-r+1)(n-r)(n-r-1)....}{(n-r)(n-r-1).......}$$

$$= \frac{n!}{(n-r)!}$$

13.6.2 Combinations

When groups of '*r*' items are selected from '*n*' items without due attention being paid to the order of the '*r*' items amongst themselves, each group is referred to as a combination and the number of groups is called the number of combinations of '*n*' taken '*r*' at a time, this can be written as:

$$^n C_r \text{ or } \binom{n}{r}$$

$$\text{where } \binom{n}{r} = \frac{n!}{(n-r)!r!}$$

It will be seen that by considering any one of the combinations, the '*r*' items can be arranged in r! different orders. If this is carried out to all the combinations, then they will have been permutated.

$$\therefore \binom{n}{r} \times r! = \,^{n}\mathrm{P_r} = \frac{n!}{(n-r)!}$$

$$\therefore \binom{n}{r} = \frac{n!}{(n-r)!r!} = \binom{n}{n-r}$$

When calculating combinations, it is found convenient to write $n(n-1)(n-2) \ldots$ to r (or $n-r$) factors, whichever is less, in the numerator and 1.2.3 ... r (or $n-r$) in the denominator

$$\text{hence}: \binom{7}{4} = \frac{7.6.5}{3.2.1} = 35 = \binom{7}{3}$$

The following examples will illustrate the use of combinations.

Example 13.8

A container contains four faulty items and seven good items. Calculate the probability of selecting at random a pair of faulty items.
   The number of ways of choosing two faulty items from four is:

$$\binom{4}{2} = \frac{4 \times 3}{2 \times 1} = 6$$

The total number of ways of selecting two items from eleven is:

$$\binom{11}{2} = \frac{11 \times 10}{2 \times 1} = 55$$

The possibility that the pair of items selected will both be faulty is:

$$\frac{6}{55} = 0.109$$

Example 13.9

From the same container, a group of five items are chosen at random. Calculate the probability that the group will contain two faulty and three good items.
   Following the Example (6.7), the number of ways two faulty items from four is:

$$\binom{4}{2} = 6$$

The number of ways of choosing three good items from seven is:

$$\binom{7}{3} = \frac{7 \times 6 \times 5}{3 \times 2 \times 1} = 35$$

Any one of the pairs of faulty items can be associated with any one of the groups of three good items; therefore, the number of possible combinations of two faulty and three good items will be:

$$\binom{4}{2} \times \binom{7}{3} = 6 \times 35 = 210$$

The total number of ways of selecting five items from eleven is:

$$\binom{11}{5} = \frac{11 \times 10 \times 9 \times 8 \times 7}{5 \times 4 \times 3 \times 2 \times 1} = 462$$

Hence, the required probability is:

$$\frac{210}{462} = 0.45\dot{4}$$

Example 13.10

Consider a hand of thirteen playing cards. Find the probability that the hand contains:

(13.10.1) Two aces
(13.10.2) Four aces

In this example there are $\binom{52}{13}$ possible different hands all mutually exclusive and equally likely.

(13.10.1) The number of ways of selecting 2 aces from the four in the pack will be:

$$\binom{4}{2} = 6$$

For each of these, the number of ways of selecting the other cards from the remaining 48 cards is $\binom{48}{11}$

The probability of choosing 2 aces in 13 cards is:

$$P_2 = \frac{\binom{48}{11}\binom{4}{2}}{\binom{52}{13}}$$

$$= \frac{\dfrac{4 \times 3}{2 \times 1} \times \dfrac{48 \times 47 \times 46 \times \ldots \ldots \times 39 \times 38}{11 \times 10 \times \ldots \ldots \times 2 \times 1}}{\dfrac{52 \times 51 \times \ldots \times 41 \times 40}{13 \times 12 \times 11 \ldots \times 2 \times 1}}$$

$P_2 = 0.216$.

(13.10.2) There is only one way that 4 aces can be selected from the 4 in this pack,

$$\text{i.e. } \binom{4}{4} = 1$$

The number of ways of selecting the remaining 9 cards from the remaining 48 cards is $\binom{48}{9}$

Thus, the possibility of 4 aces in 13 cards is:

$$P_4 = \frac{\binom{4}{4}\binom{48}{9}}{\binom{52}{13}}$$

$$= \frac{\dfrac{1 \times 48 \times 47 \times ......41 \times 40}{9 \times 8 \times.... \times 2 \times 1}}{\dfrac{52 \times 51 \times.... \times 41 \times 40}{13 \times 12 \times 11 \times..... \times 2 \times 1}}$$

$$P_4 = \frac{1}{375}, \text{ or } 0.00267$$

13.6.3 Compound Probability and Multiplication of Probabilities

13.6.3.1 Compound Events and Dependence

When an event 'A' is considered that is in association with an event 'B', the occurrence of the combined (or compound) event 'AB' consists of the simultaneous occurrences of 'A' and 'B'.

It is necessary to first determine whether 'A' and 'B' are independent or not before the probability of occurrence of this combined event can be calculated.

Take for example the two dice introduced in Example 13.7. If 'AB' is the occurrence of a '12' when throwing two dice, this will require scoring a '6' on both of them, the first dice 'A' scoring a '6' will in no way affect the probability of the second dice 'B' showing a '6'. In this case, 'A' and 'B' are considered independent.

In a second example, if 'AB' represents the drawing of two red cards in succession without replacement from a pack of 52 playing cards, the event that the first card is red will affect the probability of drawing a second red card, as the number of remaining red cards has been reduced. Therefore, in this case 'A' and 'B' are considered dependent.

If the cards are replaced after drawing the individual card, it will then be considered to be independent.

Example 13.11

A box contains 8 unused valve stems and 7 used ones. Two are drawn one at a time without replacement. Find the probability of drawing 2 unused valve stems.

Probability that the first valve stem is unused is:

$$P_A = \frac{8}{15}$$

Probability that the second selection is unused is:

$$P_{B,A} = \frac{7}{14}$$

The probability that both are unused is:

$$P_{A,B} = \frac{8}{15} \times \frac{7}{14} = \frac{4}{15} = 0.267$$

This example could also have been calculated using the method shown in example 13.11.1. Considering that the items are being drawn together, the probability will be:

$$P = \frac{\binom{8}{2}}{\binom{15}{2}} = \frac{\frac{8 \times 7}{2 \times 1}}{\frac{15 \times 14}{2 \times 1}} = 0.267$$

Example 13.12

Returning to the pack of playing cards, determine the probability of obtaining a 'flush', i.e., five cards all the same suit, in a deal of five cards.

The required probability of obtaining five cards of any particular suit is:

$$P = \frac{13}{52} \times \frac{12}{51} \times \frac{11}{50} \times \frac{10}{49} \times \frac{9}{48} = 000495$$

There are four different suits from which to choose, by the 'addition of probabilities', the probability of a flush will be $4 \times 0.000495 = 0.00198$.

This answer could have been obtained using the method outlined in Example 13.11.1.

13.7 Binomial, Poisson and Multinomial Laws of Probability

13.7.1 Series of Trials

A trial is defined as an attempt to produce, under a set of given conditions, an event 'E' that is not certain to occur. When trials are repeated they form a set or series of trials. They will be independent if the result of a trial does not depend on the outcome of previous trials.

An example of a series of independent trials could be similar to tossing a coin a number of times. To find the probability of obtaining any particular combination of results, the probability of each sequence of results, in association with the number of possible arrangements of these results, must be considered.

Considering the probability of obtaining four heads and one tail in a series of five trials, the probability of any one sequence or arrangement, such as HTHHH, will be $\left(\frac{1}{2}\right)^5$. This must be multiplied by the number of possible arrangements or orders of occurrence of the four heads and one tail in the five trials.

The number of orders is:

$$\frac{5!}{4!\,1!} = \binom{5}{4} = \binom{5}{1}$$

that is, the number of ways of arranging five objects, i.e., four alike of one kind and another of a different kind.

Thus, the probability of four heads and one tail will be:

$$\binom{5}{1}\binom{1}{2}^5$$

Similarly, the probability of three heads and two tails is:

$$\binom{5}{2}\left(\frac{1}{2}\right)^5$$

The probability of two heads and three tails is:

$$\binom{5}{3}\left(\frac{1}{2}\right)^5 = \binom{5}{2}\left(\frac{1}{2}\right)^5$$

The probability of one head and four tails will be:

$$\binom{5}{4}\left(\frac{1}{2}\right)^5 = \binom{5}{1}\left(\frac{1}{2}\right)^5$$

And for completeness, the probability of no heads and five tails is:

$$\binom{5}{0}\left(\frac{1}{2}\right)^5 = \binom{5}{2}\left(\frac{1}{2}\right)^5$$

where $\binom{5}{0} = 1$

The successive probabilities can be seen to follow a pattern; this is the sequence of terms of the binomial expansion of $\left(\frac{1}{2} + \frac{1}{2}\right)^5$.

This is a particular case of the *Binomial Law of Probability*, which states that in a series of 's' independent trials in each of which the known probability of success of an event 'E' is 'p' and $p + q = 1$, the probability that 'E' will occur 'm' times is:

$$P = \binom{s}{m} p^m q^{s-m}$$

This can be proved by considering a box containing white and black balls and a ball is chosen at random, 'p' is the proportion of white balls and 'q' is the proportion of black balls in the box.

After each trial the ball chosen is replaced in the box so that the proportions of balls remain unchanged. The probability of the first 'm' trials giving white balls and the remaining $(s - m)$ giving black balls is $p^m q^{s-m}$.

The probability of any other order is the same and the number of possible orders is:

$$\frac{s!}{m!(s-m)!} = \binom{s}{m}$$

Hence, the probability of 'm' white is $\binom{s}{m} p^m q^{s-m}$

For various values of 'm', the corresponding probabilities are the successive terms of the binomial expansion of $(q - p)^s$

$$= q^s + \binom{s}{1} q^{s-1} p + \binom{s}{2} q^{s-2} p^2 + \dots + p^s$$

Example 13.13

Five dice are thrown simultaneously (or one dice is thrown five times in succession). Determine the probability of two 'sixes' in the five results:

$$P = \binom{5}{2}\left(\frac{5}{6}\right)^3 \left(\frac{1}{6}\right)^2 = \frac{1250}{216 \times 36} = 0.1608$$

Example 13.14

Six fair coins are tossed:

(13.14.1) Find the probability of 2, 3 or 4 heads.
(13 14.2) Find the probability of 0, 1, 5 or 6 heads.
(13.14.1) The probability of 2, 3 or 4 heads is:

$$P = \binom{6}{2}\left(\frac{1}{2}\right)^2\left(\frac{1}{2}\right)^4 + \binom{6}{3}\left(\frac{1}{2}\right)^3\left(\frac{1}{2}\right)^3 + \binom{6}{4}\left(\frac{1}{2}\right)^4\left(\frac{1}{2}\right)^3$$

$$= \frac{6 \times 5}{2 \times 1}\left(\frac{1}{2}\right)^6 + \frac{6 \times 5 \times 4}{3 \times 2 \times 1}\left(\frac{1}{2}\right)^6 + \frac{6 \times 5}{2 \times 1}\left(\frac{1}{2}\right)^6$$

$$= \frac{15}{64} + \frac{20}{64} + \frac{15}{64}$$

$$= 0.781.$$

(13.14.2) The probability of 0, 1, 5 or 6 heads is:

$$P = \binom{6}{0}\left(\frac{1}{2}\right)^6 + \binom{6}{1}\left(\frac{1}{2}\right)^6 + \binom{6}{5}\left(\frac{1}{2}\right)^6 + \binom{6}{6}\left(\frac{1}{2}\right)^6$$

As $\binom{6}{0}$ is the number of ways of obtaining no heads (i.e. 6 tails) and there is only one way of achieving this, $\binom{6}{0} = 1$; and similarly $\binom{6}{6}$ the number of ways of obtaining 6 heads is 1.

$$P = \frac{1}{64} + \frac{6}{64} + \frac{6}{64} + \frac{1}{64}$$

$$= \frac{14}{64}$$

$$= 0.219$$

This result would have been achieved in (13.12.1) above as (1-0.781).

13.8 The Poisson Distribution

This distribution is used in the same manner as the binomial distribution; there are subtle differences between them.

The binomial distribution deals with events where both the probability of the event occurring and the probability of event not occurring in any one trial are real and known.

Both these outcomes are real distinct happenings that do occur in varying proportions when the series of trials are made.

The Poisson distribution deals with the occurrence of isolated events occurring at random and at unpredictable moments in time. For example, the probable number of flashes of lightning occurring in a storm or road accidents in a day or goals in a football match cannot be assessed by the binomial distribution as there is no way of accounting for the number of times the lightning did not flash or vehicles did not crash or a goal was not scored. These are intangible events and there is no way of making an estimate of their effects in a binomial distribution.

In brief, the value of 's' in the fundamental expression $(q + p)^s$ is not known.

It was found, largely by accident, in the course of experiments, that where 'x' is the expected or average number of occurrences of an event, in a series of trials, or in a definite interval of time (where the average number of occurrences with time are known), the respective terms of the series:

$$1 + x + \frac{x^2}{2!} + \frac{x^2}{3!} + \ldots\ldots etc$$

were proportional to the probabilities of obtaining the occurrences of the event 0, 1, 2, 3 … etc. times in the series of trials.

To use this as a probability distribution in the same way as the binomial distribution, the sum of all the terms must be unity, which means that each term is the actual numerical value of probability of that number of events occurring in any one series of trials.

In the binomial distribution $(q + p) = (q + p)^s$ for all values of 'x'.

Since $1 + x + \frac{x^2}{2!} + \frac{x^2}{3!} + \ldots\ldots etc. = e^x$

($e = 2.7183$ to four decimal place)

$$and \quad e^{-x} \times e^x = 1 = e^{-x}\left(1 + x + \frac{x^2}{2!} + \frac{x^3}{3!} + \ldots\ldots etc.\right)$$

This expression satisfies the requirements of a distribution and is called the Poisson probability distribution.

The Poisson Distribution: It is used extensively in medical and biological research and also for industrial quality control and engineering reliability prediction, which is covered in Chapter 6.4, Design for Reliability.

One of its first statistical uses was in the Crimean War for calculating the number of cavalrymen killed per year by horse kicks, and this showed that the accidents were the result of chance. It was also used during the latter parts of World War II when the government was trying to discover the accuracy of the V-l flying bombs that were hitting London at a frightening rate. By recording and analysing all the landing sites, it was established that the mechanism for cutting off the fuel to the engine of the bombs was not very accurate and the landing happened purely by chance.

The Multinomial Law of Probability: The multinomial distribution or probability is just a generalisation of the binomial distribution or probability. Binomial distribution is used in cases where we have only two possible outcomes. But we use multinomial distribution in cases where there are more than two outcomes.

For example, the experiment of flipping a coin has only two outcomes, while experiment of throwing a dice has six outcomes. So in case of large number of trials of throwing dice experiment, we would require the use of multinomial probability and not binomial probability.

A multinomial experiment possesses following properties:

1. There are 'n' number of repeated trials in it.
2. Every trial has a fix possible number of outcomes.
3. The probability for any trial is constant for a particular outcome.
4. All of the trials are independent of each other. This means that the results of any one of the trials do not affect any other trial.

13.8.1 Formula

A multinomial distribution is the distribution of probability in which the outcomes are coming from a multinomial experiment.

If we made 'n' number of trials in an experiment, the probability of 'k' 'types of outcomes' can then be determined by using the formula for multinomial probability given below:

$$P = \frac{n!}{(n1)(n2!).....(nk!)} \cdot (p1^{n1} p2^{n2} ...... pk^{nk})$$

Here, P is the multinomial probability for the given experiment.

'n' is the number of trials made in the experiment.

$n1n1$ is the number of occurrences of the first outcome.

$n2n2$ is he number of occurrences of the second outcome, and so on.

And similarly, $p1p1$ is the probability of occurrence of the first outcome.

$p2p2$ is the probability of occurrence of the second outcome, and so on.

$pkpk$ is the probability of occurrence of nth outcome.

The binomial probability is a special case of this multinomial probability only. When we have k = 2, then multinomial probability changes itself to binomial probability.

Example 13.15

An experiment of drawing a random card from an ordinary playing deck of cards is done by replacing it back. This was done 10 times. Find the probability of getting 2 spades, 3 diamond, 3 club and 2 hearts.

SOLUTION:

The multinomial probability is used here to solve this problem.

In this case, the number of trials, $n = 10$

Now, since four types of outputs are there, it means k = 4 with $n1 = 2$, $n2 = 3$, $n3 = 3$, $n4 = 2$

Now, the probability of drawing a spade, diamond, club or a heart is 13/52 = 0.25 for each one of them. Thus, we get that p1 = 0.25, p2 = 0.25, = p3 = p4.

Now, these values can be substituted in the multinomial probability formula with the following results.

$$P = \frac{n!}{(n1)(n2!).....(nk!)} \times (p_1^{n1} p_2^{n2} ...... p_k^{nk})$$

$$\rightarrow P = \left[\frac{10!}{(2!, 3! 3! 2!)} \right] \times (0.25)^2 \times (0.25)^3 \times (0.25)^3 \times (0.25)^2$$

$$\rightarrow P = 0.024$$

Example 13.16

A box contains 5 white, 2 black, 8 blue and 7 red balls. If balls are selected one at a time with replacement, find the probability of drawing 2 white, 4 blue, 3 red and 1 black in 10 trials.

$$P_w = \frac{5}{22}, \; P_{bl} = \frac{8}{22}, \; P_r = \frac{7}{22}, \; P_{bk} = \frac{2}{22}$$

The required probability is:

$$P = \frac{10!}{2! \, 4! \, 3! \, 1!} \left(\frac{5}{22}\right)^2 \left(\frac{2}{22}\right) \left(\frac{8}{22}\right)^4 \left(\frac{7}{22}\right)^3$$

$$= 12600 \times 0.0516 \times 0.0909 \times 0.0175 \times 0.0322$$
$$= 12600 \times 0.00000262$$
$$= 0.033 \; (\text{or one chance in 30}).$$

Example 13.17

Returning to the box containing valve stems.

Box 'A' contains 8 new and 7 old valve stems, and box 'B' contains 4 new and 8 old valve stems. A box is chosen at random and a valve stem is picked from it. Determine the probability that the valve stem chosen is new.

Probability of choosing box 'A' $= \frac{1}{2} =$ probability of choosing box 'B'

Probability of selecting a new valve stem from box 'A' is $\frac{8}{15}$

Probability of selecting a new valve stem from box 'B' is $\frac{4}{12}$

Hence, the required probability is $\left(\frac{1}{2} \times \frac{8}{15} \times \frac{1}{2} \times \frac{4}{12}\right) = \frac{13}{30} = 0.433$

14

Statistical Methods for Engineers

14.1 Definitions for Some Terms Used in Statistics

14.1.1 Population

This is the term applied to the whole group that is being studied.

14.1.2 Sample

If a number of items that are representative of the population are withdrawn for the purpose of obtaining the data of the study, the items as a group are called a *Sample*. A *random sample* is one where every item in a population has an equal chance of being selected for the sample.

14.1.3 Variate (x_r)

This is the value of a characteristic of the population. For example, height, length, weight, number of rejects, etc., are some of the many variates used. Variates may be continuous or discrete.

14.1.3.1 Continuous Variates

A continuous variable is a variable that has an infinite number of possible values. In other words, any value is possible for the variable. A continuous variate may be continuously subdivided such as length and time.

14.1.3.2 Discrete Variates

A discrete variable is a variable that can only take on a certain number of values. In other words, they don't have an infinite number of values. If you can count a set of items, then it is a discrete variable.

14.1.4 Frequency (f_r)

This is the number of occasions in which a particular numerical value of the variate occurs in a sample.

14.1.5 Mean (M) (Arithmetic Mean Average)

The arithmetic mean is a mathematical representation of the typical value of a series of numbers, computed as the sum of all the numbers in the series divided by the count of all numbers in the series. The arithmetic mean is sometimes referred to as the average or simply as the mean.

As an example: The sum of all of the numbers in a list divided by the number of items in that list. For example, the mean of the numbers 2, 3, 7 is 4 since $2 + 3 + 7 = 12$ and 12 divided by 3 (there are three numbers) is 4.

14.1.6 Mode

The mode of a set of data values is the value that appears most often. It is the value x at which its probability mass function takes its maximum value. In other words, it is the value that is most likely to be sampled.

14.1.7 Median

This is the value of the variate such that half the total number of items, or total frequency, in a sample, relates to values above, and half relates to values below it.

To find the median number:

Put all the numbers in numerical order.

If there is an odd number of results, the median is the middle number.

If there is an even number of results, the median will be the mean of the two central numbers.

14.1.8 Quartiles, Deciles, Percentiles (Partition Values)

Quartile is a useful concept in statistics and is conceptually similar to the median. The first quartile is the data point at the 25th percentile, and the third quartile is the data point at the 75th percentile. The 50th percentile is the median.

The deciles are the variate values dividing the total frequency into tenths and the percentiles divide the frequency into hundredths.

14.1.9 Dispersion

This is the spread of variate values about the mean.

There are many reasons why the measure of the spread of data values is important, but one of the main reasons regards its relationship with measures of central tendency. A measure of spread gives us an idea of how well the mean, for example, represents the data. If the spread of values in the data set is large, the mean is not as representative of the data as if the spread of data is small. This is because a large spread indicates that there are probably large differences between individual scores. Additionally, in research, it is often seen as positive if there is little variation in each data group as it indicates that the similar.

14.1.10 Standard Deviation (σ) (Variance σ^2)

The standard deviation is measure of the dispersion and is defined as the root mean square of the deviations. Using the same symbols as for the definition of the mean, then:

$$\text{deviation} = (x_r - M)$$

$$\sigma^2 = \frac{\sum_{r-1}^{n} f_r (x_r - M)^2}{\sum_{r=1}^{n} f_r}$$

14.1.11 Range

This is the difference between the highest and the lowest variate values within a distribution.

14.1.12 Kurtosis

Kurtosis is a descriptor of the shape of a probability distribution and is used to indicate the amount of 'arch' in a distribution curve.

14.1.13 Skewness

Skewness is usually described as a measure of a data set's symmetry – or lack of symmetry. A perfectly symmetrical data set will have a skewness of 0. The normal distribution has a skewness of 0.

One such measure of skewness, due to Karl Pearson, is given by the formula:

$$\text{Skewness} = \frac{\text{mean} - \text{mode}}{\text{standard deviation}}$$

Skewness may be positive or negative depending on mean, mode and median.

14.2 Frequency Distribution and Pictorial Representations

14.2.1 Bar Chart

Bar chart is used primarily for discrete variates. The bar chart or line diagram is one in which a line is drawn of length proportional to the frequency for a particular variate value (or interval of values) (see Figure 14.1).

14.2.2 Histogram

A histogram is a plot that shows the underlying frequency distribution (shape) of a set of *continuous* data. This allows the inspection of the data for its underlying distribution

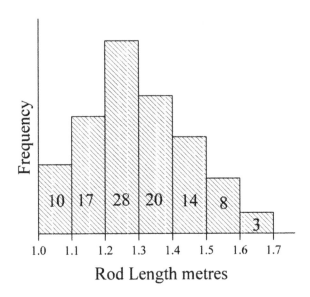

FIGURE 14.1
Bar Chart showing Frequency of Cut Lengths.

(e.g., normal distribution), outliers, skewness, etc. An example of a histogram, and the raw data, it was constructed from, is shown in Figure 14.2.

To construct a histogram from a continuous variable, the data needs to be split into intervals called **bins**. In the example above, **age** has been split into bins, with each bin representing a 10-year period starting at 20 years. Each bin contains the number of occurrences of scores in the data set that are contained within that bin. For the above data set, the frequencies in each bin have been tabulated along with the scores that contributed to the frequency in each bin (see Table 14.1).

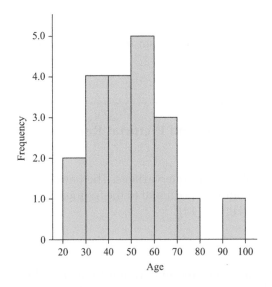

FIGURE 14.2
Histogram for Age Vs Frequency.

TABLE 14.1

Table for Age vs Frequency

Bin	Frequency	Scores Included in Bin
20–30	2	25, 22
30–40	4	36, 38, 36, 38
40–50	4	46, 45, 48, 46
50–60	5	55, 55, 52, 58, 55
60–70	3	68, 67, 61
70–80	1	72
80–90	0	-
90–100	1	91

TABLE 14.2

Frequency Table for Cut Rod Lengths

Length of Rod (m)	1.0–1.09	1.1–1.19	1.2–1.29	1.3–1.39	1.4–1.49	1.5–1.59	1.6–1.69
Frequency	10	17	28	20	14	8	3

Notice that, unlike a bar chart, there are no 'gaps' between the bars (although some bars might be 'absent' reflecting no frequencies). This is because a histogram represents a continuous data set, and as such, there are no gaps in the data.

14.2.3 Frequency Polygon

In the frequency polygon, points are plotted mid-way along the variate intervals and at distances from the horizontal variate axis proportional to the frequencies. Figure 14.3 shows the frequency polygon for Table 14.2.

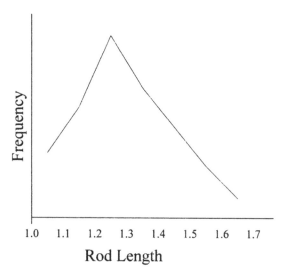

FIGURE 14.3
Frequency Polygon for Figure 14.1.

14.3 Short Method for Calculating the Mean

This method uses an assumed mean.

Let 'A' = an assumed value for the mean, such that $(x_r - A)$ gives a number, of fewer digits than x_r alone,

Let $e = M - A$ = difference between the true and assumed means,

$$\text{then } \varepsilon = \frac{\Sigma f_r (x_r - A)}{\Sigma f_r} = M - A$$

e is calculated and 'M' is obtained using the relationship M = A + e (see worked example below).

Using an assumed mean 'A' calculate the mean 'M' for the following set of values of 'x':

xr	41.3	41.5	41.7	41.9	42.1	42.3	42.5
Frequency fr	8	14	31	68	45	23	11

Let the assumed mean be 'A' = 41.9

Note: any value for 'A' could have been chosen, but it is advantageous to select a value such that the difference (xr − A) becomes 'workable' small numbers for the ensuing calculations.

Tabulations gives:

x_r	$x_r - A$	f_r	$f_r(x_r - A)$
41.3	−0.6	8	−4.8
41.5	−0.4	14	−5.6
41.7	−0.2	31	−6.2
41.9	0	68	0
42.1	+0.2	45	+9.0
42.3	+0.4	23	+9.2
42.5	+0.6	11	+6.6
		200	−16.6
			+24.8
			+8.2

$$\varepsilon - \frac{\Sigma f_r (x_r - A)}{\Sigma f_r} = \frac{+8.2}{200} = +0.041$$

From this calculation,

The mean is 'M' = A + e = 41.9 + 0.041 = 41.941

14.4 Short Method of Calculating the Standard Deviation

This method uses an assumed mean.

Let 'A' = the assumed mean.

Let $e = M - A$ as previous.

$$\text{Let } s^2 = \frac{\Sigma f_r (x_r - A)^2}{\Sigma f_r} = \text{var iance term calculated u sin g 'A'}$$

Thus $s^2 = \sigma^2 + (M - A)^2 = \sigma^2 + e^2$
hence $\sigma^2 = s^2 - e^2$ (see worked example below)

Example 14.1:

Consider the lengths of 100 assorted screws measured to the nearest mm, and the following results obtained.

x_r – screw length mm	10	20	30	40	50
f_r = frequency	5	30	40	20	5

From these results, calculate the standard deviation to the nearest mm.

x_r	f_r	$x_r f_r$
10	5	50
20	30	600
30	40	1200
40	20	800
50	5	250
	100	2900

$$M = \frac{2900}{100} = 29 \text{ mm}$$

Using this value for the mean:
The following tabulation is carried out.

x_r	$x_r - M$	$(x_r - M)^2$	f_r	$f_r(x_r - M)^2$
10	−19	361	5	1805
20	−9	81	30	2430
30	+1	1	40	40
40	+11	121	20	2420
50	+21	441	5	2205
			100	8900

$$\therefore \sigma^2 \text{ (var iance)} = \frac{\Sigma f_r (x_r - M)^2}{\Sigma f_r} = \frac{8900}{100} = 89.0 \text{ mm}^2$$

$$\therefore s = \sqrt{89} = 9.4 = 9 \text{ mm to the nearest mm}$$

14.5 Best Equation of a Curve – Method of Least Squares

The method of least squares is used to determine the best set of coefficients in an equation $y = f(x)$ such that the sum of the squares of the deviations between the true and given values of one of the variables is least. Assuming that the variable 'y' is subject to error, the sum of the squares of the deviations will be given by $E = S(y - f(x))^2$. If now the unknown constants in f(x) are say a and b, then the condition for E to be a minimum is that $\frac{\delta E}{\delta A} = \frac{\delta E}{\delta b} = 0$. This pair of equations is called the 'Normal Equations'. In practice the normal equations for 'n' observations are obtained but tabulation and summation of the given values. For an illustration of the method, see the worked Example 14.2.

The following gives the normal equations for 'n' observations of a few of the more common equations encountered, assuming that 'y' only is the subject of error.

Equation or law	Normal equations
y = ax + b	Sxy = aSx2 + bSx
	Sy = aSx + bn
y = ax² + bx + c	Sx2y + aSx4 + bSx3 + cSx
	Sxy = aSx3 + bSx2 + cSx
	Sy = aSx2 + bSx + cn
y = a + b/x	Sy/x = aS1/x + bS1/x²
	Sy = an + bS1/x
y = a + b/x + c/x²	Sy/x² = aS1/x² + bS1/x³ + cS1/x⁴
	Sy/x = aS1/x + bS1/x2 + cS1/x3
	Sy = an + bS1/x + cS1/x2
y = ax + b/x	Sxy = aSx² + bn
	Sy/x = an + bS1/x²
y = axᵇ	SXY = (log₁₀ a)SX + bSX², where X = log₁₀ x
	SY = n(log₁₀ a) + bSX and Y = log₁₀ y
y = aeᵇˣ	SxY = (logₑ a) Sx + bSx² Where Y = logₑ y
	SY = n(logₑ a) + bSx

14.6 Correlation and Lines of Regression

14.6.1 Correlation

This is defined as the connection between two simultaneously varying quantities. The coefficient of correlation, 'r', is a measure of the manner in which the correlation takes place.

Consider:

Let x bar = mean value of the variate 'x' for a set of 'n' readings.

y bar = mean value of the variate 'y' for a set of 'n' readings.

$\Sigma(x - \bar{x})(y - \bar{y}) = $ product of the deviations of x and y from their means, 'r' is defined by

$$r = \frac{\Sigma(x-\bar{x})(y-\bar{y})}{\sqrt{\Sigma(x-\bar{x})^2(y-\bar{y})^2}} = \frac{\text{Mean of product of deviations of x and y}}{\text{Product of Standard Deviation of x and y}}$$

Note: 'r' can have any value between ±1.

14.6.2 Positive Correlation

If x and y vary together in the same manner, that is an increase or decrease in one is accompanied by an increase or decrease in the other, then 'r' will be positive.

14.6.3 Negative Correlation

If x and y vary in an inverse manner, then 'r' will be negative.

14.6.4 Perfect Correlation

If x and y are directly and perfectly proportional to each other, then r = +1. For perfect inverse correlation r = –1.

14.6.5 Zero Correlation

When there is no association between x and y whatsoever then 'r' = 0.

14.6.6 Standard Error of 'r'

In order to determine the significance of 'r', the standard error is calculated.

S.E. = $\frac{1-r^2}{\sqrt{n}}$ where 'n' is the number of pairs of readings taken.

$\frac{r}{S.E.}$ > 2 Then 'r' is significant.

$\frac{r}{S.E.}$ < 2 Then 'r' is not significant and might have occurred by chance.

14.6.7 Regression Lines

If say from an experiment, a set of n readings of x and y are plotted on a graph, a scatter diagram will result. If the deviations of x and y values from their respective means are plotted on a scatter diagram, the best straight line is drawn, assuming that the y-deviations only are subject to error. This line will be the line of regression of y on x. The best straight line which is obtained assuming the x-deviations only are subject to error is called the line of regression of x on y.

Let x = mean value of x for n deviations.

y = mean value of y for n observations

σ_x = standard deviation for the x-values

σ_y = standard deviation of the y-values

r = correlation coefficient

$$\text{Then } y - \bar{y} = r.\frac{\sigma y}{\sigma x}(x - \bar{x}) \text{ line of regression of y on x}$$

$$\text{and } x - \bar{x} = r.\frac{\sigma x}{\sigma y}(y - \bar{y}) \text{ line of regression of x on y}$$

Since the events are mutually independent, the probabilities are multiplied and the probability of say 2 heads in two throws will be $1/2 \times 1/2 = 1/4$. However, the probability of say one head and one tail in two throws, regardless of order, will be $1/4 + 1/4 = 1/2$ since head followed by tail and tail followed by head are mutually exclusive events. If 'n' throws are made, it can be shown that the probability of 'r' heads, regardless of order, will be given by the (r + 1)th term of the Binomial expansion of $(q + p)^n$,

Example 14.2

Consider the following pairs of values of x and y are determined experimentally:

x	0	1	2	3	4	5
y	6.8	7.6	10.1	11.4	13.6	14.8

Determine, using the method of least squares, a law of the form $y - ax + b$ assuming that the 'y' values are only subject to error.

The normal equations for 'n' observations for the law $y = ax + b$ are:

$$\Sigma xy = a\Sigma x^2 + b\Sigma x \tag{i}$$

$$\Sigma y = a\Sigma x + nb \tag{ii}$$

A table is constructed giving the values of x, x2, y, xy, thus when n = 6

x	x2	y	xy
0	0	6.4	0
1	1	7.6	7.6
2	4	10.1	20.2
3	9	11.4	34.2
4	16	13.6	54.4
5	25	14.8	74.0
15	55	63.9	190.4

Substituting these values into equations (i) and (ii).
Therefore: $190.4 = 55a + 15b$

$$63.9 = 15a + 6b$$

Solving this pair of simultaneous equations for a and b gives:
$a = 1.751$ and $b = 6.273$
Hence, the law will be $y = 1.751x + 6.273$.

p = probability of the success of an event
q = probability of a failure of an event
n = number of trials

Then the probability of 'r' successes in the 'n' trials is $^nC_r.q^{n-r}p^r$
The probability of 'k' successes in 'n' trials is given by the summation:

$$P(k) + P(k+1) + P(k+2) + \ldots P(n) - \sum_{r-k}^{r-n} P(r) = 1 - \sum_{r=0}^{r=k-1} (Pr)$$

14.7 Binomial Distribution

The binomial distribution was first studied in connection with games of pure chance, and it is now widely used to analyse data in virtually every field of engineering. It applies to any fixed number 'n' of repetitions of an independent process that produces a certain outcome with the same probability 'p' on each repetition. For example, it provides a formula for the probability of obtaining 10 sixes in 50 rolls of a die. Swiss mathematician Jakob Bernoulli, published a proof posthumously in 1713, determined that the probability of 'k' such outcomes in 'n' repetitions is equal to the 'k' term (where 'k' starts at 0) in the expansion of the binomial expression $(\rho + q)^n$, where $q = 1 - \rho$ (hence the name binomial distribution). Using the example of the die, the probability of turning up any number on each roll is 1 out of 6 (the number of faces on each die), then the probability of turning up 10 sixes in 50 rolls is equal to the 10th term (starting with the 0th term) in the expansion of $(5/6 + 1/6)^{50}$, or 0.115586.

In 1936 the British statistician Ronald Fisher used the binomial distribution to publish evidence of possible scientific chicanery in experiments on pea genetics reported by the Australian botanist Gregor Mendel in 1866. Following W F R Weldon (1860–1906) a Cambridge biologist original critique on the report of Mendel's experiments.

Fisher perceived that Mendel's laws of inheritance would dictate that the number of yellow peas in one of the Mendel's experiments would have a binomial distribution with 'n' = 8.023 and $\rho = 3/4$, for an average of $n\rho \equiv 6.017$ yellow peas. Fisher found remarkable agreement between this number and Mendel's data that showed 6.022 yellow peas out of 8.023. One would expect the number to be close, but a figure that close should occur only 1 in 10 times. Fisher found, moreover, that all seven results in Mendel's pea experiments were extremely close to the expected values – even in one instance where Mendel's calculations contained a minor error. Fisher's analysis sparked a lengthy controversy that remains to this day on whether Mendel adjusted his observations and recordings to suit the final results.

Returning to the often used example of tossing a coin, which can land either as a head or as a tail. If only one throw is made the probability of either a head or a tail is 1/2. Let the probability of a head be $\rho = 1/2$, and the probability of not a head, i.e., of a tail, be $q = 1/2$. If more than one throw is made, then since the events are mutually independent the probabilities are multiplied and the probability of say two heads in two throws will be $1/2 \times 1/2 = 1/4$. However, the probability of say one head and one tail in two throws, regardless of order, will be $1/4 + 1/4 = 1/2$, since head followed by tail and tail followed by head are mutually exclusive events. If 'n' throws are made, it can be shown that the probability of 'r' heads, regardless of order, will be given by the (r + 1)th term of the binomial expansion of $(q + \rho)^n$. In general, if,

ρ = probability of the success of an event

q = probability of a failure of an event

n = number of trials

Then the probability of 'r' successes in the 'n' trials is $^nC_r \cdot q^{n-r}\rho^r$.

14.8 The Poisson Distribution

The French mathematician Simeon-Denis Poisson developed his function in 1830 to describe the number of times a gambler would win a rarely won game of chance in a large number of tries. Letting 'ρ' represent the probability of a win on any given try, the mean, or average, number wins (λ in 'n' tries will be given by $\lambda = n\rho$). Using the Swiss mathematician Jacob Bernoulli's binomial distribution, Poisson demonstrated that the probability

TABLE 14.3

Annual Deaths of Prussian Officers from Horse Kicks in
Prussian Army (1875–1894)

Number of Deaths	Official Record	Poisson's Prediction
1	91	97
2	32	34
3	11	8
4	2	1
5 or more	0	0

of obtaining 'k' wins is approximate to $\frac{\lambda^k}{e^{-\lambda}k!}$, where e = the exponential function and k! = $(k - 1)(k - 2) \ldots 2.1$. Noteworthy is the fact that 'λ' equals both the mean and variance (a measure of the dispersal of data away from the mean) for the Poisson distribution.

von Bortkiewicz showed how the distribution (Table 14.3) could be used to explain statistical regularities in the occurrence of rare events. As examples he considered the numbers of deaths of Prussian Cavalry officers from horse kicks in the Prussian Army studied over a 20-year period 1875–1894).

This example provided the most extensive data and has become a classical example of the Poisson distribution.

Table 14.3 compares the official records with the expected frequency from the Poisson distribution. (Source: numbers from Principles of Statistics by M. G. Bulmer).

14.8.1 Poisson Distribution of Flying Bomb Hits on London During World War II

The Poisson distribution has now become to be recognised as a vitally important distribution in its own right. A further example, in 1946 the British statistician R.D. Clarke analysed the distribution of hits from flying bombs (V1) and (V2) missiles hitting London during the World War II. It had been noted that some areas were hit more often than others and the British military wished to know if the Germans were targeting these districts (the hits indicated greater technical precision) or if the distribution was due to chance.

Clarke began by dividing an area into thousands of tiny, equally sized plots. Within each of these, it was unlikely that there would be even one hit, let alone more. Furthermore, under the assumption that the missiles fell randomly, the chance of a hit in any one plot would be a constant across all the plots. Therefore, the total number of hits would be much like the number of wins in a large number of repetitions of a game of chance with a very small probability of winning. This sort of reasoning led Clarke to a formal derivation of the Poisson distribution as a model. The observed hit frequencies were very close to the predicted Poisson frequencies (see Table 14.4). Hence, Clarke reported that the observed variations appeared to have been generated solely by chance.

TABLE 14.4

Poisson's Distribution of Flying Bomb Hits on London Suburbs During World War II

Number of hits 'k'	0	1	2	3	4	5 and over
No. of districts with 'k' hits	229	211	93	35	7	1
Poisson prediction	226.74	211.39	98.54	30.62	7.14	1.57

In the Binomial distribution, the number of trials, the number of successes and the number of failures are all known. However, there are certain cases where the number of trials is not known.

14.9 The Normal Distribution

In the Binomial and Poison distributions, the variable considered is discrete. For example, the number of trials in the Binomial distribution, or the number of calls per hour received by a telephone, exchange in a Poisson distribution. For continuous variables, the distribution that generally applies is the normal distribution (sometimes referred to as the Gaussian or error curve) see Figure 14.4.

The equation of a normal curve is:

$$y = \frac{1}{\sigma\sqrt{2\pi}} . e^{-\frac{(x-M)^2}{2\sigma^2}}$$

where x = variate

M = mean of the deviation

σ = standard deviation of the distribution

Then y = probability density of 'x'
To find the frequency density, 'F' multiply 'y' by 'N', the total number of items in the distribution, thus F = yN.

The probability that a variate lies within the range x_1 to x_2 is given by the area below the normal curve and between the ordinates at x_1 and x_2.

a. Properties of a normal curve

The curve is symmetrical about the mean 'M' Hence,

Mode = mean = median

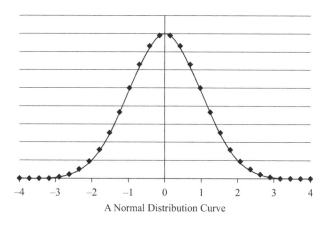

A Normal Distribution Curve

FIGURE 14.4
A Normal Distribution Curve.

b. The mean of the normal distribution is 'M' and the standard distribution is 'σ'

c. The total area under the curve is unity.

$$\text{Total area} = \frac{1}{\sigma\sqrt{2\pi}} \int_{-\infty}^{+\infty} e^{-\frac{(x-M)^2}{2\sigma^2}} \,.\, dx = 1$$

d. A 99.73% of the total area lies within ±3 standard deviations of the mean.

A 99.994% of the total area lies within ±4 standard deviations of the mean.

14.9.1 Fitting a Normal Curve to a Set of Observations

In order to plot the normal curve for a set of observations, the mean and standard deviations need to be calculated. From the normal equation for frequency density the following expression is obtained:

$$\log_e y = \log_e\left(\frac{N}{\sigma \Sigma 2\pi}\right) - \left(\frac{1}{2\sigma^2}\right).(x = M)^2$$

or using logarithms to the base 10

$$\log_{10} y = \log_{10}\left(\frac{N}{\sigma \Sigma 2\pi}\right) - \left(\frac{\log_{10} e}{2\sigma^2}\right).(x = M)^2$$

These equations may be rewritten as follows:

$$\log_e y = \log_e A - B(x - M)^2$$

$$\log_{10} y = \log_{10} A - (B\log_{10} e).(x - M)^2$$

$$\text{Where: } A = \frac{N}{\sigma\sqrt{2\pi}} \text{ and } B = \frac{1}{2\sigma^2}$$

To facilitate the calculations, a set of 'x' values are chosen so that (x − M) has as few digits as possible, these values are then tabulated and the corresponding 'y' values are calculated from them.

Example 14.3:

Fit a normal curve to the following set of figures.

x	2.1	2.2	2.3	2.4	2.5	2.6	2.7	2.8	2.9	3.0	3.1
Frequency 'f'	4	18	31	69	95	59	46	39	22	12	5

In fitting a normal curve, the values of 'x' (the variate) and 'y' (the frequency density) are plotted from the equation:

$$y = \frac{N}{\sigma\sqrt{2\pi}} e^{-\frac{(x-M)^2}{2\sigma^2}}$$

First M and σ are calculated:
Let assumed mean A = 2.5

x	f	x – A	f(X – A)	(x – A)2	f(x – A)2
2.1	4	−0.4	−1.6	0.16	0.64
2.2	18	−0.3	−5.4	0.09	1.62
2.3	31	−0.2	−6.2	0.04	1.24
2.4	69	−0.1	−6.9	0.01	0.69
2.5	95	0	0	0	0
2.6	59	+0.1	+5.9	0.01	0.59
2.7	46	+0.2	+9.2	0.04	1.84
2.8	49	+0.3	+11.7	0.09	3.51
2.9	22	+0.4	+8.8	0.16	3.52
3.0	12	+0.5	+6.0	0.25	3.00
3.1	5	+0.6	+3.0	0.36	1.80
	400		−20.1		18.45
			+44.6		
			+24.5		

$$e = \frac{+24.5}{400} = +0.06125$$

Hence: M = A + e = 2.5 + 0.06125
Therefore: M = 2.56125
Hence: $\sigma^2 = s^2 - e^2 = 0.046125 - 0.003752 = 0.042373$
$\sigma = 0.20584$
Taking logarithms of the normal equation:

$$\therefore \log_{10} y = \log_{10}\left(\frac{N}{\sigma\sqrt{2\pi}}\right) - \frac{\log_{10} e}{2.\sigma^2}(x - M)^2$$

$$\therefore \log_{10} y = 2.8895 - 5.125(x = 2.561)^2$$

As 'y' is a continuous function of 'x', then the normal curve may now be plotted using any suitable value of 'x'. The calculations will be simplified if 'x' values are chosen as 2.161, 2.261, 2.361, etc., taking values over approximately the same range as that given in the initial table.

x	x – 2.561	(x – 2.561)2	5.125(x – 2.561)2	log₁₀y	y
2.061	−0.5	0.25	1.2810	1.6085	40.6
2.161	−0.4	0.16	0.8200	2.0695	117.3
2.261	−0.3	0.09	0.4613	2.4282	268.0
2.361	−0.2	0.04	0.2050	2.6845	483.7
2.461	−0.1	0.01	0.0513	2.8382	689.0
2.561	0	0	0	2.8895	775.4
2.661	+0.1	0.01	0.0513	2.8382	689.0
2.761	+0.2	0.04	0.2050	2.6845	483.7
2.861	+0.3	0.09	0.4613	2.4282	268.0
2.961	+0.4	0.16	0.8200	2.0695	117.3
3.061	+0.5	0.25	1.2810	1.6085	40.6
3.161	+0.6	0.36	1.8452	1.0443	11.1

The normal curve plotted from these results is shown in Figure 14.5.

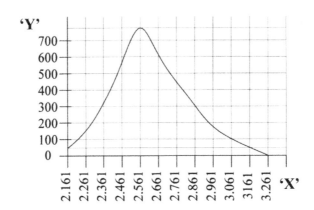

FIGURE 14.5
Normal Curve for Example 14.2.

14.10 Elementary Statistical Quality Control

In this chapter, the method of setting up and plotting control charts for the mean and range will only be discussed. Methods for sampling and sampling theory will not be considered as they are outside the scope of this chapter.

14.10.1 Seven Basic Tools of Quality

There are seven basic tools of quality given to a fixed set of graphical techniques identified as being helpful in troubleshooting issues related to quality. They are called basic as they are most suitable for engineers with little or no formal training in statistics and cover most of the problems associated with quality-related problems.

The seven tools are:

1. Cause and effect diagram (also known as the 'fishbone' or Ishikawa diagram)
2. Check sheet
3. Control chart
4. Histogram
5. Pareto chart
6. Scatter diagram stratification (also known as flow chart or run chart)

14.10.2 Cause and Effect Diagram

The fishbone diagram is a simple tool that allows quick and effective root causes to be understood, in the pursuit of corrective actions.

Often referred to as a cause and effect diagram, or Ishikawa, fishbone diagram is a simple root cause analysis tool that is used for brainstorming issues and causes of particular problems and can and often is used in conjunction with the 5 Whys tool. This is a basic root cause analysis technique used in the Analyse phase of the Six Sigma DMAIC (Define, Measure, Analyse, Improve, Control) methodology. By repeatedly asking the

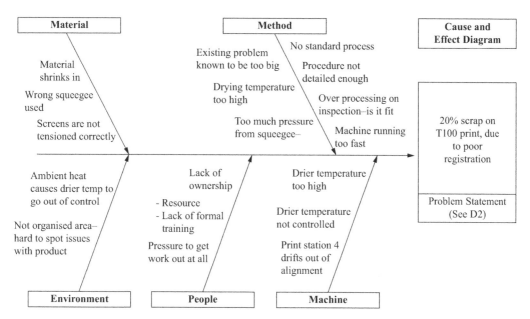

FIGURE 14.6
Cause and effect diagram (fishbone).

same question 'Why' (five times is a good rule of thumb), you can peel away the layers of the symptoms which can lead to the root cause of a problem.

14.10.2.1 An Example Fishbone Diagram

The group in the example (see Figure 14.6) had a problem with excessive scrap. They then got a cross-functional team together to understand possible reasons, listing each possible cause into categories.

The next step would be to pick the top three causes and delve deeper to find the true root causes.

In a fishbone diagram, the various causes are grouped into categories and the causes cascade from the main categories, flowing towards the effect, forming what resembles a fishbone appearance.

The prime remit is to brainstorm all the possibilities that could cause the problem and then drill down to the factor(s) that are causing this issue. Once found, eliminate them. It enables the team to focus on why the problem occurs, and not on the history or symptoms of the problem, or other topics that digress from the intent of the session. It also displays a real-time 'snap-shot' of the collective inputs of the team as it is updated.

14.10.3 Check Sheet

A check sheet is a structured, prepared form for collecting and analysing data. This is a generic tool that can be adapted for a wide variety of purposes.

A check sheet is used to record data from the same location that has been observed by the same person and includes data from a production process covering the frequency or patterns of events, problems, defect location and defect causes, etc. A typical check sheet is shown in Figure 14.7.

Dates								
Defect Type/Event Occurrence	Sunday	Monday	Tuesday	Wednesday	Thursday	Friday	Saturday	Total
Supplied parts rusted		IIIIIIIII	IIIII	IIII	II			20
Misaligned weld			III			II		5
Improper test procedure								0
Incorrect part issued		I		III				4
Voids in casting					II			2
Incorrect dimensions						II		2
Insufficient masking			II		I			3
Total		10	10	7	5	4		36

FIGURE 14.7
Brake Assembly Check Sheet.

Check sheets typically employ a heading that answers the Five Ws:

- Who filled out the check sheet
- What was collected (what each check represents, an identifying batch or lot number)
- Where the collection took place (facility, plant, apparatus)
- When the collection took place (hour, shift, day of the week)
- Why the data was collected.

14.10.4 Control Sheet

A control chart is a graph used to study how a process changes over time. Data is plotted in time order. A control chart always has a central line for the average, an upper line for the upper control limit and a lower line for the lower control limit. These lines are determined from historical data.

By comparing the current data to these lines, conclusions can be drawn about whether the process variation is consistent (in control) or is unpredictable (out of control, affected by special causes of variation).

Control charts for variable data are used in pairs. The top chart monitors the average, or the centring of the distribution of data from the process. The bottom chart monitors the range, or the width of the distribution. Figure 14.8 depicts a typical control chart.

14.10.4.1 When to Use a Control Chart

- When controlling ongoing processes by finding and correcting problems as they occur.
- When predicting the expected range of outcomes from a process.
- When determining whether a process is stable (in statistical control).

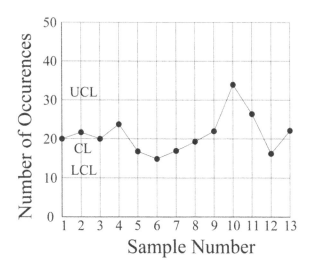

FIGURE 14.8
Control Chart Example.

- When analysing patterns of process variation from special causes (non-routine events) or common causes (built into the process).
- When determining whether your quality improvement project should aim to prevent specific problems or to make fundamental changes to the process.

14.10.5 Histograms

A histogram is a graphical tool used to visualise data.

A histogram graph is essentially a special form of bar chart, where the height of each bar represents the number of observations falling within a range of rank-ordered data values.

It allows the discovery of the underlying frequency distribution (shape) of a set of continuous date. This allows the inspection of the data for the underlying distribution (e.g., normal distribution), outliers, skewness, etc. Figure 14.9 shows an example of a histogram together with the raw data.

14.10.5.1 The Construction of a Histogram from a Continuous Variable

Prior to the construction of the histogram from a continuous variable, the data needs to be split into intervals, called 'bins'. In the example in the figure, age has been subdivided into bins, with each bin representing a 10-year period starting at 20 years. Each bin contains the number of occurrences of scores in the data set that are contained within that bin.

Bin	Frequency	Scores included in Bin
20–30	2	25, 33
30–40	4	36, 38, 36, 38
40–50	4	46, 45, 48, 46
50–60	5	55, 55, 52, 58, 55
60–70	3	68, 67, 61
70–80	1	72
80–90	0	-
90–100	1	91

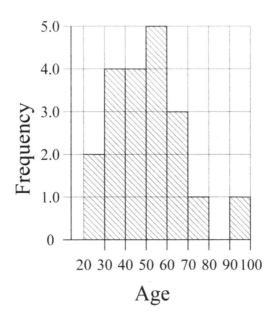

FIGURE 14.9
Example of a Histogram.

Note: unlike a bar chart there are no gaps between the bars (although some bars may be absent as the data within these bins will be zero.

In a histogram, it is the area of the bar that indicates the frequency of the occurrences for each bin. This means that the height of the bar does not necessarily indicate how many occurrences of scores there are within each individual bin. It is the product of height multiplied by width of the bin that indicates the frequency of occurrences within that bin. One of the reasons that the height is often incorrectly assessed as indicating frequency and not the area of the bar is due to the fact that a lot of histograms often have equally spaced bars (bins) and under these circumstances, the height of the bin does reflect the frequency.

There is a certain degree of confusion between the difference between an histogram and a bar chart. A histogram is only used to plot the frequency of occurrences in a continuous data set that has been divided into classes called bins. Bar charts, on the other hand, can be used for a large number of other applications including ordinal and nominal data sets.

14.10.6 Pareto Chart

A Pareto chart, named after Vilfredo Pareto, is a type of chart that contains both bars and a line graph, where individual values are represented in descending order by bars, and the cumulative total is represented by the line.

The left vertical axis is the frequency of occurrence, but it can alternatively represent cost or another important unit of measure. The right vertical axis is the cumulative percentage of the total number of occurrences, total cost or total of the particular unit of measure. Because the values are in decreasing order, the cumulative function is a concave function.

To take the example below, in order to lower the amount of late arrivals by 78%, it is sufficient to solve the first three issues.

The purpose of the Pareto chart is to highlight the most important among a (typically large) set of factors. In quality control, it often represents the most common sources of defects, the highest occurring type of defect, or the most frequent reasons for customer complaints and so on. Wilkinson (2006) devised an algorithm for producing statistically based acceptance limits (similar to confidence intervals) for each bar in the Pareto chart.

The Pareto chart is one of the seven basic tools of quality control.

14.10.7 Scatter Diagram

A scatter plot (also called a scatterplot, scatter graph, scatter chart, scattergram or scatter diagram) is a type of plot or mathematical diagram using Cartesian coordinates to display values for typically two variables for a set of data. If the points are color-coded, one additional variable can be displayed. The data is displayed as a collection of points, each having the value of one variable determining the position on the horizontal axis and the value of the other variable determining the position on the vertical axis.

A scatter plot can be used either when one continuous variable that is under the control of the experimenter and the other depends on it or when both continuous variables are independent. If a parameter exists that is systematically incremented and/or decremented by the other, it is called the *control parameter* or independent variable and is customarily plotted along the horizontal axis. The measured or dependent variable is customarily plotted along the vertical axis. If no dependent variable exists, either type of variable can be plotted on either axis, and a scatter plot will illustrate only the degree of correlation (not causation) between two variables.

A scatter plot can suggest various kinds of correlations between variables with a certain confidence interval. For example, weight and height, weight would be on the y-axis and height would be on the x-axis. Correlations may be positive (rising), negative (falling) or null (uncorrelated). If the pattern of dots slopes from lower left to upper right, it indicates a positive correlation between the variables being studied. If the pattern of dots slopes from upper left to lower right, it indicates a negative correlation. A line of best fit (alternatively called 'trend line') can be drawn in order to study the relationship between the variables. An equation for the correlation between the variables can be determined by established best-fit procedures. For a linear correlation, the best-fit procedure is known as linear regression and is guaranteed to generate a correct solution in a finite time. No universal best-fit procedure is guaranteed to generate a correct solution for arbitrary relationships. A scatter plot is also very useful when we wish to see how two comparable data sets agree to show non-linear relationships between variables. The ability to do this can be enhanced by adding a smooth line such as LOESS (Locally Weighted Scatterplot Smoothing). Furthermore, if the data is represented by a mixture model of simple relationships, these relationships will be visually evident as superimposed patterns.

A scatter (XY) plot has points that show the relationship between two sets of data.

In this example, a local ice cream shop keeps records of how much ice cream is sold vs the day time temperature. Table 14.5 shows the record of ice cream sale of 12 days. Figure 14.10 shows the distribution of points, from the figure it is clearly seen an increase in temperature results in increased sales.

TABLE 14.5

Ice Cream Sales vs Temperature

Temperature	Ice Cream Sales
°C	£
14.2	215
16.4	325
11.9	185
15.2	332
18.5	406
22.1	522
19.4	412
25.1	614
23.4	544
18.1	421
22.6	445
17.2	408

It is possible to draw a 'line of best fit' (also known as a 'trend line' on the scatter plot). For the best accuracy, the line can be calculated using the 'least squares regression'. The aim is to calculate the values 'a' (slope) and 'b' (y-intercept) for the equation of the line:

$$y = ax + b$$

To find the line of best fit for a group of (x, y) points.

Step 1: Calculate x^2 and xy for each (x, y) values.

Step 2: Sum all x, y, x^2 and xy, giving Sx, Sy, Sx^2 and Sxy.

Step 3: Calculate gradient 'a':

$$a = \frac{N\Sigma xy - \Sigma x.Sy}{N(\Sigma x2) - (\Sigma x)2}$$

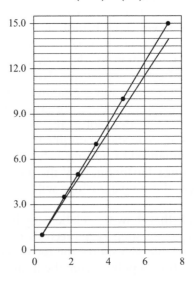

FIGURE 14.10

A trend line showing Ice Cream sales.

where 'N' is the number of points.

Step 4: Calculate intercept 'b':

$$b = \frac{\Sigma y - a(\Sigma x)}{N}$$

Step 5: Assemble the equation of a line.

$y = ax + b$

Example 14.4

Returning to the ice cream proprietor:

The proprietor had recorded the number of ice creams he sold from the shop and the number of hours of sunshine from Monday to Friday (see Table 14.6).

Calculate the best gradient (a) and intercept (b) for this data.

$y = ax + b$

For each value of (x, y) calculate x^2 and xy.

Sum x, y, x^2, and xy (giving Sx, Sy, Sx^2 and Sxy

x	y	x2	xy
2	4	4	8
3	5	9	15
5	7	25	35
7	10	49	70
9	15	81	135
Sx: 26	Sy: 41	Sx2:168	Sxy: 263

Calculate gradient: 'a'

x_1	y_1	$x_i - \bar{X}$	$y_i - \bar{Y}$	$(x_i - \bar{X})(y_i - \bar{Y})$	$(x_i - \bar{X})^2$
2	4	−24	−37	888	576
3	5	−23	−36	828	529
5	7	−21	−34	714	441
7	10	−19	−31	589	361
9	15	−17	−26	442	289
				3461	2196

$$'m' = \frac{\Sigma(x_i - \bar{X})^2(y_i - \bar{Y})}{S(x_i - \bar{X})^2} = 1.57604$$

TABLE 14.6

Ice Cream Sales vs Hours of Sunshine

'x' Hours of Sunshine	'y' No. of Ice Cream Sales
2	4
3	5
5	7
7	10
9	15

Calculate intercept 'b':

$$b = \bar{Y} - m\bar{X}$$
$$= 41 - (1.57604 \times 26)$$
$$b = 0.02277$$

Assemble the equation of a line:
$y = ax + b$
$y = 1.576\ 'x' + 0.02277$
Reviewing results:

x	y	y = 1.576 + 0.02277	error
2	4	3.1748	= 0.66
3	5	4.7509	−0.14
5	7	7.9030	0.89
7	10	11.0551	0.93
9	15	14.1844	−1.08

The final step is to graph the points and show the best-fit line through the data points.
The proprietor hears the weather forecast which states '8 hours sunshine is expected the following day' so using the new trend line he estimates the sales will be:
$y = 1.576\ x\ 8 + 0.02277$
$= 12.6$ ice creams.
so he makes fresh mixture for 14 ice creams just in case.

Note: Outliers
Be careful: least squares are sensitive to any outliers. A strange value will pull the line towards it giving rise to an incorrect trend line.

14.10.7.1 Discussion

Linear least squares regression is by far the most widely used modelling method. It is what most people mean when they refer to using 'regression', 'linear regression' or least squares to fit a model to their data.

14.10.7.2 Pareto Charts

Vilfredo Pareto (1848–1923) was an Italian economist who studied the distribution of wealth. He found that usually a small proportion of the people (about 20%) control the majority (about 80%) of a society's wealth. This 'Pareto Principle' has also been found to apply in other situations, particularly quality management. When studying things such as delays in schedules, customer complaints, employee absenteeism and accidents, Dr Joseph Juran discovered that a small number of causes are generally responsible for a large percentage of the effect.

A Pareto chart is a bar chart in which the categories are arranged in order of their frequencies from the most frequent to the least frequent. This allows you to see clearly what the most important factors are in a given situation. The Pareto chart can also include a cumulative percent graph. For each category, this shows the total percentage contribution of that category and all preceding categories.

For example, in a survey to find the main causes of lateness in a factory's work force a random sample of 200 employees who were late for work were asked the reason why. The Pareto chart in Figure 14.11 shows the results.

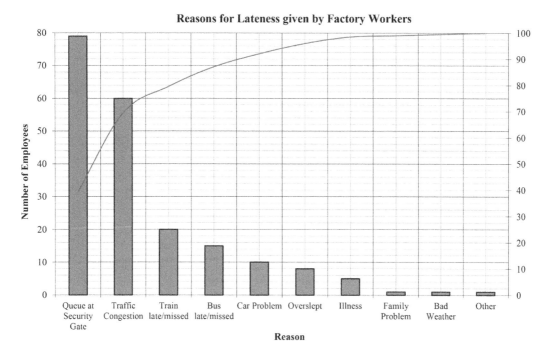

FIGURE 14.11
A Typical Pareto Diagram.

The most important factors are shown by the bars at the left-hand side of the chart. This is also where the cumulative percent graph is steepest.

In this example, the main cause of lateness was the delay caused by the security gate. On realising this, the manager introduced a new procedure at the gate to speed things up. Another random sample of 200 employees who were late for work was taken after the change in procedure.

14.10.7.3 When to Use a Pareto Chart

- When analysing data about the frequency of problems or causes in a process.
- When there are many problems or causes and you want to focus on the most significant.
- When analysing broad causes by looking at their specific components.
- When communicating with others about your data.

14.10.7.4 Pareto Chart Procedure

1. Decide what categories you will use to group items.
2. Decide what measurement is appropriate. Common measurements are frequency, quantity, cost and time.
3. Decide what period of time the Pareto chart will cover: One work cycle? One full day? A week?

4. Collect the data, recording the category each time. (Or assemble data that already exist.)

5. Subtotal the measurements for each category.

6. Determine the appropriate scale for the measurements you have collected. The maximum value will be the largest subtotal from step 5. (If you will do optional steps 8 and 9 below, the maximum value will be the sum of all subtotals from step 5.) Mark the scale on the left side of the chart.

7. Construct and label bars for each category. Place the tallest at the far left, then the next tallest to its right and so on. If there are many categories with small measurements, they can be grouped as 'other'.
   Steps 8 and 9 are optional but are useful for analysis and communication.

8. Calculate the percentage for each category. The subtotal for that category divided by the total for all categories. Draw a right vertical axis and label it with percentages. Be sure the two scales match: For example, the left measurement that corresponds to one-half should be exactly opposite 50% on the right scale.

9. Calculate and draw cumulative sums. Add the subtotals for the first and second categories, and place a dot above the second bar indicating that sum. To that sum add the subtotal for the third category, and place a dot above the third bar for that new sum. Continue the process for all the bars. Connect the dots, starting at the top of the first bar. The last dot should reach 100% on the right scale.

A Pareto chart provides facts needed for setting priorities. It organises and displays information to show the relative importance of various problems or causes of problems. It is a form of a vertical bar chart that puts items in order (from the highest to the lowest) relative to some measurable effect of interest: frequency, cost or time.

The chart is based on the Pareto principle, which states that when several factors affect a situation, a few factors will account for most of the impact. The Pareto principle describes a phenomenon in which 80% of variation observed in everyday processes can be explained by a mere 20% of the causes of that variation.

Placing the items in descending order of frequency makes it easy to discern those problems that are of greatest importance or those causes that appear to account for most of the variation. Thus, a Pareto chart helps teams to focus their efforts where they can have the greatest potential impact.

Pareto charts help teams focus on the small number of really important problems or their causes. They are useful for establishing priorities by showing which are the most critical problems to be tackled or causes to be addressed. Comparing Pareto charts of a given situation over time can also determine whether an implemented solution reduced the relative frequency or cost of that problem or cause.

Here is an eight-step method for creating a Pareto chart:

Step 1 Develop a list of problems, items or causes to be compared.

Step 2 Develop a standard measure for comparing the items.

How often it occurs: frequency (e.g., utilisation, complications, errors)

How long it takes: time

How many resources it uses: cost

Step 3 Choose a time frame for collecting the data.

Step 4 Tally, for each item, how often it occurred (or cost or total time it took). Then, add these amounts to determine the grand total for all items. Find the percent of each item in the grand total by taking the sum of the item, dividing it by the grand total and multiplying by 100.

Tallying Items in a Compilation Table		
Causes for Late Arrival	Number of Occasions	Percentage
Family problems	8	11
Woke up late	20	27
Had to take the bus	4	6
Traffic tie-up	32	44
Sick	6	8
Bad weather	3	4
Total	73	100

Step 5 List the items being compared in decreasing order of the measure of comparison: for example, the most frequent to the least frequent. The cumulative percent for an item is the sum of that item's percent of the total and that of all the other items that come before it in the ordering by rank.

Arranging Items in a Compilation Table			
Causes for Late Arrival (Decreasing Order)	Number of Occasions	Percentage	Cumulative Percentage
Traffic tie-up	32	44	44
Woke up late	20	28	71
Family problems	8	10	82
Sick	6	8	90
Had to take the bus	4	6	96
Bad weather	3	4	100

Step 6 List the items on the horizontal axis of a graph from the highest to the lowest. Label the left vertical axis with the numbers (frequency, time or cost), then label the right vertical axis with the cumulative percentages (the cumulative total should equal 100%). Draw in the bars for each item.

Step 7 Draw a line graph of the cumulative percentages. The first point on the line graph should line up with the top of the first bar. Excel offers simple charting tools you can use to make your graphs, or you can do them with paper and pencil.

Step 8 Analyse the diagram by identifying those items that appear to account for most of the difficulty. Do this by looking for a clear breakpoint in the line graph, where it starts to level off quickly. If there is not a breakpoint, identify those items that account for 50% or more of the effect. If there appears to be no pattern (the bars are essentially all of the same height), think of some factors that may affect the outcome, such as day of week, shift, age group of patients and home village. Then, subdivide the data and draw separate Pareto charts for each subgroup to see if a pattern emerges.

15

An Introduction to Material Selection

15.1 Introduction

One of the more difficult tasks encountered in engineering design is the most appropriate material to use for a specific application. With a wide choice of steels to choose from, it may seem daunting to a young engineer when faced with the decision to make the correct choice.

Obviously no designer wants to see his design fail due to an improper selection of material or processing, and selecting a material will not always save an improper geometry having high stress concentrations.

Engineering designers generally make their material choices based upon previous experiences. They prefer familiar materials but will consider unfamiliar options if they will meet the requirements.

Engineering companies will only stock the range of materials that will be used in their current production range, and the designer will be restricted to choosing from within this range unless a special case can be made to the purchasing department.

Other cases are when a current material becomes obsolete and has to be replaced by one that closely matches the properties of the previous material. Here, care has to be taken that the replacement material is not in any way inferior to the previous material. The purchasing department will, where possible, select on cost rather than physical properties.

The choice of engineering materials available to the designer is rapidly expanding. In addition to the conventional materials including the carbon steels, copper, brass, aluminium, etc., new materials such as titanium, high strength composites ceramics and silicon nitrides are becoming commercially available outside the aerospace industry.

It is necessary to employ a more structured and quantitative approach to the selection of a material to meet requirements of new components from the wide choice available without requiring a substantial knowledge of Materials Science.

The ideal material choice will become identified when a number of factors are resolved as the selection process is developed.

Material selection criteria would be based upon (but not restricted to) the characteristics and properties outlined in Table 15.1.

15.2 Stress-Strain Data

The physical properties of a metallic material used for structural purposes are determined from experimental testing. Tension and compression test coupons are manufactured to standardised designs, and these are subjected to the appropriate physical test. The test

TABLE 15.1

Summary of Material Characteristics and Properties to Be Considered for Critical Design Applications

1	**Static Characteristics**	4	**Thermal Properties**
	Strength:		Coefficient of thermal expansion
	• Ultimate strength		Thermal shock resistance
	• Yield strength	5	**Manufacturing**
	• Shear strength		Productability
	Density		Availability
	Ductility		Machinability
	Young's modulus.		Weldability
	Poisson's ratio		Heat treatment
	Hardness		Formability
	Form:		• Spinning
	• Sectional dimensions (for ruling sections)		• Deforming (forging)
2	**Fatigue Characteristics**	6	**Corrosion Resistance**
	Life required		Sea water
	Vibration and shock		Galvanic corrosion
	Fatigue strength		Stress corrosion
	Spectrum loads		
	Corrosion fatigue		
3	**Fracture Characteristics**		
	Fracture toughness		
	Flaw growth		
	Crack stability		

is repeated for a number of identical specimens manufactured from an identical batch of materials and the results are tabulated. Statistical techniques are used to determine the mean of the results.

It has to be borne in mind that the test coupons do not bear any relation with the actual shape of the component, and judgement has to be exercised when using this data. It is only to be used as a comparison with test results of other materials manufactured from a different batch for the ultimate strength and proof allowable values.

Data of importance for the analysis of structural components is derived from the stress-strain curve as shown in Figure 15.1.

15.2.1 Definitions of Terms

15.2.1.1 Proportional Limit

Proportional limit, also known as the *elastic limit*, is the point where the stress-strain curve becomes non-linear. The stress and strain values at this point are known as the proportional limit stress and strain, respectively. This can be the point beyond which Hooke's law can no longer be used to relate stress and strain in axial or shear deformation.

Figure 15.2 shows the proportional limit point associated with axial loading. A similar point also exists in shear stress-stain curves.

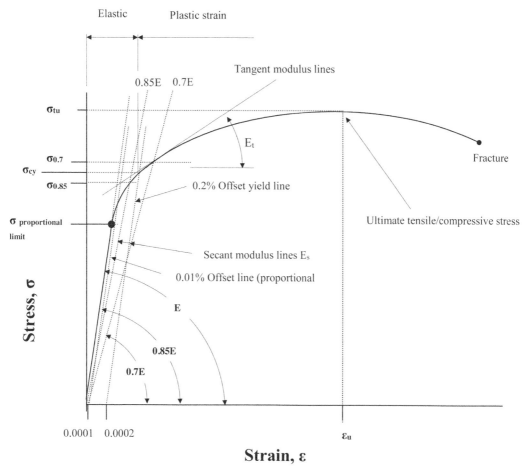

FIGURE 15.1
A typical stress-strain diagram.

15.2.1.2 Yield Strength

The yield point corresponds to the point where the material begins to have permanent (unrecoverable) deformation. Where some materials have a well-defined yield region (Figure 15.2), while others do not.

In the absence of a distinct yield point, a 0.2% offset is used to obtain an approximate yield point. Although the yield and the proportional limit points are close to each other, they do not correspond to the same location on the stress-strain curve.

The stress and strain corresponding to the yield point are called *the yield stress* and *yield strain*, respectively.

15.2.1.3 0.2% Offset

The 0.2% offset point is determined by drawing a line parallel to the linear region of the curve starting from point 0.002 on the strain axis. The intersection of this line and the stress-strain curve defines the 0.2% yield point.

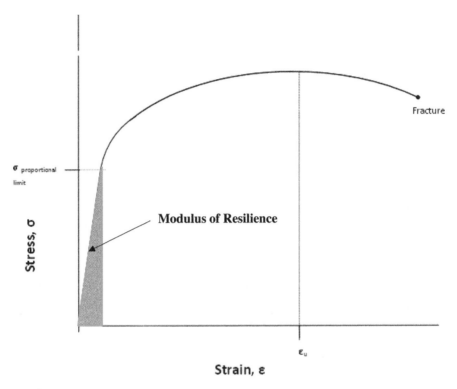

FIGURE 15.2
Modulus of resilience.

15.2.1.4 Ultimate Strength

15.2.1.4.1 Ultimate Tensile Strength

The maximum tensile stress a material is capable of carrying is known as the *ultimate tensile stress*. It corresponds to the highest point on the tensile stress-strain curve. The ultimate stress is usually denoted by σ_{tu}. The corresponding strain is known as the *ultimate tensile strain*.

A crucial point to remember is that the ultimate tensile stress is usually based on the cross-sectional area of the specimen. As such, its value on an engineering stress-strain diagram would be different from that on a true stress-strain diagram if the specimen demonstrates considerable necking prior to fracture. It is a common practice to use the value associated with the engineering stress-strain diagram.

15.2.1.4.2 Ultimate Compressive Strength

The maximum compressive stress a material specimen is capable of carrying is known as the ultimate compressive stress. Unlike in the case of tension, the compressive response of a specimen is a function of its cross-sectional shape and length. To eliminate these geometric effects, compressive specimens are usually designed to be very short with a large cross-sectional area. If the material is brittle, like concrete, then failure at the ultimate point is the form of fracture. If the material is ductile, like aluminium, then the failure is in the form of excessive yielding and as such, there is no definite value for the ultimate compressive stress of a ductile material. In the case of ductile materials it is common to assume $\sigma_{cu} = \sigma_{tu}$.

15.2.1.5 Modulus of Resilience (see Figure 15.2)

Modulus of resilience refers to the capacity of a material to absorb energy in the elastic range. Its value is simply equal to the area under the elastic region of the stress-strain curve. For any linearly elastic material, the modulus of resilience is found as:

$$U = 0.5\sigma_e \varepsilon_e$$

$$\text{or} \quad U = 0.5\frac{\sigma_e^2}{E}$$

where σ_e is the elastic-limit or proportional-limit stress of the material.

15.2.1.5.1 Toughness

Toughness refers to the capacity of a material to absorb energy prior to failure. Its value is equal to the entire area under the stress-strain curve. In most cases, the area under the elastic portion of the curve is only a small percentage of the total area and can be ignored in the calculation of the modulus of toughness. To simplify the calculation, the non-linear portion of the stress-strain curve can be approximated by a series of straight lines, as shown in Figure 15.3.

In the example shown the modulus of toughness is determined by summing the individual areas A1 to A4 using Simpson's rule. To improve the accuracy of the toughness value, the width of the individual strips can be reduced thereby reducing the error.

A ductile material with the same strength as a non-ductile material will require more energy for breaking and be tougher. Standardised methods for measuring materials for toughness include the Izod and Charpy tests. The difference is in the shape of the test piece and striker but both rely on a weighted pendulum striker.

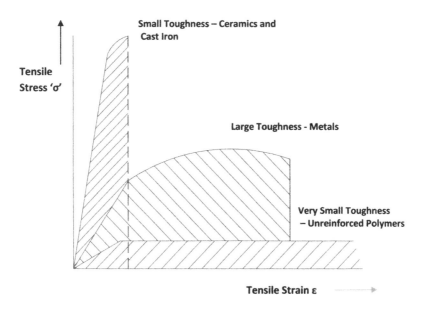

FIGURE 15.3
Toughness.

15.2.1.5.2 Modulus of Elasticity

Modulus of elasticity, also known as *Young's modulus*, is a measure of material resistance to axial deformation. Its value is obtained by measuring the slope of the axial stress-strain curve in the elastic region. It is named after the English scientist Thomas Young. It is usually denoted by E and has units M/mm^2 or lbf/in^2. Since in some materials, Young's modulus in tension is different from that in compression, subscript c or t is used to simplify the distinction.

15.2.1.5.3 Tangent Modulus (see Figure 15.4)

Tangent modulus is defined as the slope of a line tangent to the stress-strain curve at a point of interest. Tangent modulus can have different values depending on the point at which it is determined. For example, tangent modulus is equal to the Young's modulus when the point of tangency falls within the linear range of the stress-strain curve.

Outside the linear elastic region, at point 'A' shown for example, tangent modulus will always be less than the Young's modulus. Tangent modulus is mostly used to describe the stiffness of a material in the plastic range and is denoted by E_t.

15.2.1.5.4 Ramberg-Osgood Equation

This equation is used to describe the stress-strain relationship in the yield region of the stress-strain diagram. It uses three different properties of a material, i.e., E – Young's modulus, $\sigma_{0.7}$ – stress value corresponding to the secant modulus of $0.7E$ and m – shape factor describing the shape of the stress-strain diagram in the yield region.

$$m = \frac{1 + 1_n(17/7)}{1_n\left(\dfrac{\sigma_{0.7}}{\sigma_{0.85}}\right)}$$

$$\frac{E_t}{E} = \frac{1}{1 + \dfrac{3}{7}m\left(\dfrac{\sigma}{\sigma_{0.7}}\right)^{m-1}}$$

The Ramberg-Osgood equation is used in in-elastic buckling analysis of columns and plates.

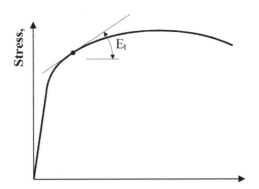

FIGURE 15.4
Tangent modulus.

15.2.1.5.5 Secant Modulus

Secant modulus is the slope of a line drawn from the origin of the stress-strain diagram and intersecting the curve at the point of interest. Therefore, the secant modulus can take different values depending upon the location of the intersect. Figure 15.5 shows how the secant modulus is obtained at point 'A' on the curve.

The secant modulus can be expressed as a percentage of the Young's modulus (e.g. $0.7E$ or $0.85E$), and it is used to describe the stiffness of a material in the in-elastic region of the stress-strain diagram. E_s commonly denotes secant modulus.

15.2.1.5.6 Secant Stress

Stress at intercept of any given secant modulus line with the stress-strain curve, F0.7, F0.85 where subscripts 0.7 and 0.85 are secant lines of 70% and 85% of Young's modulus.

15.2.1.6 Poisson's Ratio

The ratio of the lateral strain to the axial strain is referred to as the Poisson's ratio of the material. The calculation is based on the physical phenomenon shown in Figure 15.6.

The modulus of elasticity and modulus of rigidity are related to the Poisson's ratio (υ) as follows:

$$G = \frac{E}{2(1+\upsilon)}$$

15.2.1.7 Shear Rigidity

Shear rigidity, also known as modulus of rigidity, is a measure of material resistance against shear distortion. Its value is equal to the slope of the shear stress-strain curve in the elastic region.

It is usually denoted by G and has units of N/m^2 or lbf/in^2.

15.2.1.8 Ductility

The capacity of a material to undergo large in-elastic deformation prior to fracture. It is highly dependent on the operating temperature of the material. At very low temperatures, the material may lose their ductility and become brittle.

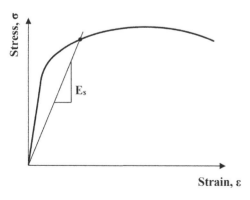

FIGURE 15.5
Secant modulus.

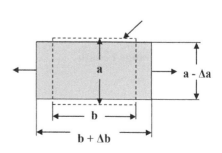

FIGURE 15.6
Poisson's ratio.

15.2.1.9 Elongation

Elongation is a measure of material ductility, it is defined as the percentage change in the specimen length at the point of fracture. Usually denoted by *e*, it can be obtained by multiplying the fracture strain by 100.

$$e = (L' - L_0 / L_0) \times 100$$

where L′ is the specimen gauge length after fracture and L_0 is the original gauge length.

A typical test coupon is depicted in Figure 15.7.

15.2.1.10 Creep

Creep is deformation that is time dependent when the material is under load at all temperatures and can lead to fracture. It is more pronounced at high temperatures but can occur at room temperatures when the applied stress level is close to the yield stress. Figure 15.8 shows a typical creep curve.

When a design is being modified or updated then the selection of material may have already been decided and the decision will not arise. There may be a case where the material normally used has become obsolete, and the material supplier has ceased to supply it. They may suggest a choice and it will be up to the designer to select the most appropriate one, or the design has had a minimal modification, say including a change in cross-section, then the original choice can be retained. But where there has been a substantial change in the component section due to a redesign to say reduce weight, then the engineer may have to consider carrying out a series of stress calculations to ensure that the life of the component is not compromised.

These notes are proposed as an aid for the young engineer when studying the important issues in material selection. Table 15.1 summarises the material characteristics and properties to be considered for new and critical design applications.

The first objective in selecting the correct material is to carry out a simple stress analysis as outlined in Section 15.3; this will then determine the approximate stress levels the component is being subject to. If the maximum stress is found to be in the order of say 450 MPa, then there is no point in selecting a material, such as say aluminium, which has an ultimate strength of, say, 450 MPa. In this case, there will be no factor of safety if the loading was to be exceeded.

A better choice would be a medium carbon steel with an ultimate strength of 620 MPa giving a minimum factor of safety of 1.3.

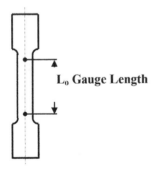

FIGURE 15.7
Typical extension test coupon.

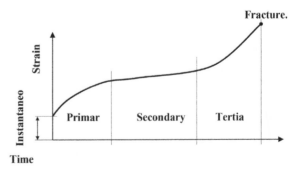

FIGURE 15.8
Conventional creep curve.

15.3 Things to Consider

The following is a basic checklist that the student engineer will need to address as the design progresses. Some or all the information may not be immediately available in the early phases of the design and will need to be acquired as the design phase progresses. It is important that the essential information is available before the initial design review.

15.3.1 Environment

It will need to be established at the earliest possible stage the nature of the environment that the component or structure will be exposed too. If the environment is in an offshore situation, then the choices will be limited to high strength corrosion resisting steels. If the component will be used in the aerospace environment, then obviously the choice will be limited to high strength lightweight materials such as aluminium but as with the off-shore industry, care will be needed to select a suitable corrosion protection package.

15.3.2 Strength

There are three principle uses of strength:

- Static strength
  The ability to resist short-term steady loads at ambient temperature.
- Dynamic strength
  The ability to resist a fluctuating load.
- Creep strength
  The ability to resist a load at elevated temperatures to produce a progressive extension over an extended period of time.

15.3.3 Durability

The dictionary definition of durability is

> 'The ability to exist a long time without any significant deterioration'.

In the context of this chapter, this will include resistance to wear and abrasion and corrosion attacks.

15.3.4 Stiffness

Stiffness is the ability of a material to maintain its shape when subject to a load or force. Consider Hooke's law, where a test material is incrementally loaded to produce an extension which is plotted against the load, and the resultant slope is used to demonstrate the relationship between stress and strain. Within the linear range of the extension, the material will return to its original size when the load or force is removed. If the test material is loaded so that this linear extension is reached, the material is said to have reached its 'proportional limit'; any further extension past this limit will then result in the test material not returning back to its original size when the applied load or force is removed. This phase is called 'the non-proportional limit'.

A material that displays a steep stress-strain curve will be stiffer than one that has a shallow curve, and a component manufactured from the first material will deflect less for a given load or force than one manufactured from the second.

15.3.5 Weight

In the transport industry, including road and aerospace vehicles, it is paramount to keep weight to a minimum. In both cases, fuel is required to propel both vehicles, and with the current high cost of fuel it is essential to maximise the distance travelled per unit of fuel used. Substantial efforts are made in the design of lightweight structures.

On the other hand, this is converse to that of a machine tool, where weight is important to minimise the effects of vibration and structural distortion when subject to cutting or forming forces.

15.3.6 Manufacturing

In the current atmosphere of high material costs, efforts are being made by manufactures to minimise material wastage. In the previous 19th and early to mid20th centuries, it was common to generate significant amounts of wastage from metal cutting machines; in the current financial climate, efforts are being made to minimise this wastage by making more use of forging, casting and other metal-forming techniques, such as pressure die casting including 'electro-forming' machines when the material properties allow its use. In the automotive and aerospace industries, significant use is made of fabrications manufactured from formed sections. There is a move now to use 3D printing technology where new materials are being developed that is a significant improvement on the early materials used. Such that NASA has installed a 3D printer on the International Space Station for printing out tools used in the maintenance of the station. These also replace any tooling that gets lost when undertaking space walks. Additionally, a 3D-printed copper combustion chamber has been ground tested and withstood the high temperatures involved.

15.3.7 Cost

In any manufacturing enterprise, whether it is large or small, every effort is made to minimise cost. If the product being manufactured is destined for the consumer market, then the selling price will be dictated by the buying public, and the manufacturing cost will have to be recovered from this; the difference will be the profit generated. When the manufacturer is selling through retailers, then the retailers will demand a percentage of the selling price, resulting in less profit for the manufacturer. The manufacturer will have to become very cost conscious and scrutinising where savings cost can be made in the product manufacture. This including material costs together with the additional cost of the manufacturing plant depreciation, and with the cost to replace obsolete plant.

15.3.8 Maintainability

A manufacturer has to make a decision whether to consider product maintenance. In the case of a low-cost consumer product, such as a hairdryer, the case may be argued that this will be a throw-away item at the end of the product's life and not to consider any maintenance. On the other hand, in a high capital cost item, such as a road vehicle, maintenance becomes a critical issue, and efforts are made to ensure the product is maintainable throughout the product lifespan with the use of replaceable modules that can be returned to either the manufacturer or companies specialising in repairing and offering the items back for replacement.

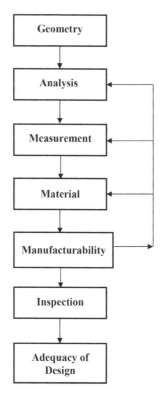

FIGURE 15.9
Model for material selection – core activities.

15.3.9 A Model for Material Selection

The author has developed a material selection model similar to the one produced by Stuart Pugh and Bill Hollins for 'total design'. Figure 15.9 shows the basic model, and it is intended to put the decision-making into a chronological order so that the important issues are dealt with in a timely manner and not considered out of order.

A brief description of the principle headings used in Figure 15.1 follows.

15.3.9.1 Geometry

The shape of the component is identified and all the boundary conditions defined. External and internal forces can then be evaluated.

15.3.9.2 Analysis

A detailed stress analysis will need to be carried out next to determine the stresses generated by the applied forces.

In the initial stages of the design, this will be to try and establish the maximum and minimum stresses to enable a preliminary selection to be made. This activity may be revisited several times as better definition becomes available.

15.3.9.3 Measurement Evaluation

Where possible, a suitable prototype is constructed and tested to confirm the measured stresses and deflections agree with the calculated values. The model can be either a full-size physical model or a mathematical finite element model if there is sufficient confidence in the model's accuracy.

15.3.9.4 Material Selection

The stage has been reached where a suitable candidate material can now be considered. Each industry will have its own specific requirements; as an example, the aerospace and automotive industry will have strength and density constraints as a high priority, whereas the agriculture industry will require cost and resistance to corrosion as their priorities.

The material properties will generally be listed on a company database covering all the materials used across the company's product lines, and it becomes a simple task to isolate a suitable material that closely fits the operating requirements criteria.

15.3.9.5 Manufacturability

The manufacture of the component will have an important influence on the final selection of the material, depending upon whether the component is machined, fabricated, cast or forged. The production department will usually reach this decision depending upon the range of machines at its disposal.

The designer may have to revisit the design and make any suitable changes to the geometry and review the stress analysis.

15.3.9.6 Adequacy of Design

In keeping with the current total design philosophy, it is important that the final design is carefully reviewed to ensure that it will meet the original design specification and that any changes made do not compromise the design integrity.

15.4 Future Developments

15.4.1 Knowledge-Based Engineering

It soon became obvious that a parametric language could be developed for use in a computer-aided design (CAD) system where the operator would simply fill in a table and the system would then generate the appropriate model. Amendments to the design could then be implemented by changes to the variables within the table. This approach will be able to save many man-hours where the design is modular.

A number of researchers have developed knowledge-based systems that could be integrated into the design process allowing domain-specific knowledge to be stored regarding a part or process, together with other associated attributes.

Further work has been extended to develop the knowledge base using a material database together with a suitable solid modelling system that uses a rule-based technique; for example, using an 'if-then' approach which is implemented to perform the material selection process. A material that satisfies all the constraints then becomes the most suitable candidate for a particular component operating within a set of specific conditions.

15.5 Material Performance Indices

Table 15.2 depicts the performance indices covering the stress limited and deflected indices used for the majority of design applications.

TABLE 15.2

Performance Indices – Stress Limited – Deflection Limited

Component	Stress Limited	Deflection Limited
Rods in tension.	$Pm\rho/\sigma_{YS}$	$Pm\rho/E$
Short column in compression.	$Pm\rho/\sigma_{YS}$	$Pm\rho/E$
Thin-wall pipe and pressure vessels under internal pressure.	$Pm\rho/\sigma_{YS}$	-
Flywheels for maximum kinetic energy storage at a given speed.	$Pm\rho/\sigma_{YS}$	-
Helical spring for a specified length and load capacity.	$Pm\rho/\tau m$	-
Thin-walled shafts in torsion.	$Pm\rho/\tau m$	$Pm\rho/G$
Rods and pins in shear.	$Pm\rho/\tau m$	-
Beams with a fixed section shape, in bending.	$Pm\rho/\sigma_{YS}^{2/3}$	$Pm\rho/E^{1/2}$
Solid shafts in bending or torsion.	$Pm\rho/\sigma_{YS}^{2/3}$ $Pm\rho/\tau m^{2/3}$	$Pm\rho/G^{1/2}$ $Pm\rho/E^{1/2}$
Long rods in compression limited by buckling.	-	$Pm\rho/G^{1/2}$ $Pm\rho/E^{1/2}$
Rectangular beams, with a fixed width, in bending.	$Pm\rho/\sigma_{YS}^{1/2}$	$Pm\rho/E^{1/3}$
Flat plates under pressure.	$Pm\rho/\sigma_{YS}^{1/2}$	$Pm\rho/E^{1/3}$
Flat plates loaded by self-weight only (e.g. ceiling tiles).	$Pm\rho^2/\sigma_{YS}$	$Pm\rho^{2/3}/E^{1/2}$
Sensitive spring elements for measuring devices.	$Pm\rho E/\sigma^2_{YS}$ $Pm\rho G/T^2m$	-
Springs for a specified load and stiffness.	$Pm\rho G/T^2$	-
Long heavy rods in tension.	$Pm\rho/(\sigma_{YS}-Lg\rho)$	-
Thick-walled piped, under internal pressure, with axial pressure balance (e.g. hydraulic cylinders).	$Pm\rho/(\sigma_{YS}-2p)$	-
Thick-walled pipes, under internal pressure, with no axial pressure balance.	$Pm\rho/(\sigma_{YS}-4p)$	-
Rollers between flat plates of the same material.	$Pm\rho E^2/\sigma_c^4$	-
Balls between flat plates of the same material.	$Pm\rho E^3/\sigma_c^{9/2}$	-

Notation	
Gravitational acceleration	g
Length	l
Internal pressure	p
density	ρ
Cost per unit weight	P_m
Young's modulus	E
Shear modulus	G
Maximum allowable Hertzian contact stress	σ_c
Tensile yield stress	σ_{YS}
Maximum allowable shear stress	τ_m

16

Mathematical Modelling and Simulation

16.1 What is Mathematical Modelling

A modelling is a powerful tool developing and testing theories and is applied to many different fields of study. Modelling together with simulation combines general methodological developments to many specific applications.

Figure 16.1 depicts the relationship between the real and conceptual worlds. In the conceptual world, observations are made of events in the real world. During the modelling phase, the observations are analysed and the model is created either to explain the results or to predict a future result.

A mathematical model can be broadly defined as a formulation or equation that expresses the essential features of a physical system or process in mathematical terms.

Models can be represented by a functional relationship between dependent variable, independent variables, parameters and forcing functions, i.e.,

Dependent variable = f (Independent variables, parameter, forcing function)

where

Dependent Variable: A characteristic that usually reflects the behaviour or state of a system.

Independent Variables: Having dimensions, such as time and space, for which the system's behaviour is being evaluated.

Parameters: Constants that are reflective of the system's properties or composition.

Forcing Functions: External influences acting upon the system.

The most common form of a model is that of the "Black Box" in which the input variables go in and response variables come out (see Figure 16.2). Engineers try to explain what is happening within the black box or to explain the relationship between the input and output variables.

16.1.1 Modelling: Newton's Second Law of Motion

The second law states that the time rate of change of momentum of a body is equal to the resultant force acting upon it.

$$F = ma$$

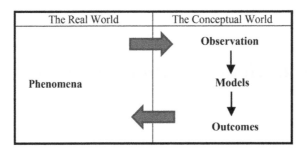

FIGURE 16.1
Real and conceptual world of modelling.

This may be rewritten in terms of 'a'

$$\Rightarrow a = \frac{F}{m}$$

where 'a' is the dependent variable (acceleration), 'm' is a parameter (mass of object) and 'F' is the forcing function (net force acting on the object).

In this case, there is no independent variable involved.

It is possible to determine the terminal velocity of a free-falling body approaching the earth's surface.

1. The law describes a natural process or system in mathematical terms.
2. It represents an idealisation and a simplification of nature.

    It ignores negligible details of the natural process and focusses on its essential manifestations.

    It excludes the effects of "relativity" that are of minimal importance when applied to object and forces that interact on or about the earth's surface at velocities and on a scale visible to humans.

3. It yields reproducible results and can be used for predictive purposes.

    Have generalisation capabilities.

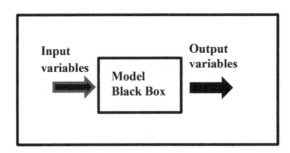

FIGURE 16.2
A black box model.

For a body falling within the vicinity of the earth's surface, the net force acting on the body is composed of two opposing forces:

$$F = F_D + F_U$$

- The downward pull of gravity 'F_D'
  The force due to gravity can be expressed as:

$$FD = mg$$

  where g is the acceleration due to gravity (9.81 m/s²)
- The upward force due to air resistance 'F_U'
  A good approximation is to express it as:

$$F_U = -c_d v^2$$

where 'v' is the velocity, c_d is the lumped drag coefficient, accounting for the properties of the falling object covering its shape or surface roughness.

The greater the velocity, the greater will be the upward force due to the air resistance.

The net force acting on the body will be the difference between the downward force and the upward force. A differential equation can be written regarding the velocity of the object:

$$\frac{dv}{dt} = g - \frac{c_d}{m} v^2$$

The exact solution for 'v' cannot be obtained using simple algebraic manipulation, but rather using more advanced calculus techniques (when v(t) = 0, t = 0):

$$v(t) = \sqrt{\frac{gm}{C_d}} \tanh\left(\sqrt{\frac{gc_d}{m}} t\right)$$

where t is an independent variable, v(t) is the dependent variable, C_d and m are parameters, and g is the forcing function.

$$\tan(x) = \frac{e^x - e^{-x}}{e^x + e^{-x}}$$

Example 16.1

A free falling skydiver having a body mass of 68.1 kg falls from a stationary hot air balloon assume the drag coefficient is 0.25 kg/m.
   Compute the velocity for the first 12 seconds of free fall
   Determine the terminal velocity for an infinitely long drop.

SOLUTION:

$$v(t) = \sqrt{\frac{gm}{C_d}} \tanh\left(\sqrt{\frac{gc_d}{m}} t\right)$$

$$v(t) = \sqrt{\frac{9.81(68.1)}{0.25}} \tanh\left(\sqrt{\frac{9.8(0.25)}{68.1}} t\right)$$

$$= 51.6938 \tanh(0.18977t)$$

$$\therefore v(12) = 50.6715$$

$$v(\infty) = 50.6938 \text{ (approx.)}$$

A graphical representation of the system is shown in Figure 16.3.

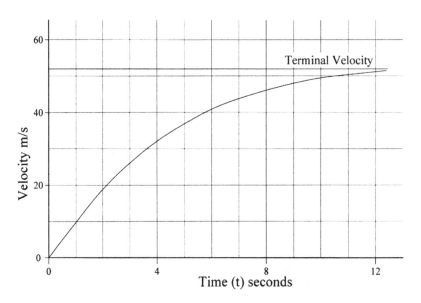

FIGURE 16.3
Graphical representation of system for Example 16.1.

16.2 Example of Numerical Modelling

Numerical methods are those problems where the mathematical problem has been reformulated enabling it to be solved using mathematical operations.

For example, the rate of change of velocity described earlier in the chapter:

$$\frac{dv}{dt} \approx \frac{\Delta v}{\Delta t} = \frac{v(t_i + 1) - v(t_i)}{t_{i+1} - t_i}$$

Note: $\dfrac{dv}{dt} = \lim\limits_{\Delta t \to 0} \dfrac{\Delta v}{\Delta t}$

Substituting the finite difference into the differential equation gives:

$$\frac{dv}{dt} = g - \frac{C_d}{m} v^2$$

$$\frac{v(t_i + 1) - v(t_i)}{t_i + 1 - t_i} = g - \frac{C_d}{m} v(t_i)^2$$

- Solve for:

$$v(t_{i+1}) = v(t_1) = \left(g - \frac{C_d}{m} v(t_i)^2 \right)(t_{i+1} - t_i)$$

$$\text{new} = \text{old} + \text{slope} \times \text{step}$$

This method is formally known as 'Euler's method'.

Figure 16.4 Applying Euler's method in 2 second intervals gives a good convergence on the required solution:

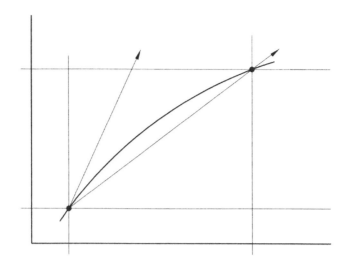

FIGURE 16.4
Example of numerical modelling 16.2.

Following the construction of the mathematical model of a dynamic situation, the next step is to see if it is a good and accurate representation for which it has been developed.

This requires running the model either manually or using a computer and submitting values and observing the results generated by the model to see if they match the results gathered following any experiments. This operation is known as 'simulation' and is an important part of the mathematical modelling verification.

16.3 Development of the Mathematical Model

16.3.1 Identify the Problem

Study the system carefully and note all activities that occur, noting the timescales.

16.3.2 Formulating the Problem

Determine which part of the activity is giving rise to the problem. Measure all physical data, accelerations, velocities, displacements, etc.

16.3.3 Collect and Process System Data

Ensure all the data collected is carefully recorded.

- Formulate and Develop a Model
- Model Validation
- Document the Model
- Interpret and Present the Results
- Further and Future Action Required
- Development of a Simulation Model

16.4 Simulation Methods

There are ways to imitate of the operation of real-world systems. It first requires that a model be developed representing characteristics, behaviours and functions of the selected system or process. The model represents the system itself, whereas the simulation represents the operation of the system over time.

The methods are widely used is Economy, Biology, Engineering and almost all sciences. It is usually done using computers making changes to variables and performing predictions about the behaviour of the system. A good example of the usefulness of computer simulation can be found in automobile traffic simulation, grocery stores checkout lines, inventory management, stock prices predictions, environmental consequences of policies and so on.

16.5 Simulation Model Validation

The goal of the validation process is:

- To produce a model that represents true behaviour closely enough for decision-making purposes.
- To increase the model's credibility to an acceptable level.

Validation is an integral part of model development:

- Verification: Building the model correctly, correctly implemented with good input and structure.
- Validation: Building the correct model, an accurate representation of the real system.

Most methods are informal subjective comparisons, while a few are formal statistical procedures.

16.6 Problems Suitable for Simulation

Applications of simulation abound in the areas of government, defence, computer and communication systems, manufacturing, transportation (air traffic control), health care, ecology and environment, sociological and behavioural studies, biosciences, epidemiology, services (bank teller scheduling), economics and business analysis.

16.7 Selecting Suitable Simulation Software

Although a simulation model can be built using general purpose programming language (such as Fortran), which are familiar to the analyst, available over a wide variety of platforms and less expensive, most simulation studies are implemented using a simulation package. The advantages are reduced programming requirements, a natural framework for simulation modelling, etc. The question how to select the best simulation software for an application arises. Metrics for evaluating a suitable package will include modelling, modelling structure, and graphic users interface, and animation, hardware and software requirements. It is always best to obtain a test program first and try it out on a segment of the program first before committing any finance to purchase the full program. Any self-respecting vendor will be happy to accommodate the companies' request.

16.8 Benefits of Mathematical and Simulation Modelling

Simulation can be used to compress a time frame, a simulation model run on a computer system can be used to investigate quickly the effects of a change in a real-life situation that take place over several years. It can be used to study complex systems that would otherwise be difficult to investigate.

Can be used in engineering and product design to investigate the effect of changes without producing a physical prototype.

Can be used to investigate situation that would be dangerous in real life.

There are disadvantages in using a simulation model.

We have a poor understanding of how some physical systems work so that we do not have sufficient data to produce a mathematical model. For this reason, it has not been possible to create simulations that can accurately predict the occurrence and effects of earthquakes and tsunami.

The formula and functions that are used may not provide an accurate description of the system resulting in inaccurate output from the simulation.

Complex simulations can require the use of a computer system with a fast processor and large amounts of memory.

16.9 Pitfalls to Guard Against When Mathematical and Simulation Modelling

Engineers tend to rush the preliminary investigation work to find an answer quickly under pressure from the project manager. It is important to proceed with caution and patience. Time spent in thinking and planning in the beginning is time well spent.

The following are other pitfalls encountered:

- Unclear objective
- Using a simulation package when an analytical solution would be more appropriate
- Invalid model
- Simulation model is either too complex or too simple
- Undocumented assumptions. This point is extremely important and it is strongly suggested that any assumptions made at any stage of the modelling and simulation are clearly identified and documented.
- Poor communication between the personnel involved in the simulation.

17

Introduction to Configuration Management

17.1 Introduction

Configuration Management Systems are considered as a subset of the overall Project Management System. It is a collection of formal documented procedures used to apply technical and administrative direction and surveillance to identify and document the functional and physical characteristics of a product, to control any changes to such characteristic, records and report each change and its implementation status and support the audit of the products to verify conformance to the requirements. It includes the documentation and defines the approval levels necessary for authorising and controlling changes.

In most design processes of any significant magnitude, a design freeze will be implemented at some point prior to completion of the project. This is the point at which the design process is formalised and design changes are implemented and placed under strict and formal control, often by some internal configuration control board (CCB). CCBs normally include membership representing all the design disciplines, project management, the customer, safety, quality control and other staff functions as appropriate. The point at which the need to control costs and configuration will be dictated by the need to inject greater discipline into the process and by the need to forcibly implement increased coordination amongst all the participants within the program. Although this is a necessary step in the overall process, it adds significant complications to the effort of the designer and restricts the ability to correct deficiencies in the design that becomes apparent after the freeze is implemented.

Configuration Management is applied throughout the lifecycle of the product and extends beyond the boundaries of the project.

17.2 Configuration Control and Change Control

Configuration Control and Change Control are often used interchangeably. Both are related activities and both are subsets of the overall Configuration Management System. They are two distinct activities with very different focus and neither is a subset of each other.

Configuration Control is the activity of managing the product (or project deliverables) and related documentation throughout the lifecycle of the product. Configuration Control ensures that

- The latest approved version of the product and its components are used at all times.
- No changes are made to the product without full authorisation.
- A clear audit trail of all proposed approvals or implemented changes exists.

17.2.1 Change Control

Change Control is the process of identifying documenting, approving or rejecting and controlling changes to the project baselines. An effective Change Control System ensures that:

- Proposed changes are reviewed and their impact is analysed prior to approving or rejecting them.
- All requests and changes are properly documented to provide a clear audit trail.
- When the organisation undertakes a change to improve performance, seize a new opportunity or address key issues, they often require changes to the way activities are carried out internal to the organisation, changes to processes, job roles and the types and uses of technology. It is the employees within the organisation who have to ultimately change that how they will undertake their roles. If these individuals are unsuccessful in their personal transitions, if they do not embrace and learn a new way of working, the initiative will fail and the organisation will be the loser. If employees embrace and adopt changes required by the initiative, it will deliver the expected results and the organisation will be the better off for it.

17.3 What Is Change Management?

Change Management is the discipline that guides how to prepare, equip and support individuals and groups to adopt changes to drive organisational successful change.

While all changes are unique and all individual are unique, decades of research shows there are actions that can be taken to influence employees in their individual transitions, Change Management creates a structured approach for supporting the individual within the organisation to move from their own current state to their new future state.

17.4 Three levels of Change Management

17.4.1 Individual Change Management

While it is natural for individuals to resist change, they are generally resilient creatures. When supported through times of change they can be adaptive and successful.

Individual change management requires understanding how individuals experience change and what is needed to change successfully. It also requires knowing what will help people make a successful transition: what messages they need to hear when and from whom, when the optimal time to teach someone a new skill is, how to coach individuals to demonstrate new behaviours and what makes changes 'stick' in someone's work ethic. Individual change management draws on disciplines such as psychology and neuroscience to apply actionable frameworks to individual change.

17.4.2 Organisational/Initiative Change Management

While changes occur at the individual level, it is often impossible for a project team to manage changes on a person-by-person basis. Organisational or initiative change management provides the steps and actions to be taken at the project level to support the large number of individuals who will be impacted by a project.

Organisational change management involves first identifying the groups and persons who will need to change as a result of the project and in what way they will need to change. Organisational change management then involves creating a customised plan for ensuring impacted employees receive the awareness, leadership, coaching and training that is needed to change successful. Driving successful individual transitions should be the focus of the activities in organisational change management.

17.4.3 Enterprise Change Management Capability

Enterprise change management is an organisational core competency that provides competitive differentiation and the ability to effectively adapt to the event changing world. An enterprise change management capability means effective change management is embedded into the organisational roles, structures, projects and leadership competencies. Change Management processes are consistently and effectively applied to initiatives, leaders have the skills to guide their teams through change and employees know what to ask for in order to be successful. The end result of an enterprise change management capability is that individuals embrace change more quickly and organisations are able to respond quickly to market changes, embrace strategic initiative and adopt new technologies more quickly and with less productivity impact. This capability does not happen by chance, however, and requires a strategic approach to embed change management across an organisation.

18

Engineering Communications

18.1 Introduction

Engineers have a bad reputation in their ability to communicate effectively outside the engineering office. Their main source of communication is through the use of drawings and sketches. Occasionally, they may be requested to produce a final report on a specific project they may be working on or produce an interim report on the work in progress they are currently involved with.

The majority of engineers have concentrated on maths and the sciences and had very limited exposure to writing and oral communications, which goes someway to explain their deficiency in this area. In general, there is little serious interest in becoming an effective writer and convincing speaker.

In today's environment, information flow is critical to business and industry. Engineers in industry often comment on the large amount of their time to writing and other forms of communication. The majority of communications in industry is verbal, in the form of face-to-face discussion, meetings and telephone conversations. Important communications are transmitted in writings so that the meaning can be precisely stated and a record can be established for future reference. This will become important in the event of a design failure, and there is a forensic investigation of the cause of the failure. Engineers who are not capable of preparing clear and concise written communications tend to be relegated to a passive role in the department. They become information receivers and not information generators and thus gradually find themselves out of the mainstream, out of touch with what is going on and out of mind when promotion comes. In effect, engineers market their skills through their ability to communicate.

18.2 The Formal Engineering Report

The engineering report is probably the greatest writing challenge that a typical engineer has to face. Engineering reports document a significant proportion of the work and is an important commitment on the part of the company in which the engineer is employed. The engineering report is usually the only document that describes in detail the work carried out and will give any recommendations and conclusions. It will be kept on file for future reference.

Engineering reports are prepared for a number of different reasons. A few of these are listed below:

- Test programs
- Experiments

- Studies
- Investigations
- Failure analysis
- Evaluations

It is evident that the format of the report should be as flexible as possible, the format being adaptable to best describe the work being undertaken. As an example, a report on a test program will require a different format for that of a failure analysis. Most companies have various customised formats depending up on the type of report being written or not familiar with the work or the author. It is very important to know the audience and to prepare the report accordingly so that it is understandable to that group of people.

An important point to bear in mind is that in some instances the report will be read by someone without any engineering knowledge.

A problem that many inexperienced writers have in preparing formal reports is establishing a logical content flow. If the reader is to have an understanding of the report, the presentation of the information must follow some thread of logic. Formal reports are normally written in the third person, past tense, so personal pronouns should be rarely used. The report should be prepared in a purely objective, impersonal manner. Results are judged on the basis of existing, applicable theory and previous experiments. Opinions should only be introduced when existing knowledge fails.

18.2.1 The Abstract

The abstract is located at the beginning of the report and consists of approximately 200 words or less. It is a brief statement of the report so that the reader is given the choice whether to read the full report or not. In larger companies that generate a large number of reports, the abstract often exists separately from the report in the technical library so that readers can make decisions to review the literature that may be relevant to their own studies.

The abstract should include a brief statement of the objective of the report, including the method used and any significant results and conclusions. Figures and tables should not be referred to in the abstract, and equations should not normally be used. It is usual to complete the report first and scanning the report for essential information and presenting this information in as few words as possible.

18.2.1.1 The Introduction

The primary purpose of the introduction is to provide the necessary background of the subject, to describe the objective(s) of the work accomplished and to define the scope of the investigation. The introduction should include the reason for carrying out the work together with any relationship that may exist between the current work and other related effort should be clearly identified. Figures and tables should not be included in the introduction, and equations and related calculations should also not be included unless absolutely necessary.

The introduction should generally be one typewritten page, the length can be either longer or shorter depending on the subject matter being introduced.

18.2.2 Technical Approach (Theory)

This section should start with a table of contents and should include an identification of the theoretical principles involved and the equations used in carrying out the calculations from any experimental data. It should also include any exoplanetary figures and tables in the sequence carried out in the experiment or review.

Consideration should be given to how the report is going to be presented and generally the following steps are carried out:

- Planning the report
- Writing the first draft
- Revising the first draft
- Diagrams, graphs, tables and calculations
- The report layout
- Headings
- References to diagrams, graphs, tables and equations
- Finalise the report and proofreading
- The summary
- Final proofreading
- References
- Bibliography
- Acknowledgements
- Appendices (if appropriate)

Note: The following section is some notes relating to the final report.

18.2.3 Structure

A technical report should in general contain the following sections, but this will depend upon the house style of the company:

Section	Details
Title page	This must include the title of the report.
Contents	Numbers and lists all section and subsection headings with page numbers.
Introduction	This states the objectives of the report and comments on the way the topic of the report is to be treated and leads into the report itself.
The sections which make up the body of the report	This divided into numbered and headed sections. These sections separate the different main ideas in a logical order.
Conclusions	A short, logical summing up of the theme(s) developed in the main text of the report.
References	The report should contain details of any published sources of material referred to or quoted within the text including addresses of any websites used for information.
Bibliography	Other published sources of material, including websites, not referred to in the text but useful for background or further reading.
Acknowledgements	List of people who helped with the preparation and research or prepare the report, including your proofreaders
Appendices (if appropriate)	Any further material which is essential for full understanding of the report (e.g., large-scale diagrams, computer code, raw data, specifications) but not required by a casual reader

18.2.4 Presentation

Very careful attention should be given to the presentation of any report as this will be a reflection of the individual writer and how well the report will be accepted by the reader. An untidy presentation will be responsible if the report is not considered acceptable even if the data is correct, whereas a tidy report will gain full acceptance.

18.2.5 Planning the Report

There are a number of excellent textbooks contain advice about the writing process and how to begin. The following is a checklist of the main stages:

- Collect the information, including all sources. Keep an accurate record of all the published references which you intend to use in your report, by noting down the following information:
  Journal articles:
  > author(s)
  > title of article
  > name of journal (italic or underlined)
  > year of publication
  > volume number (bold)
  > issue number, if provided (in brackets)
  > page numbers
  Reference books:
  > author(s)
  > title of book (italic or underlined)
  > edition, if appropriate
  > publisher
  > year of publication
- The creative phase of planning. Write down topics and ideas from your researched material in random order. Next arrange them into logical groups. Keep note of topics that do not fit into groups in case they come in useful later such as the appendix. Put the groups into a logical sequence which covers the topic of your report.
- Structuring the report. Using your logical sequence of grouped ideas, write out a rough draft of the report with headings and subheadings.

18.2.6 Writing the First Draft

Consider who is going to read the report? In professional contexts, the readers might be directors, managers, clients and project team members. The answer will affect the content and technical level, and is a major consideration in the level of detail required in the introduction.

Begin writing with the main text, not the introduction. Follow your outline in terms of headings and subheadings. Let the ideas flow; do not worry at this stage about style, spelling or word processing. If you get stuck, go back to your outline plan and make more detailed preparatory notes to get the writing flowing again.

18.2.7 Test Set-Up

In the situation when the report is describing a test. A full identification of the components or system to be tested together with all the significant test equipment should be provided.

A neat drawing or sketch and any photographs (if available) should be prepared with all the components and instrumentation clearly marked. A description should be included of the function of the major components. The reader should be able to relate how the test set was undertaken.

Make rough sketches of diagrams or graphs. Keep a numbered list of references as they are included in your writing and put any quoted material inside quotation marks.

Prepare the Conclusions next, followed by the Introduction. Do not write the Summary at this stage.

18.2.8 Revising the First Draft

This is the stage at which your report will start to take shape as a professional, technical document. In revising what you have drafted you must bear in mind the following important principle:

- The essence of a successful technical report lies in how accurately and concisely it conveys the intended information to the intended readership.

  Does that sentence/paragraph/section say what I want and mean it to say? Can it be open to misinterpretation, try writing it in a different manner. Make use of the thesaurus to help sharpen up the phrase or the sentence you are trying to write.

- Are there any words/sentences/paragraphs which could be removed without affecting the information which I am trying to convey? If so, remove them.

18.2.9 Diagrams, Graphs, Tables and Mathematics

It is often the case that technical information is most concisely and clearly conveyed by means other than words. Imagine how you would describe an electrical circuit layout using words rather than a circuit diagram. Here are some simple guidelines:

Diagrams	Keep them simple. Draw them specifically for the report. Put small diagrams after the text reference and as close as possible to it. Think about where to place large diagrams.
Graphs	As with the diagrams, keep these simple and concise. Bear in mind when the report is printed, colour may not be available, line types will be important when multiple curves are used within the graph.
Tables	Is a table the best way to present your information? Consider graphs, bar charts or pie charts. Dependent tables (small) can be placed within the text, even as part of a sentence. Independent tables (larger) are separated from the text with table numbers and captions. Position them as close as possible to the text reference. Complicated tables should go in an appendix.
Equations	Mathematical arguments, if they are really necessary, should go in an appendix. Only use mathematics where it is the most efficient way to convey the information.

18.2.10 The Report Layout

The appearance of a report is no less important than its content. An attractive, clearly organised report stands a better chance of being read. Use a standard, 12pt, font, such as Times New Roman, for the main text. Use different font sizes, bold, italic and underline where appropriate but not to excess. Too many changes of type style can look very fussy.

18.2.11 Headings

Use heading and subheadings to break up the text and to guide the reader. They should be based on the logical sequence which you identified at the planning stage but with enough subheadings to break up the material into manageable chunks. The use of numbering and type size and style can clarify the structure.

18.2.12 References to Diagrams, Graphs, Tables and Equations

- In the main text, you must always clearly identify any diagram, graph or table which you use.
- Label diagrams and graphs as follows:
  Figure 1.2 Graph of energy output as a function of wave height.
  In this example, the second diagram in Section 1 would be referred to by '... see Figure 1.2 ...'
- Label tables in a similar fashion:
  Table 3.1 Performance specifications of a range of commercially available electronic devices
  In this example, the first table in Section 3 might be referred to by '... with reference to the performance specifications provided in Table 3.1 ...'
- Number equations as follows:

$$F(dB) = 10 * \log_{10}(F) \qquad (18.1)$$

  In this example, the sixth equation in Section 3 might be referred to by '... noise figure in decibels as given by equation (18.1) ...'

18.2.13 Originality and Plagiarism

Whenever you make use of other people's facts or ideas, you must indicate this in the text with a number which refers to an item in the list of references. Any phrases, sentences or paragraphs which are copied unaltered must be enclosed in quotation marks and referenced by a number. Material which is not reproduced unaltered should not be in quotation marks but must still be referenced. It is not sufficient to list the sources of information at the end of the report; you must indicate the sources of information individually within the report using the reference numbering system.

Information that is not referenced is assumed to be either common knowledge or your own work or ideas; if it is not, then it is assumed to be plagiarised, i.e., you have knowingly copied someone else's words, facts or ideas without reference, passing them off as your own.

18.2.14 Finalising the Report and Proofreading

Your report should now be nearly complete with an introduction, main text in sections, conclusions, properly formatted references and bibliography and any appendices. The report is now ready for pagination, contents and title pages and complete the summary.

18.2.15 The Summary

The summary, with the title, should indicate the scope of the report and give the main results and conclusions. It must be intelligible and standalone from the rest of the report.

Many people may read, and refer to, a report summary but only a few may actually read the full report, as often happens in a professional organisation.

- Purpose – a short version of the report and a guide to the report.
- Length – short, typically not more than 100–300 words.
- Content – provide information, not just a description of the report.

18.2.16 References

Details of published material either in the public domain or private correspondence that is quoted within the body of the report together with any websites that are used should be included in the reference section.

18.2.17 Acknowledgements

Make sure that all the people and organisations that have helped and contributed to preparing the report are fully acknowledged in this section.

18.2.18 Appendices

Any additional material that may be referenced in the report but not fully explained and is essential for the full understanding, e.g., raw data computer codes, specifications, etc. but not immediately required by the casual reader will be covered within the appendices.

18.3 Proposed Preparation

At some time or other, the professional engineer will be tasked to write a proposal. The preparation of an engineering proposal can result from a formal request from a potential customer or from a need that is thought to exist but for which there has been no formal or informal request.

The purpose of submitting a proposal is to put an idea thought to be of interest. The proposal must first establish that the need exists and then provide information adequate to convince the prospective customer that the solution is the correct one and that the proposer is capable of accommodating the effort described within the planned schedule and budget.

It is important to be specific in regard to the product of the proposed effort. It should be clearly stated what the document covers, if the product is some form of hardware, it should be described adequately. The product is what the proposed customer is going to pay for, and it plays an important part in determining whether or not the project will be funded.

18.3.1 Background/Problem Statement

It is important for proposals to include any background information relating to the problem under discussion and this will reflect in the solution being proposed. It is important to include any background information so that the potential customer recognises that the proposer understands the problem and is capable of developing a solution.

The background should be concise but sufficiently complete enough to provide an adequate description of the sequence of events leading up to the problem recognition. The problem may not have been done before or be something that has been before but very poorly or incorrectly, or has been done only partially. The background/problem statement should address questions such as what is the problem, why is it of significance? What previous work has been done before in this area and what was discovered?

18.3.2 Objectives

After the problem has been described, a clear and concise statement of the objective of the effort is included. The objective(s) should be brief, often only of a few sentences. If the effort is to be accomplished in several phases, it is helpful to identify the objectives for each separate phase.

18.3.3 Technical Approach

This section describes the technical aspects of the proposal in how the effort will be conducted. This section is considered the most important section of the proposal, as it spells out how the proposer will go about finding a solution to the problem that has been identified. The technical approach must convince the prospective customer that the proposer fully understands the problem and that an approach is being considered that will find a completely successful solution to the problem.

The technical approach should provide an adequate level of detail so that the prospective customer can understand exactly how each of the objective would be undertaken. Individual tasks should be identified and shown on an easily understood schedule. Use of a bar chart/milestone schedule is recommended for this purpose, as it provides a clear delineation of the tasks and shows the associated schedule and important milestones.

18.3.4 Budget

The complete proposal cost is the most important element in the proposal. It is the cost that will determine whether the customer will fund the effort. Thus, the budget must follow logically from the tasks identified, and the allocations made must agree with the manner in which the effort is to be accomplished, as described in the technical approach.

18.3.5 Organisation and Capability

This section of the proposal describes how the proposer will organise the effort, describing the responsibilities of the key personnel and their qualifications, as related to the tasks for which they will be responsible for, together with the organisational support and the resources available for accomplishing the work.

18.4 Oral Communications

The ability to make a good oral presentation is an art that involves attention to the needs of the audiences, careful planning and attention to delivery. This section covers and explains some of the basics of effective oral presentation. It also covers the use of notes, visual aids and computer presentations.

18.4.1 The Audience

Some basic questions to ask about an audience are:

- Who will I be speaking to?
- What is known about the topic I will be speaking about.
- What is it they want to know about my topic.
- What do I want them to know at the end of my talk?

By basing the content and style of the presentation following the answers to these questions, you can make sure that what has to be said regarding the topic will be less important than what the audience wishes to hear.

18.4.2 Planning the Presentation

In an effective presentation, the content and structure of the presentation is adjusted to the medium of speech. When listening, it is not possible to go back over a difficult point to understand it or easily absorb long arguments. A presentation can easily be ruined if the content is too difficult for the audience to follow or if the structure is too complicated.

As a general rule, expect to cover much less content than in a written report. Try to make difficult points easier to understand by preparing the listener for them, using plenty of examples. Leave time for questions within the presentation.

Give the presentation a simple and logical structure. Within the introduction, outline the points intended to cover followed by a conclusion where the main points will be covered.

18.4.3 Delivering the Presentation

Presenters vary in their ability to speak confidentially in public, but everyone gets nervous and everyon can learn to improve their presentation skills by applying a few simple techniques.

The three main points to consider are the quality of your voice, your rapport with the audience, the use of notes and visual aids.

Voice quality involves attention to volume, speed of speech and fluency, clarity and pronunciation. The quality of your voice will improve dramatically if it is possible to practice beforehand in a room of similar size to the one that the presentation will take place in.

Rapport with the audience involves paying attention to the audience and trying to make eye contact with them, sensitivity to how the audience is responding to your talk and your appearance from the point of view of the audience. These can be improved by practicing in front of a few friends or videotaping your rehearsal.

One important point to bear in mind is to try and keep humour at a minimum and do not be frivolous during the presentation as it will destroy your image of that you want to present to the audience.

18.4.4 Effective Use of Notes

Presentation speakers vary a great deal in their use of notes. Some are able to deliver a whole presentation without any use of notes, while others write out their speech in great detail. If you are one who lacks the confidence, it is not a good idea to speak without notes as you will soon lose the thread of the talk. Also avoid reading a prepared text aloud or memorising the speech as this will be boring.

The ideal solution may be to use notes with headings followed by points to be covered. It may be appropriate to write down key sentences. Notes may be on either paper or cards. It is not unknown for some presenters to use the overhead transparencies (OHRs) as notes. The important thing is to avoid shifting your attention from the audience for too long. The notes should be written large enough to avoid moving your head to much.

18.4.5 The Use of Visual Aides

The use of visual aids help make the presentation more interesting. They can also help to present information that would be very difficult to follow through speech alone.

The two common forms of visual aids are 'overhead transparencies' and computer slide shows, using, for example, 'PowerPoint'. These allow the speaker to project an image while facing the audience. The images may be a picture or graphic.

Other methods used include:

- Flip charts
- Blackboard
- 35 mm slides
- Video and sound tape recordings
- Motion picture (with or without sound)

It may be possible that objects that can be displayed can also be passed around the audience; this can be very effective and often helps to relax an audience. Some presenters also give printed handouts during the presentation to follow the discussion, while others prefer to give the handouts at the end of the talk, as they can distract the audience from the presentation. As soon as someone starts taking notes, tell the audience that they do not need to do so as they will get the information on the handout.

Index

Note: Locators in *italics* represent figures and **bold** indicate tables in the text.

Printed and bound by CPI Group (UK) Ltd, Croydon, CR0 4YY

18/10/2024

01776204-0016